Also by Bill Lucarelli

THE ORIGINS AND EVOLUTION OF THE SINGLE MARKET IN EUROPE

Monopoly Capitalism in Crisis

Monopoly Capitalism in Crisis

Bill Lucarelli
University of Western Sydney, Australia

palgrave
macmillan

First published 2004 by
PALGRAVE MACMILLAN
Houndmills, Basingstoke, Hampshire RG21 6XS and
175 Fifth Avenue, New York, N.Y. 10010
Companies and representatives throughout the world

PALGRAVE MACMILLAN is the global academic imprint of the Palgrave Macmillan division of St. Martin's Press, LLC and of Palgrave Macmillan Ltd. Macmillan® is a registered trademark in the United States, United Kingdom and other countries. Palgrave is a registered trademark in the European Union and other countries.

ISBN 1–4039–3255–7

This book is printed on paper suitable for recycling and made from fully managed and sustained forest sources.

A catalogue record for this book is available from the British Library.

Library of Congress Cataloging-in-Publication Data
Lucarelli, Bill.
Monopoly capitalism in crisis/Bill Lucarelli.
p. cm.
Includes bibliographical references and index.
ISBN 1–4039–3255–7 (cloth)
1. Capitalism. 2. Monopolies. 3. Business cycles. 4. Marxian economics. I.Title.

HB501.L896 2004
330.12′2—dc22 2003058120

10 9 8 7 6 5 4 3 2 1
13 12 11 10 09 08 07 06 05 04

Printed and bound in Great Britain by
Antony Rowe Ltd, Chippenham and Eastbourne

Contents

List of Tables

List of Figures

Acknowledgements

First and foremost, I should acknowledge a debt of gratitude to my long-time partner in life and crime, Katherine Bowe, for her practical and emotional support in the long and arduous process of writing this book.

The other usual suspects that I owe a long legacy of intellectual support and inspiration are my close academic colleague at the University of Western Sydney, Steve Keen, and my friend and mentor Joseph Halevi at the University of Sydney.

Much of my recent motivation and renewed passion for intellectual engagement has sprung from the rise of the post-autistic movement in economics. I therefore dedicate this book to those scholars and students who share the vision of a more heterodox and tolerant approach in the study of economics.

Introduction

The ideas for this study have been distilled from the simple proposition that an unregulated market economy is subject to recurrent phases of growth and stagnation. Yet for the neoclassical economist, these alternating phases of boom and slump merely reflect temporary disturbances, or exogenous shocks to the system. If left to its own devices, neoclassical theory asserts that the market economy will eventually gravitate back to its "normal" state of long-run equilibrium. The aim of this book is to debunk this conventional wisdom and to suggest that in the market economy, these recurrent crises are not only an inherent characteristic, but also tend to be more endemic and entrenched under the conditions of oligopolistic competition.

In this context, the aim is twofold. In the first part of this study, a theoretical critique is developed and alternative theories will be evaluated from post-Keynesian and Marxian perspectives. It is not sufficient, however, merely to construct a theoretical critique. The real problem is to formulate a theory that can explain the general economic dynamics of a specific phase of historical development. In other words, the problem of historical specificity needs to be addressed. The object of economic theory should ultimately be to reveal the "deeper" structures operating as threshold historical tendencies (Lawson, 1997). Accordingly, several tentative hypotheses will be articulated in order to shed light on recent historical developments. The second part of this study is therefore devoted to a more concrete historical analysis of these inherent "tendencies." The essential kernel of the argument is that under the mature stages of the evolution of monopoly capitalism and in the absence of powerful countervailing forces (i.e. technical innovation, market expansion), the natural tendency is toward economic stagnation. This conclusion is doubtless the very antithesis of the neoliberal claim that the market economy tends toward full employment equilibrium in the long run.

Over the past two decades, most Western countries, especially the English-speaking world, have experienced a revival of neoliberal economic doctrines. Proponents of these neoliberal doctrines sought to completely dismantle the postwar regimes of accumulation and national modes of regulation. Their theories were informed by standard textbook microeconomics, which had supported the view that to improve international competitiveness and more efficient resource allocation, countries should be exposed to the rigors of free trade. Neoliberals believed that it was essential to deregulate both the financial and labor markets and to privatize, wherever possible, state enterprises. The Chicago school of economics, which had elevated small government and lower taxes as high virtues so that the market would allocate resources and prevent the "crowding out" of private investment, influenced their ideas. Their ideology was imbued with a profound distrust of government intervention and an equally blind faith in the efficacy of the unfettered free market.

From the standpoint of the neoliberal paradigm, the prevailing Keynesian policies had exhausted themselves. Neoliberal critics argued that these national policies could no longer be legitimized. This paradigm shift away from the prevailing corporatist forms of state regulation (e.g. the welfare state, financial regulation and industry intervention) coincided with the demands of transnational corporations that these national modes of regulation and protectionism should be gradually abolished. National deregulation, privatization of public corporations and market liberalization became the neoliberal mantra. Most of these ostensible "efficiency" gains would be secured through cost reductions and rationalization in order to promote static Pareto-efficiencies and improve competitiveness. However, the efficacy of the neoliberal strategy ultimately confronts the limits of its own narrow economism. It is just as plausible to contend that the liberal and deregulationist logic will merely accentuate regional disparities, erode established social legislation and norms, and severely limit the scope for traditional Keynesian policies of fiscal stabilization and full employment.

The neoliberal strategy not only implied the dismantling of national modes of regulation but the curbing of the power of organized labor in order to foster greater labor market flexibility and mobility. The basic theoretical contention was that market liberalization would generate an increase in the level of productive investment and economic restructuring through the purgative forces induced by competition. The most powerful advocates of neoliberalism came from the World Bank, the International

Monetary Fund (IMF), the US Treasury and from the reconstituted World Trade Organization (WTO), and are reflected in the so-called Washington consensus. Some writers refer to this globalization drive as the Wall Street–IMF–US Treasury complex.[1]

Within the neoliberal revival, two strands emerged. *Public choice theory* argued that government intervention encourages rent-seeking behavior by private firms and "moral hazard" risks in the form of cronyism and corruption. Free markets were the most efficient means by which resources should be allocated. Hence, governments should play a minimal role in economic life. The second dominant current, emanating from the World Bank, advocated *market-friendly* policies and argued that there is a role for government on the grounds of market failure. Government policies, however, should be "non-selective" and should be focused on the provision of public goods in terms of a social and physical infrastructure and an appropriate regulatory environment to encourage private investment. Neoclassical economists generally favored comprehensive change towards liberalization, an immediate "big bang," or "shock therapy" treatment.[2] However, these policies have failed to take into account the critical role performed by institutions in the determination of transaction costs (North, 1990). In other words, neoclassical theory is concerned primarily with the operation of markets, not with how markets develop. Markets are perceived as impersonal abstractions rather than complex institutions governed by a set of legal and political rules and regulations.

In the absence of countervailing modes of state regulation and governance, market fundamentalism will inevitably destroy social cohesion (Boyer, 1996, p. 108). The persistence of high levels of unemployment, more volatile financial panics and the emergence of semipermanent overcapacity have characterized the neoliberal era since the mid-1970s. Polanyi (1957) developed a powerful and radical critique by posing the question: can social life be governed exclusively by the abstract principles of supply and demand? Needless to say, his answer was in the negative: "The commodity description of labour, land and money is entirely fictitious. Nevertheless, it is with the help of this fiction that actual markets for labour, land and money are organised" (Polanyi, 1957, p. 72). Doubtless, the most visible legacy of the neoliberal counterrevolution has been the growing income inequalities, both between the rich and poor countries and within those countries themselves.

The centrifugal forces generated by the neoliberal strategy have also sharpened regional disparities. The spatial dimension of economic development has been characterized by a core/periphery configuration. One of the seminal theories of this process of uneven development was developed by Myrdal, who argued that capital movements tend to increase regional inequality by concentrating in the more developed regions (Myrdal, 1957). These are identified as the centrifugal, "spread effects":

> In the centers of expansion, increased demand will spur investment, which in turn will increase incomes and demand and cause a second round of investment and so on. Saving will increase as a result of higher incomes but will tend to lag behind investment in the sense that the supply of capital will steadily meet the brisk demand for it. (Myrdal, 1957, p. 28)

However, the opposite logic of cumulative causation is evident in the less-developed regions. These are identified as the "backwash effects" which merely reinforce the structural and socioeconomic disadvantages of these regions.

Capital will tend to migrate from the less profitable to the more profitable sectors and regions of a spatially defined economy. According to Emmanuel, if labor remains relatively immobile, wages in the more technically advanced sectors of the economy will be generally higher than those in the less-developed regions:

> Since equivalence in capitalist production relations signifies not the exchange of equal quantities of labour, but that of equal aggregates of factors (labour and the use of capital), non-equivalence (unequal exchange) can only signify the exchange of unequal aggregates of the same factors. (Emmanuel, 1972, p. 325)

Uneven development can thus be defined as a sectoral disparity between different branches of production, which exhibit differing capital/labor ratios. A dualism has evolved between the high wage, high productivity regions/countries, on the one hand, and the low wage, low productivity regions/countries, on the other hand.

A common theme throughout this study is that neoclassical theories of growth have attempted, unsuccessfully, to abolish the trade cycle. Orthodox neoclassical theories have assumed that the capitalist economy naturally gravitates toward a steady state of full employment equilibrium. Crises are merely transitory exogenous events, which momentarily disturb this equilibrium. Yet a cursory analysis of the recent historical evidence would suggest that in the capitalist economy, booms and slumps govern the growth trajectory. Say's law of the market implies the impossibility of general gluts. However, as soon as money is construed as a store of value, rather than a means of payments or as a "veil over barter," the whole logic of Say's law breaks down. This is particularly so with the development of credit institutions. Money is increasingly an endogenous function of private financial institutions. Credit tends to incessantly expand the limits of accumulation. With the issuing of bank money, credit supersedes the limits imposed by the level of savings. It follows that, under a finance-led regime of accumulation, crises become endemic. "Every crisis in the realisation of exchange-value assumes a global character and appears as a *financial crisis*. It affects financial circulation as a whole, but its epicentre is necessarily the banking system as the site where private credits are given liquidity" (Aglietta, 1979, pp. 336–7). This paradox is cogently summarized by Hilferding:

> The general possibility of a crisis arises from the dual existence of the commodity, as commodity and as money. This involves the possibility of an interruption in the process of commodity circulation if money is hoarded instead of being used to circulate commodities.... But as long as money functions only as a means of circulation, as long as commodities exchange directly for money and money directly for commodities, the hoarding of a sum of money need only be a single isolated occurrence which would make it impossible to sell some particular commodity, but would not involve a general slump in sales. The situation changes, however, when the function of money as a means of payment and commercial credit develop. A slump in sales now makes it impossible to meet previously contracted debts.... The chain of debtors resulting from the use of money as a means of payment is broken, and a slump at one point is transmitted to all others, so becoming general.... Only capitalist production generalises commodity production, allows all possible products to assume the commodity form, and finally – this is the crucial point – makes the sale of the commodity a precondition for the resumption of reproduction. (Hilferding, 1981, pp. 239–40)

Under the conditions of monopoly capital, there is an inherent tendency toward chronic stagnation. This study generally supports the Baran/Sweezy thesis that the central problem, which confronts the monopoly stage of capitalism, is the absorption of the economic surplus. The problem of effective demand becomes the ultimate barrier to the accumulation of capital and also implies the concomitant dilemma of the utilization and absorption of excess capacity. This phenomenon usually takes the form of a crisis of overaccumulation (Chapter 3). One of the great tragedies that accompanied the rise of neoliberalism over the past two decades has been the loss of historical memory and the deep insights offered by Keynes, Kalecki and their later adherents. It is as if economic theory has gone full circle. Say's law, the very cornerstone of orthodoxy's articles of faith, was reinstated 50 years after it had been demolished by Keynes's General Theory and discredited by the bitter experience of the Great Depression. More than ever, it is the innate failure of conventional, neoclassical theories to explain the alternating phases of growth and stagnation in economic life, which has provided the basic rationale for this study.

It will be argued that the prevailing neoclassical theories of growth fail to articulate the dynamics of innovation and technological change. Technology is still treated as a "black box," as though it were *in vacuo* and exogenous to the economic system as a whole. These theories lack a coherent explanation of endogenous technological change and are quite devoid of a systematic treatment of long-term structural change. The myth that the market economy will move toward a steady state of full employment equilibrium is not only pre-Keynesian but also entirely inappropriate on simple empirical grounds. In this study, it will be assumed that the market economy is inherently unstable and that *disequilibria* dominate its behavior.

Indeed, there is something quite perverse about the deductive methodology of modern economic theory in general. Neoclassical models are based upon a comparative static methodology and are essentially devoid of any sense of historical time and the very notion of *dynamics* (Keen, 2001). In this steady state world of equilibrium, linear production functions, characterized by perfect competition and perfect substitutability in the factors of production, constitute the means by which a supply-side theory of growth is articulated. The growth accounting method assumes constant returns to scale, elevates price effects over income effects, stresses substitution over complementarity and regards technical change and factor endowments as *exogenous*. By assuming the exogeneity of factor endowments and technical change, the theory abstracts from the most interesting and critical driving forces of the growth process itself. It can be surmised that neoclassical theories tell us very little about the stylized facts of the dynamics of growth. In order to account for these stylized facts, an alternative approach, informed by post-Keynesian theories of growth, will be developed (Chapter 2).

Post-Keynesian critiques have challenged the monetarist assumptions of an exogenous money supply and the doctrine of monetary neutrality in the long run. Post-Keynesian economists such as Minsky, Kaldor, Kalecki and others have argued that the money supply is endogenous and is governed by the demand for credit and by the Keynesian notion of liquidity preferences. These heterodox theories also reaffirm the original insights by Keynes over the critical issue of uncertainty in the behavior of investors and consumers, which contradict the assumptions of rational expectations. Minsky once remarked that Keynes without the notion of uncertainty was akin to Hamlet without the Prince. Unfortunately, public policy is still informed by ideas that have ceased to have much relevance in the real world. Translated into the political arena, moribund ideas are more difficult to overcome: "Practical men, who believe themselves exempt from any intellectual influences, are usually the slaves of some defunct economist. Madmen in authority, who hear voices in the air, are distilling their frenzy from some academic scribbler of a few years back" (Keynes, 1936, p. 293).

The dominant view in macroeconomic policy over the past two decades has been informed by the monetarist-inspired expectations-augmented Phillips curve. The emphasis has therefore shifted from the conventional postwar Keynesian policies of full employment to the macroeconomic objective of price stability. However, the imposition of restrictive monetary and fiscal policies in order to curtail inflation have led to historically high levels of unemployment and the underutilization of productive capacity. Indeed, the legacy of high levels of unemployment in order to achieve price stability can no longer be justified on both social and scientific grounds. A more recent critique by James Galbraith (1997) questions the empirical validity of the non-accelerating inflation rate of unemployment (NAIRU), which has become the cornerstone of modern macroeconomic theory.

> Friedman supplied no theory for a short-run Phillips curve, yet he affirmed that such a relation would "always" exist. And Friedman's argument depends on it. If the Phillips curve fails empirically – that is, if levels of unemployment do not in fact predict the rate of inflation in the short-run – then the construct of the natural rate of unemployment also loses meaning. (Galbraith, 1997, p. 94)

In his influential 1943 article on the political aspects of full employment, Kalecki argued that the "captains of industry" would oppose full employment policies because this would lead to a breakdown of discipline in the factories. The capitalist system demands that there always exist a "reserve army of labor" in order to contain wage rises and maintain discipline in the workforce even though this might inevitably lead to a fall in the level of effective demand (Kalecki, 1972). The Phillips curve can therefore be interpreted as a political struggle waged over the distribution of income between profits and wages. The objectives of price stability should also be viewed from the standpoint of the conflicting interests of debtors and creditors. High levels of inflation would benefit debtors at the expense of creditors and vice versa. The anti-inflationary policies favored by monetarists therefore benefit finance capital and rentiers at the expense of industrial capital. Such an outcome would doubtless evoke a sense of grave misgivings from those economists steeped in the Keynesian tradition of financial "repression" and Keynes's own declaration of the "euthanasia" of the rentier.

Perhaps the most contentious proposition that informs the NAIRU is the neoclassical assumption of a perfectly competitive labor market and the implication that involuntary unemployment does not exist (the so-called "natural" rate of unemployment). This theory is pre-Keynesian in that the supply and demand for labor cannot be modeled in terms of the real wage. A nominal wage cut will not restore equilibrium but will affect the level of effective demand. Furthermore, there is a close relationship between money wages and nominal wage increases. Therefore, workers are unable, as a general rule, to negotiate for their real wages. In the general Keynesian scheme, aggregate demand for output rather than the supply and demand for labor, will ultimately determine the level of employment. Nor is it empirically plausible to suggest that inflation is caused solely by wage rises. Indeed, most of the inflationary pressures over the past two decades have been caused by supply shocks such as the recurrent oil price rises. The other major source of inflation in the United States can be attributed to successive exchange rate depreciations, which have increased import prices. It can be argued that in recent years, the onset of deflation as a result of chronic excess capacity and stagnant effective demand has emerged as the real danger to growth and recovery in the global economy.[3] If the debt-deflation theory developed by Fisher (1933) and elaborated by Minsky (1982) is borne out by history, then the real problem over the next decade could prove to be deflation rather than inflation.

What does remain pertinent, however, is the extent to which the disinflationary policies pursued over the past two decades have contributed to the possible onset of debt deflation:

> A high rate of inflation during a crisis enables debts which were based on unrealistic expectations to be nonetheless validated, albeit over a

> longer period than planned and with far less real gain to investors. A low rate of inflation will mean that those debts cannot be met, with consequent "domino" effects even for investments which were not unrealistic. (Keen, 1993, p. 10)

In other words, will the monetary authorities – most of whom are still imbued with the ideology of monetarism – respond to the crisis by pursuing reflationary policies or will they continue to be obsessed by the inflationary demons? If we assume the latter, then the consequences could prove to be quite deleterious.

The broad outlines of this slump syndrome are already evident with the severe curtailment of effective demand in most OECD countries and the emergence of quite serious financial retrenchment after the end of the 1990s speculative financial boom in the United States. The ultimate economic consequences of this monetarist-inspired process of severe disinflation are rising unemployment and a decline in productive investment. As tax revenues shrink as a result of the slump, each government will be confronted by a fiscal crisis. Since the ability to resort to foreign borrowings has been constrained by the penalties imposed by deregulated financial markets, there has been an overwhelming trend toward public sector expenditure cutbacks and the privatization of public assets in order to balance the national budget over the economic cycle. Taken as a whole, these policies amount to a radical dismantling of the post-war system of regulation, a weakening of the "automatic stabilizers" performed by the state sector and the winding back of traditional Keynesian countercyclical policies.

The basic structure of the book is divided into two parts. In the first part, the general aim is to develop a theoretical framework to interpret the dynamics of growth and crisis under oligopolistic conditions. Chapter 1 will revisit some of the controversies that have informed Marxian economics over the dynamics of accumulation and crisis. This will provide a useful theoretical "compass" in the sense that these debates were quite seminal and continue to resonate in modern discourses. Chapters 2 and 3 develop an analysis of alternative theories of accumulation under the conditions of oligopoly. In the former, post-Keynesian theoretical renovations of circular and cumulative causation will be introduced as a critical alternative to the prevailing neoclassical theories of growth. In the latter, the stagnationist tendencies inherent under the conditions of oligopolistic competition and rivalry will be examined from a Kalecki, Steindl, and Baran/Sweezy perspective. Recent developments of the Fisher/Minsky dynamics of "debt deflation" embodied in the preeminence of a finance-led regime of accumulation are also introduced. Chapter 4 critically surveys long-run phases of capitalist accumulation and the Schumpetarian waves of "creative destruction" as possible countervailing forces to the inherent tendency toward stagnation.

In the second part of this study, the dynamics of stagnation and crisis will be analyzed from a more concrete historical standpoint. The final three chapters provide a historical contextualization of the most recent developments in the international capitalist economy from the mid-1970s to the onset of the East Asian financial meltdown in 1997–98. The breakdown of the postwar system of *Pax Americana* and the emergence of chronic stagnation in Europe and Japan will form the core narrative in the possible onset of a global crisis of overaccumulation. These chapters intend to highlight the inherent and systemic tendencies of the processes of globalization and interimperialist rivalries, which threaten to hasten a severe and prolonged phase of crisis over the next decade. Needless to say, the diagnosis does not lend itself to optimism. However, one of the great tragedies of the history of economic thought is that prevailing orthodoxies are only overthrown in the event of a major crisis. After all, it was the Great Depression of the 1930s which gave birth to the Keynesian revolution. We could soon witness a similar "great transformation" to borrow from Polanyi's powerful and seminal study.

Part I

A Theoretical Critique

1
Accumulation and Crisis: Marxian Controversies

Introduction

The controversies within Marxian economics over the causes of capitalist crises and the issue of effective demand provide a fertile terrain in the study of the dynamics of growth and crisis. Despite the different language and theoretical categories that inform Marxian economics, the issues and problems that the leading theorists had encountered still resonate with the modern concerns of mainstream economics since the publication of Keynes's *General Theory*. Indeed, it is quite astounding just how these controversies have withstood the test of time and continue to inform the contemporary discourse. The debates sparked by the publication of Rosa Luxemburg's *Accumulation of Capital*, appear to have prefigured the theoretical issues that had tempered the Keynesian revolution in modern economic thought.

Marxian economics views capitalist crises as inherent and necessary characteristics of the market economy. These crises take several forms: (1) the disproportionality between the different branches of production, (2) crises of the realization of surplus value into profit, which can act as a catalyst for a general financial panic, and (3) the tendency for the rate of profit to fall in the long run. The latter implies the eventual demise of capitalism. Since this prediction has failed to materialize, Marxian economics has lost much of its legitimacy. However, this does not mean that Marxian economics is irrelevant. It might simply mean that since the time of Marx, capitalism itself has been transformed. After all, it was the Keynesian revolution that ultimately rescued capitalism from crisis and collapse in the 1930s. Since the turn of last century, capitalism has evolved into its present monopoly stage of development, which signifies that the central problem that confronts the system is the "absorption" of a rising economic surplus, rather than a falling rate of profit (Baran & Sweezy, 1966).

In this chapter we will explore some of the controversies within Marxian economics over the dynamics of growth and crisis. Marx's original theory of the tendency for the rate of profit to fall will be critically examined as well as the schemes of reproduction in Volume 2 of *Capital*. The debates over the problem of markets, sparked by Rosa Luxemburg's *Accumulation of Capital*, will be revisited. Finally we will examine the later contributions of Baran and Sweezy to these perennial controversies.

1 The law of value revisited

Before we explore the laws of motion, which characterize the Marxian dynamics of growth and crisis, the natural point of departure involves no less than a revitalization of the Marxian theory of value. The law of value is based upon the appropriation of surplus value. The central problem for Marx was to develop a theory which explained the origins of surplus value. Under the conditions of generalized commodity production, Marx contends that surplus value is a function of labor power, which is performed above the socially necessary labor-time required to produce commodities and is appropriated by the owners of the means of production. Realized in its various historical forms as profit, rent, interest, dividends, etc., surplus value acquires a logic of its own and the incessant struggles waged over its distribution and appropriation constitute the very logic of class struggle.

Whereas simple commodity production is merely an idealized expression in which values exchange for their equivalents in terms of simple use values, generalized commodity production is based upon the realization of exchange value. Simple commodity production can be defined by the general formula C–M–C in which commodities (C) are both the starting point and end result of circulation. In stark contrast, generalized commodity production is the sine qua non of capitalism, which is characterized by the circuit M–C–M′ where money (M) undergoes a metamorphosis into capital (M′). In other words, surplus value is transformed into profit. The mediation of money acquires a seemingly independent power and presupposes a more advanced stage in the development of capitalism. Under the conditions of generalized commodity production, the process of exchange increasingly determines the *real* limits of production and enlarged reproduction. Use value constitutes a universal end of productive activity, independent of historical forms of social organization. Under capitalist relations, however, exchange value in order to realize surplus value, becomes the sole and compelling motive of production itself.

The incessant tensions and contradictions generated between the use value and exchange value of commodity production constitute the root causes of capitalist crises. A crisis occurs when there is a violent rupture between the use value and exchange value of generalized commodity production. The social character of production previously concealed beneath the "phenomenal" form of exchange value now comes to the forefront. Crises are therefore an inherent feature of the capitalist mode of production. Capitalist crises possess a dual character: on the one hand there emerge recurrent crises of overproduction and relative disproportion between the different branches of production, on the other hand there is always the possibility that these crises could assume the form of a generalized crisis of *realization*.

> The real barrier to capitalist production is capital itself. It is that capital and its self-expansion appear as the starting and closing points, the motive and the purpose of production, that production is only production for capital and not vice versa, the means of production are not mere means for a constant expansion of the living process of the society of producers ... The means – unconditional development of the productive forces of society – comes into conflict with the limited purpose, the self expansion of the existing capital. The capitalist mode of production is, for this reason, a historical means of developing the material forces of production and creating an appropriate world market and is, at the same time, a continual conflict between this its historical task and its own corresponding relations of social production. (Marx, 1978, Vol. 3, p. 250)

2 The tendency of the rate of profit to fall

In classical Marxian terminology, the general formula for capital is $c+v+s$, in which c denotes constant capital (means of production), v denotes variable capital (labor power) and s represents surplus value (unrealized profit). In this simple formula, the rate of surplus value can be calculated as a ratio to variable capital (s/v). The rate of profit, however, is expressed as the ratio of surplus value to total capital [$s/(c+v)$]. From this formula, Marx introduced the critical concept of the *organic composition of capital*. In other words, an increase in the constant component of capital relative to the variable component (c/v) induces a rise in the organic composition of capital. In Marx's own words:

> The composition of capital is to be understood in a two-fold sense. On the one side of value, it is determined by the proportion in which it is divided into constant capital or value of the means of production and living labour-power, the sum total of wages. On the side of the material, as it functions in the process of production, all capital is divided into means of production and living labour-power. This latter composition is determined by the relation between the mass of the means of production employed, on the one hand, and the mass of labour necessary for their employment, on the other. I call the former the *value composition*, the latter the *technical composition* of capital. Between the two there is a strict correlation. To express this, I call the value composition of capital, in so far as it is determined by its technical composition and mirrors the changes of the latter, the *organic composition of capital*. (Marx, 1978, Vol. 1, p. 574)

Accordingly, Marx highlights the crucial distinction between *absolute* and *relative* rates of surplus value. The former can be defined as an increase in the intensity of exploitation in terms of increasing the working hours or an increase in the physical tempo of the labor process. The latter implies a rise in the technical composition of capital as machines and technology are introduced in order to improve labor productivity. Compelled by competitive forces, capitalists can increase profitability by substituting capital for labor. Hence, technical progress in the Marxian schema is always labor-saving.

A rise in the organic composition of capital will induce a fall in the average rate of profit. It is precisely this *tendency* of a falling rate of profit, which forms the theoretical basis of the Marxian theory of crisis and has fuelled controversy since the publication of *Capital*. Every growth cycle, or phase of capital accumulation, carries with it the *possibility* of crisis. In this context, the fall in the rate of profit will be determined by a rising capital/labor ratio in relation to a specific profit/wages ratio. In order to prevent a decline in the rate of surplus value, capital would need to either (a) increase the absolute rate of exploitation, or (b) increase investment in the means of production by improving labor productivity. If we assume a constant rate of surplus value, then a rise in the organic composition of capital induces a fall in the average rate of profit insofar as it is only the variable component of capital that yields surplus value, whereas profit is measured in terms of total capital.

In the long run, a rise in the technical composition of capital inevitably reduces the value composition of capital. Expressed in its mathematical formula, the falling rate of profit, r, can be calculated as $r = e/(d + 1)$, where e is the rate of exploitation and d is the social organic composition of capital. In the process of capital accumulation, d will inevitably rise as c expands in proportion to v. Although the organic composition of capital rises, the rate of profit falls as a result of a rise in the capital/output ratio: "This continual relative decrease of the variable capital vis-à-vis the constant, and consequently the total capital, is identical with the progressively higher organic composition of the social capital in its average" (Marx, 1978, Vol. 3, p. 212).

The latent tendency for the rate of profit to fall will only manifest itself if it is not counteracted by a corresponding expansion in the rate of surplus value. These countervailing forces operate as the threshold historical conditions in the process of capital accumulation. In Volume 3 of *Capital*, Marx identifies six countervailing tendencies:

1. *Cheapening the elements of constant capital*: An increase in the organic composition of capital may lower the value of constant capital thereby offsetting the tendency for the rate of profit to fall.

   > In short, the same development which increases the mass of the constant capital in relation to the variable reduces the value of its elements as a result of the increased productivity of labour, and therefore prevents the value of constant capital, although it continually increases, from increasing at the rate as its material volume, i.e. the material volume of the means of production set in motion by the same amount of labour power. In isolated cases the mass of the elements of constant capital may even increase, while its value remains the same, or falls. (Marx, 1978, Vol. 3, p. 236)

2. *Increasing the intensity of exploitation*: This can be achieved either through the prolongation of the working day or by reducing wages through the mechanism of the reserve army of unemployed labor. Increasing the intensity of the labor process can also accelerate the rate of absolute surplus value.
3. *Relative overpopulation*: The strategic mechanism, which arises from relative overpopulation, is the reserve army of labor. The ebbs and flows of capital accumulation during the early stages of industrialization are conditioned by the reserve army of labor, which regulates the level of wages and its proportion in relation to profits. Indeed, the Marxian schema is similar to the type of predator–prey model developed by Goodwin (1982). A large pool of unemployed or the existence of a large rural population will act as a means of dampening wages in the industrial sector.[1]

4. *Foreign trade*: During the colonial era, raw materials were acquired more cheaply from the colonial regions by exploiting a relatively inexpensive and abundant labor force, which cheapened the elements of constant capital. Colonialism and foreign trade therefore acted as an outlet, which counteracted the tendency toward a falling profitability in the metropolitan centers.
5. *An increase in the stock of capital*: This is especially relevant under the conditions of monopolistic competition in which the degree of the concentration and centralization of capital allows the mobilization of large reserves of capital and the emergence of economies of scale and scope, which increases the mass of surplus value. In other words, the law of increasing returns is set in motion.[2]
6. *The depression of wages below the value of labor power*: This category can be included in that of raising the intensity of exploitation.

The dynamics of capital accumulation cannot be depicted in the neoclassical sense as a prosaic, linear movement toward a steady state of full employment equilibrium. To the contrary, its volatile, cyclical motion can more accurately characterize the process of accumulation. Marx was the first classical economist to emphasize these cyclical dynamics. At a given moment in the business cycle, a crisis of overproduction is hastened and has its immediate origins in the investment cycle. The volume of investment becomes too large in relation to a falling profitability. Whereas Keynes captured this tendency in the short run, referring to it as the falling marginal efficiency of capital, Marx grasped the long-run tendencies of a falling rate of profit. A falling rate of profit will sharpen the competition between individual capitalists, especially in those sectors of the economy experiencing a severe overproduction crisis. "The antagonism between each individual capitalist and the capitalist class as a whole, then comes to the surface, just as previously the identity of their interests operated in practice through competition" (Marx, 1978, Vol. 3, p. 253).

A paradox emerges during a cyclical slump: either the rate of return of investment cannot realize expected future profits, or it is not sufficient to overcome the problem of the lack of effective demand. It follows that "crises are always but momentary and forcible solutions of the existing contradictions. They are violent eruptions which for a time restore the disturbed equilibrium" (Marx, 1978, Vol. 3, p. 249). The supreme paradox of this recurrent state of irrationalism manifests itself when the private ownership of the means of production comes into conflict with the existing social relations of production. "Centralisation of the means of production and socialisation of labour at last reach a point where they become incompatible with their capitalist integument. This integument is burst asunder. The knell of capitalist private property sounds. The expropriators are expropriated" (Marx, 1978, Vol. 1, p. 715). If the revolution is not consummated and capitalist relations are restored once again, then the problem of the expanded reproduction of the system is encountered. "Now however the question is where will the workers and capitalists obtain their articles of consumption and the capitalists obtain their means of production, how will the finished product meet all of these demands and enable production to expand?" (Lenin, 1967, p. 52). As long as the rate of exploitation can be intensified either absolutely or relatively, the process of capital accumulation will continue on an expanded scale.

The movement of capital from one sphere of production, which has experienced a falling rate of profit to other branches of production with a relatively higher rate of profit, creates the tendency for the equalization of profit in the economy as a whole. Competition is the driving force behind this tendency. In this sense, the concept of the "prices of production" constitutes the empirical foundation of the theory of value. From a strictly logical standpoint, the average rate of profit is derived from surplus value in which values are transformed into "prices of production." Beyond this ceaseless fluctuation of prices and insofar as surplus value is transformed into profit, the general law of value asserts itself as a complicated and approximate average of the sum total of existing values.

> What competition does not show, however, is the determination of value, which dominates the movement of production; and the values that lie beneath the prices of production and that determine them in the last instance. Competition, on the other hand shows:
> 1. The average profits, which are independent of the organic composition of capital in the different spheres of production and therefore also of the mass of living labour appropriated by any given capital in any sphere of exploitation;
> 2. The rise and fall of prices of production caused by changes in the level of wages, a phenomenon which at first glance completely contradicts the value relation of commodities;
> 3. The fluctuations of market-prices, which reduce the average market-price of commodities in any given period of time, not the *market-value*, but to a very different market price of production, which diverges considerably from this market-value. All these phenomena seem to contradict the determination of value by labour-time as much as the nature of surplus value consisting of unpaid surplus

labour. *Thus everything appears reversed in competition.* [italics added] (Marx, 1978, Vol. 3, p. 209)

The law of value thus acts as the center of gravity insofar as it mediates an equilibrium between the distributions of labor within different branches of production. This can be defined as the *magnitude* of value, which functions as a regulatory mechanism in the distribution of labor between different organic compositions of capital. Marx refers to this aspect as the *quantitative* dimension of value. Conversely, from a purely *qualitative* standpoint, the law of value exhibits a social relation between wages and profits, or between capital and labor. In other words, it reflects the productive intercourse between people rather than between things or objects, as the classical economists were habitually prone to fall into.

Consequently, the law of value inherits a twofold nature: the quantitative aspect concerned primarily with the *magnitude* of value, on the one hand, and the qualitative form defined as a social relation, on the other hand. This fundamental distinction is based upon the commodity fetishism characteristic of capitalist relations, which is viewed in orthodox economics entirely from the standpoint of exchange value rather than from the use value of commodity production. Concrete and abstract labor correspond respectively to this twofold movement of value and its transformation into the prices of production.

Without the incessant turnover of capital investment, existing plant and equipment would be rendered obsolete. However, in order to increase the rate of surplus value in a relative magnitude, necessarily implies the progressive socialization of production through mechanization and economies of scale. Capitalists are compelled to transform a portion of realized surplus value into constant capital, which is divided into fixed and circulating capital so that the cycle is repeated. "The periodical depreciation of existing capital – one of the means immanent in capitalist production to check the fall of the rate of profit and hasten accumulation of capital value through formation of new capital – disturbs the given conditions within which the process of circulation and reproduction of capital takes place, and is therefore accompanied by sudden stoppages and crises in the production process" (Marx, 1978, Vol. 3, p. 249). On the one hand, a recovery of investment spending carries with it a reaction in the form of a crisis of overproduction, which could hasten a prolonged slump. A prolonged slump as it swells the ranks of the unemployed, however, acts as a catalyst in the restoration of the rate of profit insofar as wages fall and investment in new plant and equipment is curtailed. In the final analysis, overproduction appears at the very moment of the cycle when the gulf between the creation of surplus value and its realization widens. The emergence of a generalized glut and excess capacity signifies the saturation of existing markets and the exhaustion of future, potential investment outlets. "A crisis appears as a catharsis as well as retribution: as a sole mechanism by which, in this economy, equilibrium can be restored, once it has been extensively broken" (Dobb, 1973, p. 103).

It can be surmised that an increase in the technical composition of capital (technological progress, economies of scale, labor-saving techniques, etc.) will increase the ratio of constant capital relative to variable capital and induce a fall in the general rate of profit. From a historical perspective, however, the evidence suggests that this tendency has not asserted itself. In an authoritative but neglected study, Gillman (1957) concludes that a rapid increase in the organic composition of capital did actually occur from the second half of the nineteenth century until the First World War. This period was characterized by the transformation of small-scale industry into large-scale mechanization of industry and the rapid migration of the workforce from traditional agriculture to industry. These years before the outbreak of the First World War, had experienced a growing prosperity; the ostensible "golden era" of burgeoning Victorian affluence. However, the system of laissez faire also bred vicious and often violent slumps and recurrent crises. As the organic composition of capital steadily rose, a falling rate of profit, most notably during the 1890s depression, began to assert itself, which led to two profound developments. On the one hand, the increased concentration of capital prefigured the rise of monopoly capital. On the other hand, the increased centralization of capital hastened the rise of finance capital, which would soon occupy the commanding heights of the economy (Hilferding, 1981). Gillman sums up the general conclusions from these empirical observations: "While Marx's law of the falling rate of profit applies to capitalism in its stages of rapid development and mechanization, it gradually ceases to apply and asserts itself but feebly as industry becomes fully developed and fully mechanized" (Gillman, 1957, p. 59).

Indeed, it would seem to be counterintuitive to suggest that a relative rise in constant capital would lead to a fall in the rate of profit. Marx's original theory appears to be informed by the Ricardian law of diminishing returns. From a historical standpoint, however, the law of increasing returns has been set in motion with the introduction of new technologies and techniques, the emergence of large-scale production and the evolution of oligopolistic competition as the dominant modes of capitalist accumulation. Consequently, under monopoly capital, there has been an increase in aggregate profits. The problem is therefore one of effective demand: how does the system dispose of the increasing surplus value? The issue of markets and the *realization* of surplus value becomes the central problem that confronts the monopoly stage of capitalism. This theoretical issue informed Rosa Luxemburg's critique in the *Accumulation of Capital* early last century and remains one of the most insightful and controversial contributions to the debates within Marxian economics.

3 Simple and expanded reproduction

In Volume 2 of *Capital*, Marx develops a complex two-sector model in the exchange relations between the consumer goods sector and the capital goods sector. The causes of capitalist crises are attributed to the problem of the disproportionality between the two main sectors of the economy. In the case of simple reproduction in which the social surplus is consumed, total social product is equivalent to:

Department 1: $c + v + s$
Department 2: $c + v + s$

If we express values in the two departments of production, total social product would be:

1: $4000c + 1000v + 1000s = 6000$
2: $2000c + 500v + 500s = 3000$
$= 9000$ total social product

In department 1, the 1000v and 1000s are produced as means of production but also represent the wages of the workers and the consumption of the capitalist class. In order to obtain the means of production in department 2, there must be an equivalent exchange with the 1000v and the 1000s in department 1 (workers' and capitalists' means of consumption). This means that department 1 exchanges 1000v + 1000s for 2000c in department 2. Capitalists and workers in their respective departments consume the rest. The 4000c in department 1 is consumed productively and reconstituted as constant capital, while the workers and capitalists of that department consume the 500v and 500s in department 2. Hence the equilibrium condition under simple reproduction is[3]

$$C2 = V1 + S1$$

where C2 is the constant capital produced in the consumption goods sector (department 2), V1 denotes variable capital and S1 represents surplus value in the capital goods sector (department 1) respectively. In this closed system, the possibility of crisis cannot occur because the entire surplus is consumed and all markets are assumed to clear. Simple reproduction embodies an abstraction, or the ideal conditions necessary for the reproduction of the means of production and means of consumption. If population increases, economic growth must be capable of producing value in direct proportion in order to achieve the conditions of steady state. Any social surplus that is generated will be directly absorbed into mainstream social consumption.

> Simple reproduction on the same scale appears as an abstraction inasmuch as on the one hand, the absence of all accumulation or reproduction on an extended scale is a strange assumption in capitalist conditions, and on the other hand, conditions of production do not remain exactly the same in different years (and this is assumed). (Marx, 1978, Vol. 2, pp. 398–9)

Expanded reproduction, on the other hand, is a dynamic process by which investment expands production and drives the process of capital accumulation. Using Marx's own schemes, Appendix 1A provides a more detailed exposition of the process of expanded reproduction. Marx poses the problem of how the capitalists in the consumption goods sector can dispose of their commodities. If the circuit of productive capital ceases to realize surplus value into profit, the expanded reproduction of capital will be interrupted and trigger a generalized crisis. However, the crisis is not necessarily caused by a lack of effective demand because the exchange between the two main departments of production also reveals the distribution of income between workers and capitalists. Accumulation could proceed without a rupture in the sphere of exchange as long as consumption constitutes the sole motive of production. Yet this case would correspond to simple commodity production for use values. The critical rationale of capitalist production, however, is the realization of surplus value into money capital, that is to say, the maximization of profit rather than the fulfillment of social needs. In Marx's own words:

> The problem that confronts us directly is this: how is the capital consumed in production replaced in value out of the annual product and how does the movement of this replacement entwine with the consumption of the surplus-value by the capitalists and of the wages by the labourers? (Marx, 1978, Vol. 2, p. 397)

The object of Marx's reproduction schemes is to analyze the process of accumulation inasmuch as the expansion of department 1 creates the real limits to capital accumulation in department 2. Having established this condition, department 1 is seen as the driving force in the dynamics of expanded reproduction. If, however, department 1 expands production, the problem of realization could be encountered. Since capitalism is founded upon the appropriation of surplus value, its continued reproduction involves the progressive capitalization of its accumulated surplus value. Quite apart from the portion of surplus value that is consumed unproductively by the capitalist class, a proportion must be capitalized and reinvested in the means of production in order to increase output.

> According to Marx, accumulation is possible, realisation is possible, expanded reproduction is possible. However these processes do not run smoothly, but complete themselves in contradictions, both those that reveal themselves in the permanent variations of the capitalist system, and the others, which express themselves in violent convulsions. In the final analysis, the process of capitalist reproduction itself represents an expanded reproduction of capitalist contradictions. (Bukharin, in Tarbuck, 1972, p. 203)

4 The problem of effective demand

Rosa Luxemburg argues that Marx's reproduction schemes constitute a closed system and as soon as some of the restrictive assumptions are removed, the problem of the realization of a growing surplus of production in department 2 is encountered. This is necessarily the case if one assumes a rise in the organic composition of capital induced by technical change. Luxemburg therefore argues that the system is dependent upon a *third market* to absorb the social surplus. She identifies this third department as the noncapitalist sector. In other words the problem of effective demand occupies the center stage. Marx's model merely reinstates Say's law in which supply is assumed to create its own demand.

> So the surplus product of department 1 and 2 must be bought – by whom? On the above showing, there will have to be an "effective demand" outside 1 and 2, merely in order to realize the surplus value of the two departments, just so that the surplus product can be turned into cash. Even then, we should only have got to the stage where the surplus value is further to be employed in the process of enlarging reproduction, in accumulation, and even larger demand

> must be expected in the future, a demand which is again to come from outside the two departments. Either the demand for the surplus product will therefore have to increase annually in accordance with the rate of increase of accumulated surplus value or – vice versa – accumulation can only proceed in so far as the demand outside 1 and 2 is rising. (Luxemburg, 1971, pp. 137–8)

When one views the entire process of accumulation from the standpoint of the numerous individual capitalists in both departments, it becomes evident that if capitalist A from department 1 converts his surplus value into money capital, capitalist B in department 2 is deprived of the ability to reconvert constant capital into productive capital. Consequently we would expect a deficit in the process of reproduction as a whole. Under simple reproduction, the formation of surplus money capital in the hands of capitalist A in department 1 will represent an "underconsumption," or a deficit in the hands of capitalist B in department 2. It therefore seems that from the premise of simple reproduction, permanent underconsumption tends to dominate its movement. This logic leads Luxemburg to argue that the problem of enlarged reproduction, viewed as a closed system, cannot provide a solution for the additional source of money capital required for accumulation. Marx attempts to resolve this dilemma by assuming that the production of gold occurs in department 1 and provides the additional money capital for the purposes of either hoarding (saving) or investment. Gold embodies both the universal equivalent of exchange value and also takes the form of a commodity as it enters into the process of circulation. Yet Luxemburg remains unconvinced and contends that the solution cannot be found in the additional source of money capital but should be found in the sphere of effective demand. Effective demand, in turn, implies the problem of realization. Luxemburg argues that the problem, which had eluded Marx's efforts to discover the source of that additional money required for expanded reproduction, was the fact that the reproduction schemes form a closed system. The solution lies outside the two main departments.

> Once accumulation has been established for some time, when increasing amounts of value are thrown upon the market in every period of production, buyers of these additional values cannot fail to become a problem. And on this point the preferred solution breaks down. For that matter, it was never more than a seeming solution; *not a real one*. On closer scrutiny, it fails us even at the precise instant that it appears to have smoothed the way for us. For if we take accumulation just at

> the very moment of its emergence from simple reproduction, the prime condition it demands is a decrease in the consumption of the capitalist class. No sooner have we discovered a way to expand reproduction with the means of circulation already at hand, than we find previous consumers trickling away at the same rate. [italics added] (Luxemburg, 1971, p. 146)

However, Luxemburg is incorrect when she assumes that consumption alone mediates production. Her assumptions appear to be based on the schema for simple reproduction. The simple fact remains that capitalism does not produce for the sake of satisfying social needs (i.e. use value), nor is this its compelling motive. Its primary motive from the standpoint of the individual capitalist is the production of surplus value in order to realize profits. The problem of effective demand can be resolved on the basis that expanded reproduction calls forth additional workers and the concomitant increase in additional wages, which increases the level of effective demand. In this sense, there is a fallacy of composition: what is rational and optimal for the individual capitalist (i.e. the expansion of output) may not be socially optimal in terms of effective demand. Hence, there emerges the problem of relative over-production. Money only serves as a means of exchange, or as a "veil over barter" between the two main departments of production. Consequently the problem resides at the very core of the theory of value, namely, the paradox between use value and exchange value. The function of gold can be grasped from this dual character.

> The division of the pure commodity function of gold from its money function finds its main and fundamental expression in the fact that the product of the gold-mining industry appears on the one hand as a raw material for industrial ends, on the other hand, is converted into money and functions in the quite specific form of a general commodity equivalent. (Bukharin in Tarbuck, 1972, p. 184)

An important objection to Luxemburg's three-sector model is that it assumes a constant rate of investment. In reality, this is far from the truth as the unpredictable fluctuations of the business cycle demonstrate. Moreover, according to Sweezy (1946), it is not possible to sell to noncapitalist consumers without also having to buy from them. Capitalist expansion into these precapitalist regions cannot be sustained until the historical conditions for the rise of generalized commodity production have come into being. Otherwise the circuit M–C–M′ ceases to function. The logical conclusion of Luxemburg's position is that capitalism will inevitably collapse as soon as these noncapitalist markets are exhausted. In other words, a "breakdown" tendency is inherent from the moment that a world capitalist market is more fully developed and capitalism encounters a *permanent* crisis. Indeed, the conception of a third market as the "engine" of capital accumulation, appears to contradict the law of value itself. Surplus labor power ceases to be the source of surplus value.

Let us reconsider the premises from where the Marxian schemes of reproduction acquire their theoretical content, quite apart from their historical form of development. Marx assumes that there are two conditions required for accumulation on an enlarged scale (Vol. 2, Ch. 11). First, the volume of capital must be sufficient under the given technical conditions either to expand constant capital or to accumulate for the purpose of hoarding (saving), until favorable conditions for investment appear. Second, production merely for the sake of reproduction (i.e. recapitalization), has its immediate origins in past accumulation and is not simply the moment of transition from simple to enlarged reproduction: "The money on the one side then calls forth extended reproduction on the other because the possibility of it exists *without* money. For money in itself is not an element of real reproduction" (Marx, 1978, Vol. 2, p. 494). Hence, the aim of expanded reproduction is not the expansion of money capital, as Luxemburg assumes, but the increase in real output. Yet money assumes a latent form of potential money capital as it enters into the circuit of productive capital. This is precisely the unique condition that differentiates the capitalist mode of production from other economic systems and therefore carries with it the possibility of realization crises: "Conditions which change into so many conditions of abnormal movement, into so many possibilities of crises since a balance is itself an accident, accruing to the spontaneous nature of this production" (Marx, 1978, Vol. 2, p. 499).

Kalecki (1990a) provides a succinct solution to the problem of effective demand posed by Luxemburg. The problem is not so much the existence of a "third market" but is the result of excess capacity induced by a fall in the rate of investment. Kalecki assumes that the rate of accumulation (i.e. net investment) is 4 percent per annum and that the means of production and labor are fully utilized. Depreciation is 3 percent per annum (i.e. gross investment is 7 percent); there is a constant share of gross profits (including depreciation) in the national product and constant ratios in the distribution of capitalist consumption and gross investment. It follows that given the constant share of gross accumulation in the national product, income (wages and capitalist consumption) would increase by the equivalent rate of 4 percent. Under the conditions of full capacity utilization, the problem of effective demand would cease to exist.

Accumulation therefore proceeds on the basis of past expectations of profits and returns to investment. However, if these conditions change (i.e. an exogenous shock, a shift in future expectations), and the rate of gross investment declines to only 6 percent, the problem of effective demand will manifest itself. In other words, the ratio of investment to the stock of capital falls by one-seventh (14 percent). If the proportion of capital invested to that consumed by capitalists remains constant, the fall in investment will curtail the demand for wage goods and thus workers' aggregate income by a corresponding 14 percent. The multiplier effect of a fall in effective demand will further induce a decline in investment and income. It can be surmised that expanded reproduction assumes full employment equilibrium but as Keynes highlighted in the *General Theory*, this is not the natural state of the capitalist system. The irony is that Luxemburg was one of the first theorists to identify the problem of effective demand but was misguided in that expanded reproduction is not necessarily driven by the search for "external" markets in the noncapitalist sector.

Baran and Sweezy (1966) developed a novel argument in terms of the problem of effective demand. In the absence of price competition under the conditions of oligopolistic rivalry, there is a tendency for the social surplus to increase. In stark contrast to Luxemburg, the main problem confronting monopoly capital is not so much the realization of surplus value but the disposal or the "absorption" of the economic surplus. The surplus is defined as: "The difference between what a society produces and the costs of producing it" (Baran & Sweezy, 1966, p. 9).

> For monopoly capital generates not only profits, rent and interest as elements of the economic surplus, but conceals an important share of surplus under the rubric of costs. This is due to the ever-widening gap between productivity of the *necessary productive workers* and the share of the national income accruing to them as wages. (Baran & Sweezy, 1966, pp. xix–xx)

The mechanism by which this growing surplus is absorbed includes armaments spending, the "sales effort" (e.g. advertising, marketing) and other elements of "wasteful" state expenditure. Hence, quite contrary to the neoclassical myth of Pareto optimality in the efficient allocation of resources, monopoly capital resembles the mercantilist era of trade monopolies. When viewed from the standpoint of the growing social surplus devoted to unproductive consumption, the parallels are indeed striking. To be sure, far from the rate of profit falling as the original Marxian orthodoxy had envisaged, monopoly capital encounters a *rising* economic surplus. In order to counteract the inherent tendencies toward stagnation, the system requires outlets for the absorption of the economic surplus.

The lack of effective demand is therefore a problem of rising labor productivity spurred by technical innovations, which set in motion the law of increasing returns and a rising social surplus. Yet, at the same time, the wellsprings of growth do not necessarily flow into higher wages. The investment of oligopolistic capital will depend on the level of effective demand, which determines the degree of utilization of their productive capacity and on their level of profits. As soon as the state of full capacity utilization is reached, the main problem that confronts the process of capital accumulation is the lack of effective demand. Despite the methodological problems involved with the articulation of the problem of "surplus absorption," the insights offered by Baran and Sweezy appear to coincide with the development of the monopoly stage of capitalism. The original Marxian doctrine of a falling rate of profit under the conditions of a competitive capitalism and a rising organic composition of capital ceases to have any real empirical validity.

Conclusion

In stark contrast to the prevailing neoclassical treatment of the dynamics of growth and crisis, Marxian economics offers very important insights into the workings of the capitalist economy. Indeed, the critical issue of recurrent crises is completely ignored in conventional neoclassical theories of growth. In the idealized world of general equilibrium, these recurrent crises are either impossible if one assumes Say's law, or are the product of anomalous "exogenous shocks." Marxian economics, by contrast, suggests that these crises are endemic and are a natural consequence of the inherent anarchy of the market. The Marxian framework continues to provide invaluable contributions to our understanding of the dynamics of growth and crisis. To be sure, growth and crisis are simply opposite moments in the dialectical movement of capital as a whole. As long as the market continues to govern economic life, these crises will continue to reappear. The real problem, however, is to develop a coherent theory that can explain the causes and distinguish the various historical forms that these crises tend to assume.

Appendix 1A Expanded reproduction

Using Marx's original schemes of expanded reproduction in Volume 2 of *Capital*, we can derive the following values:

1: $5000c + 1000v + 1000s$
2: $1430c + 285v + 285s$ = total social product of 9000

It is assumed that the ratio of variable capital to constant capital is constant at 1 : 5 and that there is no technical progress. It is also assumed that capitalists reinvest 50 percent of their surplus value and consume the other 50 percent. After the first round of accumulation, total capital set in motion is:

1: $5000c + 1000v$
2: $1430c + 255v$ = 7715

If we assume a rate of surplus value of 100 percent, then total social product is:

1: $5000c + 1000v + 1000s$
2: $1430c + 285v + 285s$ = 9000

If capitalists in department 1 reinvest 50 percent of their surplus value (500*s*), the other 1500 in department 1 (worker and capitalist consumption) must be exchanged for consumption goods in department 2. Hence, the total social product is:

1: $5000c + 1000v + 500s$
2: $1430c + 285v + 285s$ = 8500 (500*s* is capitalized)

However, for the equilibrium condition $2c = 1v + 1s$ to be fulfilled, 70*s* of department 2 must be transformed in order to set in motion the accumulation of capital in department 2:

2: $(1430c + 70s) + 285v + 215s$

In order to generate 70*s* as constant capital, a variable capital of 14 is required (i.e. the ratio of *c* to *v* is 5 : 1) from 1:

2: $(1500c + s) + (285v + 14s) + 201s$
Or 2: $(1500c + s) + 299v + 201s$

When the capitalists in department 1 reinvest their 500*s* at a ratio of 5 : 1, we have the following:

1: $(5000c + 417c) + (1500v + s + 83v)$
2: $(5000c + s) + 299v + 201s$

However, the equilibrium $1v + 1s = 2c$ is not satisfied and an additional 83 is deducted from the surplus value in department 2 to enable v and s of department 1 to be exchanged for consumption goods:

1: $5417c + 1583v + s$
2: $1583c + 299v + 118s$

Once again, a proportion (5 : 1) of v is set in motion, which equals 17 and is deducted from $2s$:

1: $5417c + 1583v + s$
2: $1583c + 316v + 101s$

The final round represents an expanded reproduction of capital:

1: $5417c + 1083v = 6500$
2: $1583c + 316v = 1899$ $\quad = 8399$ capital value

500s is consumed unproductively in department 1 and 101 (2000 − 1899) is consumed unproductively in department 2. Consequently, the cycle began with 7715 capital values and ended with an increased 8399. Expanded reproduction has therefore increased the total capital value by 684.

2
Circular and Cumulative Causation

Introduction

Recent debates, which have informed modern growth theories, have centered on the issue of technical progress. In the original Solow/Swan model, most of the growth was attributable to exogenous technical change, or the so-called Solow residual. As a result, neoclassical growth theories were based on a model in which the greater part of the sources of growth occurred "outside" the model. Technology was analogous to a black box. The problem for the new growth theorists was to endogenize technical progress. However, the basic analytical framework remained essentially neoclassical. In other words, the growth process continued to be a peculiarity of the neoclassical production function with all of its special and restrictive assumptions. Neoclassical and general equilibrium models have been subjected to quite rigorous critiques by post-Keynesian theories. The general rationale for these critiques is that the heuristic assumptions, which inform neoclassical theories of growth, are designated to be entirely unrealistic. In order to account for the "stylized facts," post-Keynesian approaches emphasize the law of increasing returns, endogenous technical change and the role performed by effective demand as the major sources of long-run, sustainable growth. A more dynamic theory of circular and cumulative causation informs these critiques.

1 Neoclassical and the "new" endogenous growth theories

In the standard Solow/Swan model, the aggregate production function is represented by the equation

$$Y = A\,e^{ut}K^{\alpha}N^{1-\alpha} \tag{2.1}$$

where Y is gross domestic product, K is the stock of physical capital, N is unskilled labor, A is the constant that reflects the base level of technology, and e^u denotes the constant exogenous rate at which technology grows over time (t). Thus α represents the elasticity of output in relation to capital (the percentage increase in GDP resulting from a 1 percent increase in physical capital). Growth is basically a function of capital accumulation. The model therefore assumes *diminishing returns* to labor and capital. Consequently, any increases in aggregate output that cannot be attributed to endogenous factors are ascribed to the *Solow residual*, which represents more than 50 percent of recorded growth rates in the industrial countries (Solow, 1956). In other words, most of the growth is attributed to *exogenous* factors. The amount of inputs (labor, capital, raw materials, etc.) required to produce a given output depends on technology and this will be reflected in the form of the function. For instance it may be linear or nonlinear. A linear function reflects *constant returns to scale* and thus no real technical innovation. *Diminishing returns to scale* would reflect the rundown of capital stocks and *increasing returns to scale* would exhibit the investment of new plant and equipment, which embodies technical innovation.[1]

Empirical estimates of growth in the US economy during the period 1909–49 by Robert Solow (1957), found that over 80 percent of the growth in output per labor hour over that period was attributed to technical progress. Using the growth accounting method similar to equation (2.1), Solow estimated that in the same period, the average annual growth of total GDP in the United States was 2.9 percent. Decomposing the 2.9 percent annual growth rate, Solow estimated that 0.32 percent was due to capital accumulation, 1.09 percent was attributable to increases in labor inputs and the remaining 1.49 percent was the result of technical progress. Consequently more than 50 percent of multifactor productivity could be attributed to technical progress.

Equilibrium models assume that the system tends to gravitate toward full employment equilibrium in the long run. It would be plausible to suggest that equilibrium models have acquired the status of an immutable law, analogous to the law of gravity in the study of physics before the discovery of relativity.[2] It follows from this logic that public policy which attempts to stimulate growth by increasing investment or the level of domestic savings will, in the long run, encounter diminishing returns and be unable to influence the long-run rate of growth. Indeed, it is argued that such policy interventions will have "level" effects but not "growth" effects (Romer, 1986). Long-run economic growth can be augmented to these models but the factors that influence secular growth are viewed as essentially *exogenous*. The basic problem for new growth theories then is to identify an endogenous source of long-run growth.

In order to account for long-term growth, new growth theories assume the law of *increasing returns*. Rather than a static equilibrium model based on perfect competition and constant returns to scale, a more dynamic long-run theory informed by increasing returns to capital is proposed. If returns to deferred consumption are sufficiently high and cease to diminish, then there might be enough incentive for high rates of saving, which it is assumed, could generate continual growth.[3] The focus of analysis therefore shifts to factors such as returns to physical investment in education and R&D expenditure as the crucial variables that generate long-term increasing returns.

According to one of the leading proponents of recent endogenous growth theories, technical and scientific knowledge can be designated as a public good which induces a cumulative spillover effect in the economy as a whole (Romer, 1986, 1994). Even though knowledge can be viewed as a commodity and appropriated through a regime of intellectual property rights and patents, every blueprint increases the common stock of knowledge. These incremental, cumulative changes in the stock of knowledge constitute an input to the accumulation of capital and the long-term rate of economic growth. The new focus becomes the issue of identifying the potential of increasing returns through innovation. The engine of long-term growth is therefore governed by the accumulation of human capital, which generates a cumulative increase in the level of productivity. In this critical sense, human capital should be viewed as a *public good* that contributes to an increase in social returns over and above those appropriated by private investment. In the long run, the process can be regarded as being *endogenous* rather than arising from a technological "black box."

There is also overwhelming evidence of the strategic importance of investment in core, nonmilitary infrastructure. These forms of investment contribute to long-term economic growth by increasing the returns to private capital formation. As a result, the gains from policy intervention are potentially much greater than those gains identified by static analysis of market failure and externalities. The basic contention of the new growth theories is that private returns to innovation and investment in physical and human capital is, as a general rule, less than the social returns. Market failures and the underinvestment in the private sector will inevitably lead to suboptimal growth. It is from this empirical observation that the case for public investment is justified.

Although the new growth theories associated with the pioneering work of Romer (1986) provide a convincing case for public policy interventions on the grounds of market failure, the general tenor of this approach is still governed by neoclassical assumptions. Neoclassical production theory describes the employment of factors of production as a process of factor combinations rather than a process in which these factors are developed and changed. The focus of the analysis is static rather than dynamic. Furthermore, the behavior of firms is short term, governed by price competition, which compels them to substitute factors of production in order to maximize profits. This kind of competitive model rests on the assumption of a smooth and rapid adjustment by firms in their production configurations in response to market competition. Within growth theory, the trajectory of rising productivity can be conceptualized from both movements of the production function and movements along the production function.

In the orthodox Walrasian system, equilibrium is a function of prices that ensure a Pareto optimum in the allocation of resources. In this steady-state world of equilibrium, constant returns to scale are assumed to operate along a linear production function, governed by perfect competition and perfect substitutability in the factors of production. Movements along the production function are governed by relative price changes in the factors of production, while shifts in the production function are caused by exogenous technological change. The basic assumption of equilibrium theory is the existence of a homogeneous and linear production function that constitutes one of the necessary axioms required to reconcile perfect competition and profit maximization. In this schema, however, the *law of diminishing returns* will manifest itself in the long run as the increase in the stock of capital will cause a fall in the marginal product of capital.

Most neoclassical theories tend to treat the problem of growth in terms of static models of competitive equilibrium that assume a supply-side theory based on aggregate production functions (Solow, 1956; Swan, 1956).[4] Consequently, the neoclassical approach does not distinguish between industries in terms of their differential effects on growth. The growth accounting method applied by the Solow/Swan model assumes constant returns to scale, elevates price effects over income effects, stresses substitution over complementarity and regards technical change and factor endowments as *exogenous*. Worse still, the critical issue of effective demand is completely ignored. By contrast, post-Keynesian growth theories, inspired to a large extent by the work of Nicholas Kaldor (1957, 1972, 1985, 1996), identify manufacturing as the primary impetus in productivity and per capita income growth. The accent is on increasing returns, endogenous technical change and the role of effective demand as the major determinants in long-term aggregate growth. Post-Keynesian theories of growth offer one of the most rigorous and coherent critiques of the competitive equilibrium model. The theory of *circular and cumulative causation* reaffirms the preeminent role of manufacturing and the capital goods sector as important catalysts in aggregate growth (Toner, 1999; Kaldor, 1985; Hirschman, 1958; Myrdal, 1958; Young, 1928). The theoretical rationale is based on three propositions that run counter to conventional neoclassical assumptions:

1. *The role of increasing returns*: Productivity gains through increasing returns are cumulative. Manufactures are assumed to have a high price and income elasticity of demand, that is to say, a fall in real prices as a result of increasing returns is assumed to result in a more than proportionate increase in demand. Productivity growth arising from an increase in the capital–labor ratio is usually embodied in technological change (i.e. the introduction of labor-saving techniques). Furthermore there is assumed to be a strong positive correlation between the rate of economic growth and the rate of technological change.
2. *Endogenous technical change*: Within equilibrium theory, technology and innovation are basically exogenous. Technological externalities occur when there are direct linkages between individual firms. However, this process of technological diffusion is not transmitted through the market mechanism but is a peculiarity of the neoclassical production function. With the formation of vertically integrated sectors and greater specialization, complementarity between individual firms tends to supersede the neoclassical theory of perfect competition. The development of economies of scale and scope increasingly govern economic behavior (Chandler, 1990). Indeed, complementarity in the factors of production is far more pervasive and significant than the neoclassical principle of substitution. Two aspects of complementarity should be assumed: (1) fixed-factor coefficients in production with the emphasis on the indivisibility of factors, and (2) the neoclassical notion of diminishing returns to a factor of production should be suspended to capture increments to a capital stock. New technology embodied in new capital goods and intermediate goods improves their productivity and may also improve the productivity of existing capital goods and other inputs. This approach is the very opposite to the neoclassical view that each additional unit of capital, by definition, competes with the existing stock and the marginal productivity of capital necessarily declines as the stock of capital grows.

3. *The role of effective demand and net exports*: The theory of *circular and cumulative causation* proposes that a circular relation exists between growth in productivity and growth in total output. The Keynesian concept of effective demand explains how the long-run rate of growth of manufacturing output is determined by demand outside this sector (Kaldor, 1985). Given the high elasticity of demand for manufactured output, the standard Keynesian multiplier would have the effect of increasing the demand-induced level of investment. Hence, the critical role performed by manufacturing in generating increasing returns and higher levels of income in the dynamics of growth.

2 The law of increasing returns

The formulation of the law of increasing returns has its origins in the seminal theories of Adam Smith and Alfred Marshall. Smith formulated the dictum that "the division of labor is limited by the extent of the market." In other words, every increase in aggregate output, by widening the market, yields beneficial externalities. Marshall's formulation of the law of increasing returns was informed by the observation that, accompanied by internal economies, external economies represent one of the wellsprings of growth (Marshall, 1961). However, external economies only offered a provisional answer to the problems posed by partial equilibrium analysis. Increasing internal economies implied the rejection of the assumption of perfect competition because economies of scale would inevitably lead to oligopoly and monopoly. On the other hand, external economies were at least immune to the implication of imperfect competition.

Yet the Marshallian notion of increasing returns was quite narrow and ultimately contradicted the competitive equilibrium model which had assumed a given demand curve for a specific product of an industry and consequently, since changes in factor incomes would affect the demand curves, the assumption of a perfectly elastic supply of factors would contravene the conditions for competitive equilibrium (Arndt, 1995). The Marshallian dichotomy of internal and external increasing returns was a partial view and thus could not reconcile the assumptions that had governed Walras's system of competitive equilibrium. It is quite evident that increasing returns to scale is difficult to reconcile with a theory of relative prices based on competitive equilibrium between supply and demand.

A more critical aspect of increasing returns was highlighted by the influential Cambridge economist – Allyn Young – who noted in his seminal paper in 1928, that the law of increasing returns does not necessarily imply the tendency toward monopoly (Young, 1928). It is not the size of the individual firm as such but the fact that the larger the market for a good, the greater the propensity toward specialization and a more complex division of labor. Increasing returns is also a function of specialization rather than exclusively the product of economies of scale. The emphasis, in the Marshallian tradition, therefore shifted to *external economies* as a result of the concentration of specialized industries:

> Over a large part of the field of industry an increasingly intricate nexus of specialised undertakings has inserted itself between the producer of raw materials and the consumer of the final product...With the extension of the division of labour among industries the representative firm, like the industry of which it is a part, loses its identity. Its internal economies dissolve into the internal and external economies of the more highly specialised undertaking, which are its successors and are supplemented by new economies. In so far as it is an adjustment to a new situation created by the growth of the market for the final products of industry, the division of labour among industries is a vehicle of increasing returns. (Young, 1928, pp. 537–8)

It can be surmised that Young had inverted Adam Smith's original axiom by claiming that the division of labor not only depends upon the extent of the market but *the extent of the market also depends on the division of labor*. In this sense, Young was one of the earlier exponents of the theory of circular and cumulative causation (Harcourt, 1997, p. 3).

In his neglected article of 1926, Sraffa suggested that the entire Marshallian theory of increasing returns should be abandoned (Sraffa, 1926). Manufacturing industries are governed by the law of decreasing costs based on a profit "mark-up" similar to the Kaleckian notion of the "degree of monopoly."[5] The level of mark-up will depend on the conditions of entry (e.g. the extension of the market, the elasticity of demand, technology, product differentiation, advertising, raw material prices). In stark contrast to marginalist theory, the aggregate mark-up will tend to vary inversely with changes in direct costs (Sylos-Labini, 1993, p. 37). "It is necessary, therefore, to abandon the path of free competition and turn to the opposite direction, mainly, towards monopoly" (Sraffa, 1926, p. 542). Sraffa also stressed the critical dimension of time in the dynamics of increasing returns. Stated simply: "the shorter the period of time allowed for the adjustment, the greater the likelihood of decreasing returns, while the longer that period, the greater is the probability of increasing returns" (Sraffa, 1926, p. 538).

Increasing returns are primarily set in motion by the application of new technology and the embodied and disembodied knowledge, which are diffused in the production process. These normally take the form of *positive feedbacks* in which the incremental nature of most process and product innovations are diffused and improved upon through the application of *learning by doing* (Arthur, 1990, p. 84). Rather than a static equilibrium model based on perfect competition and constant returns to scale, a more dynamic long-run theory informed by oligopolistic markets and increasing returns to scale appears to be a more useful approach in the manufacturing sector (Sylos-Labini, 1969). While agriculture and mining are subject to diminishing returns, manufacturing exhibits increasing returns. The focus of analysis therefore shifts to factors such as returns to physical investment in capital equipment ("sunk costs"), technological externalities and market expansion as the primary impetus in the cumulative logic of long-run increasing returns.

The organization of industry and the indivisibility in factor inputs also tend to reinforce the law of increasing returns. According to orthodox theory, given the structure of demand for final goods and the state of technological innovation, the marginal productivity of capital will be high or low depending on the relative "mix" of factors. The introduction of more efficient methods or technologies will not only induce an increase in aggregate output but will also bring about changes in relative factor inputs. These backward linkages, in terms of inputs, generate a multiplier effect that tends to improve efficiency in the production chain upstream (Hirschman, 1958). With an increase in the scale of output, there are efficiency gains due to improvements in the organization of industry. In other words, *static* increasing returns are realized.

Internal economies are determined by large-scale production and the concomitant increase in the size and scope of the firm. Large-scale production tends to stimulate the introduction of new machines and new techniques of production which are, as a general rule, labor-saving. In classical Marxian terminology, constant capital will increase relative to variable capital. Economies of scale and scope are often associated with the indivisibility of fixed factors of production. These usually take the form of "sunk" costs in capital equipment. Consequently, indivisibility of specific factors accounts for increasing returns because a certain cost must be incurred regardless of whether it is fully utilized or not. Indivisibility of some factors of production (mostly capital goods) not only explains the large scale of a production unit but is also an essential concept in understanding the dynamics of increasing returns. This proposition runs counter to the neoclassical notion of factor substitution in response to changing demand conditions and price elasticities. If a factor of production is indivisible, it combines with the other elements through a process of *complementarity* rather than substitutability; that is to say, a fixed coefficient type of production prevails (Morroni, 1992, p. 28). The economic problem involves choosing a combination of production processes that are characterized by the *indivisibility of inputs*, rather than allocating resources in terms of an ideal Pareto optimality.

Productivity gains by means of increasing returns are cumulative. Manufacturers are assumed to have a high price and income elasticity of demand. This self-reinforcing expansionary process is governed by the investment accelerator, which sets in train increases in output and demand. The whole dynamic is therefore cumulative and perpetuates *disequilibria*. In the long run, rates of technological innovation and capital investment are linked in a circular and cumulative way (Toner, 1999, p. 45). An increase in the stock of capital (investment) and aggregate output accelerates the rate of technical diffusion, which raises the marginal productivity of capital and thus creates new investment opportunities (Arndt, 1995). Technological innovation is therefore *endogenous*. Investment in new capital and intermediate goods involves the successive replacement of old vintages that directly increases the productivity of capital and generates beneficial externalities in terms of new scientific knowledge (i.e. dynamic economies of scale). On the other hand, only economies of scale that assume technical knowledge as given, can be regarded as the source of *static* increasing returns (Sylos-Labini, 1993, p. 29).

3 Endogenous technical change

Despite the belated attempts to endogenize technical progress, technological innovation is still treated as an exogenous factor by neoclassical theorists, while the process of innovation usually equates the production of "technology" with "science." From the standpoint of technological knowledge, the conventional neoclassical theories make some rather heroic assumptions. A critique of the neoclassical/endogenous growth approach can be briefly summarized as follows:

1. Equating science and technology can be misleading. Technological development does not necessarily follow scientific discoveries but might in fact lead the latter. Indeed, technology depends far more on other technology than it does on science and science depends more on other science than it does on technology. In other words, the internal connections are much stronger than the cross-connections.

2. Innovation is an endogenous condition for market economies to adapt to change.
3. Information asymmetries cannot be treated solely as market failures but more fundamental *systemic failures*.
4. Pareto optimality and innovation are incompatible because innovation requires high levels of initial investment in order to resolve the problem of market entry. In this sense, Schumpeterian profits are an essential precondition for the development of economies of scale and innovative capacity.
5. The production of knowledge is characterized by increasing returns, which take the form of external spillover effects. In other words, knowledge is diffused to multiple consumers independently of the market.
6. Technological knowledge involves a high degree of uncertainty and it is difficult for the producers of knowledge to appropriate the full benefits. In this sense, technological knowledge has more in common with a public good than with a tradable commodity.

From this fundamental critique of the neoclassical paradigm, the new evolutionary economics develops a sophisticated theory of innovation and technological change, which has its genesis in the seminal research undertaken by Kondratiev (1935) and Schumpeter (1939).[6] At present, the research in this new school is still in its infancy and comprises an eclectic mixture of diverse theories and approaches. One of the leading schools of thought in this growing literature can be loosely designated as the theory of innovation systems. Most of the perennial debates center on the institutional dynamics of growth and the role of government intervention in national economic development, which were derived from the seminal ideas of Thorstein Veblen, the German Historical School and in the writings of Frederich List.[7] This tradition stands in stark contrast to the neoclassical school, which has dominated economic discourse in the English-speaking countries. The literature on national innovation systems focuses on the interindustry technological regimes based on the dynamic interaction between suppliers and users of capital and intermediate goods in order to establish an international competitive advantage (Porter, 1990). In contrast to the individualist ethos of the free market, clusters of firms engage in cooperative, interactive learning through the development of technological complexes that form part of a national innovation system. Close linkages with public research infrastructures augment these clusters. These linkages are critical for the development, diffusion and use of new technology and the new tacit and codified knowledge required for its reproduction (Boyer, 1992). In this schema, the role of human capital is absolutely pivotal in the development of industry clusters and national innovation systems.

The *raison d'être* of these clusters is the recognition that innovation is the most critical factor in the international competitiveness of the firm and ultimately underpins economic growth on the national level. A similar analysis was developed by the French *regulationist* school, which was based on the concept of the *filière* (Aglietta, 1979). A *filière* can be described as a social regime of national regulation and innovation that comprises a specific set of infrastructures, technologies, institutions, practices and actors. The technological structure of an economy is therefore embedded in the development of vertically integrated sectors, which accommodate the diffusion of innovations and reinforce inter-firm specialization through the evolution of industry clusters, supply chains and networks.

> The existence of an industrial district – characterised by infrastructures, skills and professional abilities specific to some particular manufacture – favours the external growth of firms. This model of growth of firms, "from the inside out" is the opposite of the traditional view of a firm's growth from within, through increasing both direct investment and employment. The external model of a firm's growth through cooperative inter-firm linkages is often based on a "constellation" of firms with a leading firm and a cluster of complementary organisations or a "network" of independent firms with collaborative relationships. In spite of the small dimension of single firms, these cooperative linkages enable certain economies of scale to be achieved through high overall production volumes. (Morroni, 1992, p. 66)

Clusters are also networks that link private firms with public institutions (universities, research institutes, etc.) to form a national innovation system. The concept of a cluster therefore goes beyond that of an intrafirm network and captures all forms of knowledge sharing and exchange. The analysis of a cluster also supersedes traditional sectoral analysis since it accounts for the interconnection of firms outside their traditional sectoral boundaries. Some clusters are closely linked to the science system (i.e. pharmaceuticals, semiconductors and biotechnology), while others act as intermediaries between science and other sectors (information technology). Still others are quite independent of the science system (mechanical engineering). Regional clusters are often based on certain local strengths such as strong knowledge infrastructure, geographical location or the presence of a major firm or industry.

Industry clusters and national innovation systems are the institutional bases of human capital investment or what has become known as the "knowledge" economy. Reich describes this subtle shift as the rise of the "symbolic analyst" in which the ownership and development of human capital are beginning to supersede the ownership of physical capital (Reich, 1991). There is a fundamental dichotomy in the determination of demand for information and knowledge. The value for the purchaser is not known until after the information is acquired. Similarly, the appropriation of knowledge can be reproduced at a fraction of the cost required for it to be produced. Reverse engineering is always possible once the prototype is sold. Consequently, the market is the least efficient means by which knowledge can be produced and allocated. If the producers cannot appropriate the full benefits, then they have no real incentive to produce knowledge. The market is, in this sense, the very antithesis of the Pareto theorem of optimality in relation to the production of knowledge. In short, the production of knowledge is not only a public good but constitutes the very core of a national innovation system.

4 The role of effective demand and net exports

The theory of circular and cumulative causation contends that increasing returns contribute to an enlargement of the overall size of the market. Most consumption-goods industries are *complementary* in that they provide a market for each other. Kaldor applied the Keynesian concept of effective demand to explain how the long-run rate of growth of manufacturing output is determined by demand outside this sector (Kaldor, 1985). Endogenous demand is automatically stimulated by production. However, this does not necessarily correspond with Say's law, nor with the neoclassical theorem of long-run steady state. In a money economy, as Keynes had shown in the *General Theory*, aggregate demand can be a function of aggregate supply but this rarely, if ever, corresponds with full employment; the problem of excess capacity utilization will be encountered. It was precisely this critique of the "classical" doctrine of Say's law under the conditions of competitive equilibrium, which still remains one of the most enduring insights of the *General Theory*.

In the *General Theory*, Keynes argued that expenditure decisions govern aggregate demand and thus provide the primary determinant in the level of output. In growth theories informed by Keynesian economics, the chain of causation between saving and investment is reversed: the investment decisions of entrepreneurs represent a prior claim on output, since business expenditure will determine the share of profits. Thus the primacy accorded to business profits, which must always be sufficient to provide the residual amount of saving required to finance investment. "To state the matter in a different way: profits *ex post* will always be sufficient to generate residual savings which means that *ex post* savings will equal *ex post* investment" (Kaldor, 1985, p. 34). Contrary to the Chicago School exponents of rational expectations, Keynes regarded investment decisions in any given period to be determined by the prevailing state of expectations (i.e. "business confidence") under the conditions of radical uncertainty. It was from this theorem that one ascribes Keynes's famous statement about the "animal spirits" of entrepreneurs.

A dynamic growth path can be conceptualized as a process of demand inducement caused by changes in productivity. Both the rate of growth of induced investment and the rate of growth of consumption are the function of the growth of the *autonomous* component of demand, which will govern the rate of growth in the economy as a whole. Given the high elasticity of demand for manufactured output, the standard Keynesian multiplier would have the effect of increasing the demand-induced level of investment. If one assumes that manufacturing is the main current of productivity growth, it is evident that it constitutes the "engine" of growth. In short, the theory supports the proposition that a circular, cumulative relation exists between growth in productivity and growth in total output. Increased demand will spur investment, which in turn will increase income and demand and cause further rounds of increases in investment via the multiplier effect. A virtuous circle is thus set in motion as saving will increase as a result of higher incomes but will tend to lag behind as the supply of capital will steadily meet the rising demand (Myrdal, 1957).

The multiplier determines the extent to which income increases as a result of an increase in investment, which in turns depends upon the propensity to save out of income. The accelerator, on the other hand, determines the rate at which additional capital is required to cover the expected increase in consumption. In the Keynesian schema, there is a reciprocal feedback mechanism; net investment generates additional income, which induces expectations of an expansion of effective demand and hence new investment with each new round of expenditure. Consequently, the rate of investment and the propensity to save will tend to vary over time. Other factors also feed into this cumulative process: the distribution of income, exogenous technical change, the rate of interest and so forth.

If a country encounters chronic balance of payments disequilibria as it expands domestic demand before the economy has reached full capacity utilization, then it has encountered a balance of payments constraint to its growth potential. Consequently, the economy will operate at levels well below full capacity, effective demand will be curtailed, employment growth will stall, which then dampens investment and ultimately puts a brake on the rate of embodied technical innovation. In this case, the logic of circular and cumulative causation operates in reverse. A prolonged recession has a similar effect.

Adverse terms of trade could set in motion a vicious circle. It is this structural argument that supports the advocacy of export-led growth in the manufacturing sector. Indeed, within a relatively open economy at a highly developed stage of industrialization, the most important driver in manufacturing output growth is the expansion of industrial exports. Export-led growth, as the economies of East Asia have recently testified, creates a virtuous circle of cumulative increases in output and productivity, which in turn, sets in train an expanding share of export markets. These multiplier and accelerator effects can be explained by the application of the Harrod foreign trade multiplier.[8] In Harrod's schema, exports are denoted as the exogenous variable and imports as a function of income:

$$Y = E/m \tag{2.2}$$

Y is the rate of growth of output, which is a function of the rate of growth of the volume of exports (E) over the income elasticity of demand for imports (m). Harrod's trade multiplier has been verified empirically; international statistical comparisons have supported the thesis that differences in growth rates of GDP are mainly explicable in terms of differences in the growth rates of the manufacturing sector. Moreover, countries whose exports of manufactures have grown at an even faster rate have experienced the highest GDP rates of growth.

The simple policy conclusion for most countries is that a higher rate of GDP growth can be accomplished by overcoming the balance of payments constraint on domestic demand. To increase productive capacity through improvements in productivity, while not being able to expand effective demand because of the balance of payments constraint, suggests that the economy is operating below full capacity utilization. If the balance of payments equilibrium can be raised, however, by either making exports more attractive or by reducing the income elasticity of demand for imports, domestic demand can be expanded. This would set in train a virtuous circle of demand-induced investment, increased productivity growth and the absorption of under-employed productive capacity.

Thirwall (1979) has demonstrated that a simple formula based on the ratio of a country's rate of growth of exports to its income elasticity of demand for imports explains much of the greater part of the differences in recorded growth rates of the industrialized countries. The results reveal a very close correspondence between the actual and predicted growth rates. Thirwall's findings support Kaldor's hypothesis that the balance of payments is an effective constraint on growth.[9] In effect, either increasing the level of exports or reducing the income elasticity of demand for imports can overcome the limits to growth. "Thus, the explanation of growth rate differences must be primarily in differences in the rate of growth of demand, and the major constraint on the rate of growth of demand in most countries is the balance of payments" (Thirwall, 1979, p. 57).

> The growth of a country's exports thus appears to be the most important factor in determining its rate of progress and this depends on the outcome of the efforts of its producers to seek out potential markets and adopt their product structure accordingly. The income elasticity of foreign countries for a particular country's product is mainly determined by the innovative ability and the absorptive capacity of its manufactures. In the industrially developed countries, high-income elasticities for exports and low-income elasticities for imports frequently go together, and they both reflect successful leadership in product development. (Kaldor, 1985, p. 69)

The accumulation of trade surpluses is therefore closely associated with the export of high value-added industrial goods. Trade surpluses in turn generate the export of capital in the form of foreign investment. Surplus countries thus enjoy the benefits of foreign trade disproportionately as well as being net exporters of capital. According to Vernon, direct investment abroad is governed by the product cycle in which the temporary monopolistic advantages conferred by the firm's ownership of technological innovation, generates demand for exports. As these foreign markets are saturated and the innovations are diffused, however, overseas corporations lose their oligopolistic advantages. In order to prevent the loss of these foreign markets, oligopolistic competition compels multinational firms to establish subsidiaries in close proximity to local markets (Vernon, 1966). Manufacturing exports not only overcome the balance of payments constraint on growth but also provide the basis for long-term sustainable growth based on rising incomes, technological progress and increasing returns.

Conclusion

From this brief survey of modern growth theories, it has become increasingly evident that prevailing neoclassical theories are inadequate in providing a coherent and rigorous analysis of the dynamics of technological change and innovation. Prevailing neoclassical competitive equilibrium analyses have encountered widespread critical scrutiny. Post-Keynesian growth theories challenge the assumption that the market economy moves toward a state of equilibrium in the long run. To the contrary, the system is propelled from one state of disequilibrium to another. This process of discontinuity originates from the internal logic of investment cycles and the endogenous shocks experienced from the introduction and diffusion of new technologies. The study of long-run economics is necessarily one that highlights structural change and technological innovation (Clark & Juma, 1987).

If the theoretical arguments presented in this chapter are assumed to be valid, then the wellsprings of growth emanate from the law of increasing returns, which generates a process of circular and cumulative causation in terms of increasing productivity growth and output per capita. Similarly, growth can be increased through an expansion in the volume of industrial exports, which tend to be highly income-elastic. The theory of circular and cumulative causation reaffirms the preeminent role of manufacturing and the capital goods sector as the primary catalysts for growth in the economy as a whole. In contrast to the static a priori assumptions, which govern conventional neoclassical accounts, these theories are based on the "stylized facts" that the economic system is characterized by increasing returns, endogenous technological change and a circular complementarity in production and consumption. Yet it should be conceded that the main currents of circular and cumulative causation fail to fully grasp the profound implications of growth and stagnation under the conditions of oligopolistic competition. These theoretical issues will be analyzed in the next chapter.

Appendix 2A The Solow/Swan Model

The cornerstone of the Solow/Swan model is the neoclassical *production function*, which measures the relationship between the output of a firm or economy and the inputs used to produce that output. In simple mathematical notation it is written:

$$Y = A\,f(N, K, t\,...) \tag{2A.1}$$

where Y is the dependent variable (output) and N (unskilled labor), K (capital), t etc. are independent variables (inputs). A is a variable that reflects the available production technology. If A rises, the economy produces more output from any given combination of inputs. Most production functions assume constant returns, which means that a doubling of all inputs causes the amount of output to double as well. For example: $xY = A\,f(xN, xK)$ if $x = 2$, then both the left-hand side and right-hand side of the equation will show output doubling. Labor productivity can be denoted as $x = 1/N$. Therefore: $Y/l = A\,f(1, K/l)$ where Y/l represents output per worker or a measure of productivity which depends on physical capital per worker (K/l). Productivity is also a function of technology denoted by the variable A. We assume a given and constant rate of labor force growth (i.e. $\delta N/N = n$) and assume that there is no technical progress (i.e. $\delta A/A = 0$). Hence growth is determined by the accumulation of capital. The growth of the capital stock is determined by the savings ratio.

An economy with population growth will reach a *steady state* in which output growth per head and capital per head will remain constant. If output per head is to remain constant, output and population must grow at the same rate (i.e. $\delta Y/Y = \delta N/N = n$). Therefore the growth of the capital stock is equal to the growth rate of the workforce (i.e. $\delta K/K = n$). The higher the capital–labor ratio, the higher is output per head. However, the increment to output that results from raising the capital–labor ratio grows progressively smaller as the ratio rises. In order to achieve and maintain a steady state, investment must equal saving.

To obtain an increase in the capital stock, depreciation would need to be deducted. Hence, δK = saving – depreciation. It is assumed that saving is a constant function of income (sY). Depreciation is a constant rate of d percent of the capital stock (dK). Consequently, in the steady state, saving is just sufficient to provide for enough investment to offset depreciation and to equip new members of the labor force with capital. If saving is larger than this amount, capital per head would grow, leading to rising income per head. Conversely, if not enough is saved, capital per head would fall and with it, income per head. An increase in the saving rate increases growth in the short run but does not affect the long-run growth rate of output. However, an increase in the saving rate will increase the long-run level of capital and output per head. In other words, there will be *level* effects but not *growth* effects.

Equation (2A.1) can be transformed into a very specific relation between input growth to output growth. This is expressed by the growth accounting equation

$$\Delta Y/Y = [(1 - \beta) \times \delta N/N] + (\beta \times \delta K/K) + \delta A/A \tag{2A.2}$$

Or

Output growth = [labor share × labor growth] + [capital share × capital growth] + technical progress

where $(1 - \beta)$ and β are the weights equal to labor's share of income and capital's share of income respectively. Equation (2A.2) therefore summarizes the contribution of input growth and of the improved productivity of the growth of output. We can surmise that labor and capital contribute an amount equal to their respective individual growth rates *multiplied* by the share of that input in total income. The rate of technical progress, or the growth of total factor productivity, is the third term in equation (2A.2). The growth rate of total factor productivity is the amount by which output would increase as a result of improvements in the methods of production, with all inputs assumed to be unchanged. For example, labor's share of income is 0.75 and that of capital is 0.25. We assume that the labor force grows by 1.2 percent, growth of capital stock by 3 percent and total factor productivity grows by 1.5 percent per annum. Applying equation (2A.2) we obtain

$$\Delta Y/Y = (0.75 \times 1.2\%) + (0.25 \times 3\%) + 1.5\% = 3.15 \text{ percent}$$

Growth in inputs is weighted by factor shares which means that if capital and labor *both grow* by an extra 1 percent, so too does the growth of output. Technical progress can be measured by rearranging equation (2A.2):

$$\Delta A/A = \delta Y/Y - [(1 - \beta) \times \delta N/N] + (\beta \times \delta K/K) \tag{2A.3}$$

The changes in total factor productivity are therefore attributed to the Solow residual.

So far we have been concerned primarily with the growth in total output. However, a more accurate measurement of an increase in living standards is the growth of per capita GDP. Per capita GDP is the ratio of GDP to the population. Hence, the growth rate of GDP equals the growth rate of per capita GDP as well as the growth rate of the population:

$$\Delta Y/Y - \delta N/N = \beta \times (\delta K/K - \delta N/N) + \delta A/A \tag{2A.4}$$

Equation (2A.4) can be rewritten in per capita terms as

$$\Delta Y/Y = \beta \times \delta k/k + \delta A/A \tag{2A.5}$$

where k is the capital/labor ratio. Since β is about 0.25, equation (2A.4) suggests that a 1 percent increase in the amount of capital available to each worker increases output by only about 0.25 percent.

3
Overaccumulation and Crisis

Introduction

> The mature capitalist economy is subject to and dominated by a basic contradiction: the very growth of its productive potential puts insuperable obstacles in the way of making full use of available human and material resources for the satisfaction of the needs of the great mass of the population. What this means is (1) that in the absence of sufficiently powerful countervailing forces, the normal state of the economy is stagnation; and (2) that the real history of the system in its monopoly capitalist phase is determined by the interaction of the tendency to stagnation and the forces acting counter to this tendency. (Magdoff & Sweezy, 1988, p. 24)

One of the major structural causes of the contemporary crisis of monopoly capitalism can be attributed to the problem of surplus absorption. The problem of semipermanent excess capacity utilization relative to the diminution of the level of effective demand can be diagnosed as the fundamental malaise that afflicts the current phase of stagnation in the "mature" capitalist countries. The aim of this chapter is to develop a theory of accumulation under the conditions of oligopoly. In so doing, an enormous intellectual debt is acknowledged to the seminal theories of Kalecki, Steindl and Baran/Sweezy. It will be argued that in the absence of countervailing forces (i.e. technical innovation, new markets), the mature stage of monopoly capitalism inherits a natural tendency toward chronic stagnation.

The system therefore incessantly seeks out new profitable outlets in order to overcome the problem of overaccumulation. Over the past two decades, a growing proportion of aggregate profits have been channeled into the financial markets, which has led to an unprecedented phase of instability and volatility in international financial markets. In this context, Fisher's seminal theory of debt deflation and Minsky's financial instability hypothesis provide an extremely useful theoretical framework by which to interpret the contemporary phase of stagnation.

1 The determination of national income: a Kaleckian model

Neoclassical theories assume that all profits are reinvested in productive capacity. However, the myth of the Weberian capitalist, motivated by frugality and abstinence, should be debunked. Kalecki developed a stylized, realistic model of the determination of national income. The model uses a simplified two-sector economy based on the capital goods sector, on the one hand, and the wage goods sector, on the other hand. In other words, the model is divided into wage-earners and capitalists (the former spending all their income and the latter responsible for investment). In a closed system, aggregate profits determine the rate of investment. Since workers spend all their wages on consumption, capitalists and rentiers account for aggregate saving.[1] National income is therefore defined as *wages plus profits* or equal to the value of consumption and investment output in a closed economy.

The model makes certain assumptions for the sake of simplicity or in economic jargon, uses the *ceteris paribus* condition. Unlike standard neoclassical models, however, these assumptions are quite realistic. First, the analysis does not assume full employment equilibrium but might assume *excess capacity*. Second, the analysis is based on the short term, that is to say, investment is assumed as given and is determined by past investment decisions by firms or rentiers.

Kalecki starts with a closed model in the absence of a government sector with wages (W) spent currently on the consumption of wage goods (Cw). The national income gross of depreciation Y can be defined as aggregate value-added or the value of final goods

$$Y = P + W \tag{3.1}$$
$$Y = \mathrm{Cw} + \mathrm{Cc} + I \tag{3.2}$$

where P, Cc and I denote profits gross of depreciation, capitalist consumption and investment gross of depreciation respectively. Since workers are assumed not to save, aggregate profits (P) are equal to capitalist consumption (Cc) plus investment (I), or

$$P = Cc + I \tag{3.3}$$

It is assumed that both kinds of decisions are made in real terms and consequently all aggregates are measured in constant prices. From (3.3) by subtracting Cc from both sides, we get

$$S = I \tag{3.4}$$

or the equality between saving and investment. Investment is the independent variable while saving is the dependent variable. Thus investment tends to "finance itself." Kalecki emphasized that (3.4) is independent of the short-term rate of interest.

If spending by businesses increases or decreases, a shift in the marginal revenue curve will occur; employment or prices change as a result of this change in demand until P is once again equal to the level of business spending. $P = Cc + I$ is therefore the fundamental equation of the analysis; the causality runs from spending to profits. In other words, business expenditure determines profits in the short run because they can influence their spending decisions but not their incomes.

> The conclusion that the increase in capitalists' consumption increases in turn their profits, contradicts the common conviction, that the more is consumed the less is saved. This approach which is correct with regard to a single capitalist, does not apply to the capitalist class as a whole. If some capitalists spend money, either on investment or consumer goods, their money passes to other capitalists in the form of profits. Investment or consumption of some capitalists creates profits for others. Capitalists as a class gain exactly as much as they invest or consume, and if – in a closed system – they ceased to construct and consume they could not make any money at all. Thus capitalists as a whole determine their own profits by the extent of their investment and personal consumption. In a way they are "masters of their own fate"; but how they "master" is determined by objective factors, so that fluctuations of profit appear after all to be unavoidable. (Kalecki, 1966, p. 14)

The problem with supply-side neoclassical theories of growth is that they neglect the critical role performed by effective demand. The increase in consumption caused by an increase in investment is possible if there is idle capacity which can be resolved by an increase in effective demand. The assumption is quite Keynesian in that excess capacity rather than full employment equilibrium is assumed to be the norm and that investment is the main factor driving effective demand. As Kalecki has eloquently stated: "The tragedy of investment is that it causes crises because it is useful. Doubtless many people will consider this theory paradoxical. But it is not the theory that is paradoxical, but its subject – the capitalist economy" (1966, p. 94). Accordingly, it can be argued that a rise in aggregate profits implies the problem of the *realization* of profits into investment which is determined by the level of effective demand. It can be surmised that a rise in wages will induce an increase in the level of effective demand. Workers will increase their demand for consumption goods which are generally produced on the domestic market.

If one assumes an open system with a government sector, aggregate profits would be

$$P = I + Cc + G + \mathrm{NX} \tag{3.5}$$

where G equals government spending and NX denotes net exports. Aggregate profits are therefore equal to investment, *plus* an export surplus *plus* budget deficits. An increase in the export surplus will induce a rise in aggregate profits, all things being equal. A budget deficit has a similar effect to that of an export surplus. By incurring successive budget deficits, governments can increase the level of aggregate profits as long as government spending is devoted to the provision of public goods and services to the private sector, rather than in pursuing policies which subsidize private consumption. Spending on armaments and wars is the classical means by which budget deficits tend to increase aggregate profits.

In order to stimulate investment through an increase in domestic net profits, the balance of trade component of profits must increase. In other words, a trade surplus must be achieved. Kalecki makes a crucial distinction between an increase in the export surplus (exports minus imports) and absolute exports. An increase in exports would lead, *ceteris paribus*, to a rise in the surplus of foreign trade but would also hasten an increase in demand for imports, most notably in raw materials and intermediate goods required for an expansion in production.

The balance of trade is denoted by s and the corresponding increase in imports and exports by i and e respectively:

$$e = i + s \tag{3.6}$$

Consequently only a proportion of the total increase in exports contributes to the increase in the balance of trade and thus to aggregate profits. The remainder is used for additional imports necessary for higher levels of output. If the relative share of profits in the aggregate value of production is denoted by the symbol β, production will increase by s/β. Moreover, if the ratio of imports to the value of aggregate production is denoted as α, then the increase in imports will be:

$$i = \alpha(s/\beta) \tag{3.7}$$

Thus we obtain

$$s/i = \frac{e-i}{i} = \beta/\alpha \tag{3.8}$$

For instance, if there is an increase in the balance of trade and total exports only a proportion of this total will increase the balance of trade, while another part is used to cover the imports of goods required for the expansion of production. The ratio between these two components is the same as that between the relative share of profits in the value of aggregate production. In the period of expansion of investment, aggregate profits increased because of the rise in the item "investment" by k, but fell by s as a result of the decline in the item "balance of trade." As a general rule, the increased profits amounted to $k - s$.

Thus if one denotes β as the relative share of profits in the value of aggregate production and the ratio of imports to this value as α, the following conclusions can be drawn:

1. The increase in the value of production corresponding to the increase in profits by $k - s$ is equal to $(k - s)/\beta$ and the corresponding rise in imports to $[(k - s)/\beta]\alpha$.
2. If imports decline by the same amount as the decline in the balance of trade, we obtain $[(k - s)/\beta]\alpha$.

It follows directly that:

$$k = s(1 + \beta/\alpha) \tag{3.9}$$

"It is now clear what are the advantages of an upswing stimulated by means of securing a surplus in foreign trade" [italics added] (Kalecki, in Osiatynski, 1990, p. 173).

> It is from this point of view that the fight for foreign markets may be viewed. The capitalists of a country which manages to capture foreign

> markets from other countries are able to increase their profits at the expense of the capitalists of the other countries. Similarly, a colonial metropolis may achieve an export surplus through investment in its dependencies. (Kalecki, 1971, p. 51)

2 Oligopoly and stagnation

One of the great virtues as well as one of the major limitations of orthodox theories of imperfect competition is that the existence of excess capacity can be explained in terms of equilibrium. The traditional theory is based on the notion of "surplus" profits generated as a result of the degree of excess price above marginal cost. Under the assumption of full capacity utilization, it is argued that these abnormal profits will eventually be eliminated as new entrants into the market have the effect of dampening prices. As a result, excess capacity and surplus profits are only temporary and the system gravitates toward a new equilibrium governed by perfect competition.

Traditional neoclassical theory, however, soon encounters serious problems in relation to the process of adjustment. One of the more intractable problems arises from the assumption that there are no sunk costs and that individual plants are easily divisible. In other words, the theory fails to take into account the existence of economies of scale and scope. The adjustment of capacity could only proceed if the Schumpeterian process of "creative destruction" occurs over a relatively short interval. The existence of both static and dynamic economies of scale implies that investment decisions are taken over a long time span and that in order to ensure profitability, large oligopolistic firms are characterized by: (1) high sunk costs in which average costs fall as output increases, (2) the indivisibility of inputs and (3) relative price rigidity. This confers market power and is a natural barrier to entry. These conditions are inimical to the traditional theory of imperfect competition in which the existence of excess capacity in a state of equilibrium generates temporary surplus profits. It can be argued and supported empirically that abnormal profits can be maintained over long periods by the deliberate holding of excess capacity. New entrants can be effectively excluded by adjusting capacity utilization and by adopting a strategy of price fixing.

In stark contrast to traditional price theory in which firms maximize profits when marginal cost equals marginal revenue under the conditions of perfect competition, the Kaleckian theory of the "degree of monopoly" offers a more realistic framework. According to the Kaleckian formula, oligopolistic firms adopt a policy of a profit "mark-up" in which price p is determined by the firm in relation to prime costs u (wages, raw materials, etc.). In order to counter price competition, each firm will exploit their degree of monopoly by adjusting the ratio of p to the weighted average of all firms, p^*, so that the price does not become too high. If u rises, the firm can adjust their price by increasing p proportionately but only if the weighted average p^* also increases. On the other hand, if p^* increases less than u the firm's price p will also rise less than u. In the simple Kaleckian schema these conditions are represented by the formula

$$p = mu + np^* \tag{3.10}$$

in which m and n are positive coefficients. It logically follows that the coefficients m and n characterize the price-fixing strategy of oligopolistic firms and reflect the firm's "degree of monopoly." The higher the degree of monopoly, the higher is $m/(1 - n)$. If the degree of monopoly increases, p^* also increases in relation to u^*.

> Such a firm (oligopolist) knows that its price p influences appreciably the average price p^* and that, moreover, the other firms will be pushed in the same direction because their price formation depends on the average price, p^*. Thus, the firm can fix its price level higher than would otherwise be the case. The same game is played by other big firms and thus the degree of monopoly increases substantially. This state of affairs can be reinforced by tacit agreement (such an agreement may take inter alia the form of price fixing by one large firm, the "leader," while other firms follow suit). Tacit agreement, in turn, may develop into a more or less formal cartel agreement which is equivalent to full scale monopoly restrained merely by fear of new entrants. (Kalecki, 1971, p. 17)

The "mark-up" will tend to vary between different industries and is, in the final analysis, dependent on the degree of competition. The degree of monopoly therefore depends upon the relation of the individual firm's price p to the weighted average price p^* for the industry as a whole:

$$(p - u)/u = f(p^*/p) \tag{3.11}$$

where f is an increasing function: the lower p is in relation to p^*, the higher the mark-up will be fixed. From formula (3.11) we derive

$$p = u[1 + f(p^*/p)] \tag{3.12}$$

Consequently, the function *f* will be different for individual firms in an industry and will reflect the degree of monopoly.

It can be surmised that the phase of monopoly capital is dominated by "price regulated" industries characterized by tacit cartels and price leadership. Indeed, the existence of oligopolistic competition tends to impart a higher degree of price rigidity. Inelastic prices tend to dampen the amplitude of the trade cycle in these industries. Oligopolistic firms will be reluctant to reduce prices during the phase of slump in the trade cycle. As a result, prices and profits will be set high enough to keep potential new entrants at bay but low enough to counter existing competitors. To be sure, the degree of monopoly will tend to increase during the slump as the price leaders attempt to squeeze out existing competitors. These tendencies have quite profound implications in the duration and magnitude of the slump, generating a powerful undercurrent toward chronic stagnation.

> Thus a new type of cumulative process becomes possible; any reduction of the rate of capital growth will reduce the degree of utilization, and this will further reduce the rate of growth of capital. Thus, a given reduction in capital growth will lead to a further decrease in the rate of growth. This cumulative process may again tend to a definite limit, so that the rate of growth will settle down at a new lower level, but it is not certain whether it might not continue, theoretically, without limit. (Steindl, 1976, p. 137)

Confronted by a fall in the level of effective demand, oligopolistic firms have the ability to resort to a curtailment of the degree of capacity utilization. Capacity utilization, x, can be defined simply as the level of output, y, divided by capacity, c. Excess capacity, e (whether planned or unplanned), can be denoted as $1 - e$. A fall in the degree of capacity utilization will result in a fall in the rate of profit. However, market power confers the advantages of attracting a higher volume of internal savings generated by a higher share of profits in a specific industry or market. The ability to maintain higher prices in relation to costs implies that profit margins become inelastic in a downward direction (Steindl, 1976, p. 135).

In terms of effective demand, an increase in the degree of monopoly might be accompanied by a fall in nominal wages. This is most evident during the course of a slump. The fact that aggregate profits are inelastic in a downward direction as a result of relative price rigidity under the conditions of oligopoly, implies that pressure will intensify to reduce the level of wages in order to reduce prime costs. Class struggles are thus waged between capitalists and workers over the distribution of national income. A fall in nominal wages, however, does not lead to a rise in the level of employment as the conventional wisdom so often proclaims. The slump in employment will have an adverse effect on the wage-goods sector as the real purchasing power of workers declines. A fall in wages will therefore curtail the level of effective demand.

If the degree of monopoly remains unchanged, aggregate profits would tend to fall in the same proportion as prime costs. At the same time, in the course of a slump, aggregate profits tend to fall less than prime costs. These conditions are therefore quite favorable for the inducement of tacit agreements between oligopolists not to reduce prices in the same proportion as prime costs (Kalecki, 1990, Vol. 2, p. 18). In Marxian terms, the degree of concentration will increase as capital is attracted away from those sectors of the economy with a low profitability to those sectors that exhibit higher levels of profitability. In this case, investment funds are redistributed from the smaller, more competitive firms and sectors, to the larger, oligopolistic enterprises and industries.

In the simple two-sector, closed model, profits and wages are the only forms of income and wages (W) are linked to the national product by a linear function:

$$W = \alpha Y + \beta Z \quad (Y \leq Y^*) \tag{3.13}$$

where βZ denotes wage costs as a fixed proportion of the capital stock Z. In other words, we assume a constant capital/labor ratio as a first approximation. The formula (3.14) is limited by the full capacity utilization Y^*. Hence, profits can be denoted as

$$P/Y = 1 - \alpha - \beta Z/Y = I/Y + Cc/Y \quad (Y \leq Y^*) \tag{3.14}$$

where I and Cc denote investment and capitalist consumption respectively. It follows directly that the marginal profit share $(1 - \beta)$ equals the aggregate of the average profit ratio and the mark-up ratio. Kalecki's formula can be modified by assuming, as Steindl does, that the mark-up ratio depends on the utilization of capacity and varies inversely with it, but is ultimately constrained by the full capacity barrier. Steindl also assumes that the coefficients α and β are given. The latter is determined by the cost structure, while the former is determined by the degree of monopoly. In this context, the mark-up, u, can be represented as $(1 - \alpha)/\alpha$. Given $1 - \alpha$ and β, aggregate investment and capitalist consumption in a closed, two-sector model will determine the degree of utilization and the mark-up ratio.

Steindl's model therefore builds on the Kaleckian foundations by introducing a more dynamic interpretation of the degree of capacity utilization. In this sense, two critical variables are introduced. First, oligopolistic firms will plan the degree of utilization over a long time span in the course of the trade cycle as a result of high sunk costs, economies of scale and the indivisibility of inputs. Given their high degree of market power, capacity utilization can be deployed as a competitive weapon to push out potential rivals, if this tactic does not prove to be too costly. Second, if capacity utilization is below the desired level, investment in new capital stock will be curtailed. It is quite evident that under these conditions of oligopolistic competition, stagnationist tendencies become the norm rather than the exception. Each recurrent slump will tend to be amplified in the course of the trade cycle.

> It was shown that the excess capacity might lead to an intensified competition between capitalists, and that should tend to bring the rate of "surplus value produced" down again. To this a modification has to be added now: with the growth of oligopoly, the competition between capitalists works less and less well, and the excess capacity can persist long without leading to the forcible ejection of superfluous capital. The excess capacity remaining, it exerts then a depressing influence on the investment decisions of capitalists, and the rate of growth of capital slows down. (Steindl, 1976, p. 245)

3 The credit cycle and the onset of debt deflation

The problem of the trade cycle was abandoned in the neoclassical literature in favor of the Solow/Swan growth accounting model. Consequently, neoclassical theory has been unable to adequately explain the recurrence of booms and busts as an endogenous process of capital accumulation itself. These disturbances to steady-state growth were attributed to temporary "exogenous" shocks. The economy would, it was assumed, gradually gravitate toward full-employment equilibrium.

At the same time, however, there emerged a growing and influential literature within the post-Keynesian paradigm, which reaffirmed the general *dynamic* framework of Keynes's *General Theory*. The most influential of these theories was Kalecki's *Theory of Economic Dynamics*. Kalecki's theory of investment is based on the notion of "aggregate profits." In other words, the propensity to invest is determined by the realization of past profits. Since profits represent a return to capital, the distribution between profits and wages constitutes the central mechanism in the dynamics of the trade cycle. In Kalecki's model $D(t)$ represents the investment decision and $I(t)$ denotes the actual investment of capital equipment:

$$I(t + \beta) = D(t) \tag{3.15}$$

or

$$I(t) = D(t - \beta) \tag{3.15a}$$

The symbol β denotes the fixed time interval required between the investment decision and the installation of the investment equipment. The decision to invest is positively related to profits $P(t)$ and negatively to the capital stock $K(t)$. Income is divided between profits appropriated by the capitalists and the wages received by the workers. As a general rule, workers consume all of their income and capitalists save and invest most of their income. Hence, profits $P(t) = sY(t)$, where s represents the share of income appropriated by the capitalists or in the Keynesian form of $s = (1 - C)$, which is equivalent to the marginal propensity to save by capitalists.

Investment is therefore unstable and performs a determinant role in the fluctuations of the business cycle. "The main determinants of investment were the ability of firms to internally finance investment, the size of the capital stock and profits. These, in turn, were determined by the level and rate of change of economic activity" (Kriesler, 1995, p. 18). In stark contrast to Hicks's IS/LM analysis, Kalecki made the crucial observation that investment is influenced by the long-term rate of interest, which tends to be cyclical, rather than by the short-term rate. Given the time lags and the planned investment decisions undertaken by oligopolistic firms, this assumption is quite realistic. "The economy is activated by capitalists' expenditures which – when it comes to investment spending – are the expression of their bets on the future" (Halevi & Taouil, 1998, p. 3).

Kalecki assumes imperfect competition. Hence if money wages fall, the "mark-up" between prices and wages would increase. This implies a redistribution of income from wages to profits. However, capitalists, as a general rule, have a lower propensity to consume than workers, which means that the level of effective demand will tend to fall in the economy as a whole. A fall in the wages share of national income therefore leads to higher levels of unemployment and unused capacity. This conclusion is diametrically opposed to the neoclassical assumption of increasing the level of employment by reducing wages.

The Kaleckian relationship between profits and investment has been further refined and elaborated by Minsky (1982). According to Minsky, a capitalist economy is characterized by two sets of relative prices: (1) current output and (2) capital assets. On the one hand, prices of capital assets depend upon expectations of future rates of return to capital and the Keynesian notion of liquidity preferences. On the other hand, the prices of current output will be determined by existing perceptions of short-term demand conditions: "Capital assets and current output prices are based upon expectations over quite different time horizons: capital asset prices reflect long-run expectations and current output prices reflect short-run expectations" (Minsky, 1982, p. 95).

The implication of Minsky's argument is that the simple relationship between profits and investment in the Kaleckian schema should be modified in the light of the "financial instability" hypothesis. To restate Kalecki's profit–investment relationship, we get

$$\pi = I \quad \text{(profits equal investment)} \tag{3.16}$$

However, I is a function of (Pk, $P_I(I)$, Eπ, Ext. Finance) where Pk = price of capital assets, $P_I(I)$ = supply price of investment goods as functions of investment price, Eπ = expected profits and Ext. Finance = external financing conditions. Hence

$$I \longrightarrow \pi \tag{3.16a}$$

in which the causation runs from investment to profits. From this simple theorem, Minsky develops the financial instability hypothesis:

> Keynes insisted that the main propositions of the *General Theory* centre around the disequilibrating forces that operate in financial markets. These disequilibrating forces directly affect the valuation of capital assets relative to the price of current output, and this price ratio, along with financial market conditions, determines investment activity (p. 60).... Once financial considerations are integrated into the investment decision, it is evident that capitalism as we know it is endogenously unstable.... Contradictions and tensions associated with the accumulation of wealth come to the forefront of the analysis. Instability becomes normal rather than abnormal. (Minsky, 1982, p. 81)

The immediate cause of a general financial crisis can therefore be attributed to a fall in asset prices and a shift in long-run expectations. In this process, the role performed by the credit cycle is absolutely critical.

Since credit consists of obligations assumed during a period of high asset prices, the contraction of credit is tantamount to a depreciation of credit money (Hilferding, 1981, p. 65). In contrast to prevailing neoclassical accounts, an analysis of the credit cycle provides the most useful framework to interpret the crisis of excess capacity and overaccumulation. According to Keynes: "We can define the credit cycle to mean the alternations of excess and deficit in the cost of investment over the volume of saving and the accompanying see-saw in the purchasing power of money due to these alternations" (Keynes, 1930, Vol. 2, p. 277). In his seminal *Treatise on Money*, J.M. Keynes described four phases through which the credit cycle progresses in the general trajectory of the business cycle:

> The order of events is, therefore, as follows. First, as Capital Inflation leading to an increase of Investment, leading to Commodity Inflation; second, still more Capital Inflation and Commodity Inflation for approximately one production period of consumption goods; third, a reaction in the degree of the Commodity and Capital Inflations at the end of this period; fourth, a collapse of Capital Inflation; and finally, a decrease of Investment below normal, leading to Commodity Deflation. (Keynes, 1930, Vol. 2, p. 304)

The primary phase of the credit cycle is characterized by speculative windfall profits generated by rising expectations and the emergence of a "bull" in the stock market (Kindleberger, 1978). Prices tend to rise and are further induced by the upsurge of commodity inflation. A secondary stimulus to the expansion of output originates with rising incomes as the primary boost to investment spurs consumption. Thus, the secondary phase is characterized by both commodity and income inflation. A shortage in the factors of production, especially those of labor, causes a rise in money wages. The combined effects of windfall profits and rising money wages accelerates the multiplier effect through excess investment and the emergence of excess capacity.

Since the secondary phase stimulates the production of consumption goods, an overproduction crisis is set in motion. Prices will tend to fall as markets become saturated. Individual enterprises will be impelled to curtail output and investment. As bankruptcies multiply in the course of the business cycle downswing, financial institutions find themselves burdened by an avalanche of nonperforming loans.

> The banks find themselves in the presence of an increased demand for credit, while there is no longer any repayment of earlier credits.

> Since everyone needs liquidity, settlement demands flow in from all sides. The debt chain breaks at several points where the banks are no longer able to meet their commitments. A financial crisis breaks out and credit contracts, while money appears in its function as a store of value. The sudden devalorisation of credits gives rise to bankruptcies and destruction of capital. Market prices then fall at an even faster rate than they previously rose. (Aglietta, 1979, pp. 341–2)

Consequently, the downturn is characterized by commodity and income deflation and a collapse in capital inflation. The ensuing recession is a necessary, though irrational means by which profitability is restored. The general rate of profit begins to rise again at the bottom of the slump as wages growth is curtailed and new expenditure in capital goods is temporarily postponed.

> The position at the bottom of the slump is analogous to that at the top of the boom. While the rate of profit is falling at the top of the boom because of additions to the stock of capital equipment, it is rising at the bottom of the slump because depreciation of capital equipment is not being made good.
>
> But it may be questioned whether this situation is symmetrical with that of the top of the boom. It may indeed be claimed that the effect of capital destruction upon investment decisions during the slump is much weaker than that of capital accumulation in the boom because the equipment "destroyed" in the slump is frequently idle in any case. As a result, slumps may be very long. (Kalecki, 1971, p. 126)

The conditions for a renewed recovery are therefore established through the Schumpeterian dynamic of *creative destruction*. Yet there is no automatic or endogenous mechanism that ensures that the recovery will occur any time soon. In the absence of powerful stimulatory forces, the system could be mired in a state of long-term stagnation. The onset of a severe phase of debt deflation could characterize this phase of debilitating and chronic stagnation.

Irving Fisher formulated the original debt-deflation theory of great depressions in 1933. Fisher argues that there are two central factors in the cumulative causation of economic depressions: (1) the accumulation of debt and (2) the diminishing purchasing power of the monetary unit. The onset of deflation sets off a chain of events, which leads to the cessation of debt validation and the emergence of a severe economic slump. This chain of events is summarized by Fisher in the following order (Fisher, 1933, p. 372):

1. Debt liquidation and stress selling of assets.
2. The contraction of deposit currency and the money supply (a fall in the velocity of circulation).
3. A fall in the level of prices and the rise in the value of the currency.
4. Rising levels of bankruptcies and financial indebtedness.
5. A fall in the rate of profit.
6. A sudden contraction in output and employment.
7. The onset of pervasive pessimism and the loss of confidence by investors and consumers.
8. Hoarding and a further contraction of the money supply.
9. A fall in the nominal interest rate but a rise in the real rate of interest.

Consequently, the liquidation of debts acts as both a cause and a catalyst for the onset of deflation. The more that debtors attempt to validate their obligations, the more difficult it becomes to liquidate their assets because of falling prices. The whole process becomes self-defeating:

> The very effort of individuals to lessen their burden of debt, increases it, because of the mass effect of the stampede to liquidate in swelling each dollar owed. Then we have the great paradox which, I submit, is the chief secret of most, if not all, great depressions: the more that debtors pay, the more they owe. (Fisher, 1933, p. 374)

The preceding boom is activated by the expansion of investment into new markets; new opportunities offered by innovations, which are driven by the prospect of capturing Schumpeterian profits; or by the discovery of new natural resources. Whatever the causes of the boom, it is the lure of expected high profits and dividends, which ignites the speculative frenzy. These future expectations are reflected in the emergence of a "bull" in the equity markets. Share prices, in turn, determine the market valuation of capital assets owned by firms. "Thus the ability to debt finance new investment depends upon expectations that future investment will be high enough so that future cash flows will be large enough for the debts that are issued today to be repaid or refinanced" (Minsky, 1982, p. 65). Hence, the issue of uncertainty in the original Keynesian sense of the word, can be seen as performing the central role in this financial drama. In Keynes's own words:

> Of the maxims of orthodox finance none, surely, is more anti-social than the fetish of liquidity, the doctrine that it is a positive virtue on

> the part of investment institutions to concentrate their resources upon the holding of "liquid" securities. It forgets that there is no such thing as liquidity of investment for the community as a whole. The social object of skilled investment should be to defeat the dark forces of time and ignorance, which envelop our future. The actual, private object of most skilled investment today is "to beat the gun," as the Americans so well express it, to outwit the crowd, and to pass the bad, or depreciating, half-crown to the other fellow. (Keynes, 1936, p. 155)

In the course of the trade cycle, an expansion of investment could, under the conditions in which finance capital prevails, degenerate into a speculative mania. These speculative manias are an inherent feature of the market economy but assume a critical dimension with the development of finance capital and circuits of credit. It follows, therefore, that in the course of the slump, the fall in asset prices is always accompanied by a contraction in the volume of credit money. Indeed, as prices fall, returns to investment also fall, but the validation of past debts will fall due precisely at the same time when profits and sales remain depressed (Hilferding, 1981, p. 65).

Minsky (1982) distinguishes between hedge and speculative finance. Hedging operations are based on the assumption that cash flows and revenue are large enough to cover debt repayments. Speculative finance, on the other hand, is based upon the ability to validate its current interest payments but must also raise new capital, either by selling assets or by issuing bonds in order to pay the principal of its outstanding loans (Henword, 1998, p. 222). Investors place bets on future valuations and expected rates of return on the assumption that these expectations will be greater than the current debt obligations (Minsky, 1982, p. 66). A third type of financial player, which usually appears during the final stages of the speculative boom, is the over-leveraged *Ponzi* financier in which investment becomes akin to the casino. In this tragi-comedy, Ponzi financiers soon find that they are caught in the horns of a dilemma. On the one hand, a rise in interest rates will cause debt repayments to increase relative to their earnings and cash flows. On the other hand, their earnings are normally based on a longer-term expectation of future returns to investment, but their liabilities must be validated in the short term. A rise in both short- and long-term interest rates will therefore have the effect of inducing a greater depreciation of their assets than their liabilities. Ultimately, however, the greatest vulnerability lies in the sudden fall in asset prices, which leaves the speculator exposed to the accumulation of debt. When this occurs, bankruptcies and payment defaults feed into the process of debt deflation.

> It is, therefore, precisely the uncertain, incalculable factor which speculators are obliged to take into consideration. In short, no certain foresight is possible in speculative activity, which is essentially a groping in the dark. Stock market speculation is like a game of chance or a wager, but for insiders it is a wager *à coup sûr*. (Hilferding, 1981, p. 137)

Consequently, a sudden shift in expectations, caused by uncertainty, could trigger a severe stock market crash. What ultimately prevents the descent into a depressive spiral is the operation of automatic stabilizers made possible by the existence of a substantial state sector. At the same time, central banks are capable of injecting liquidity and temporarily acting as a lender of last resort to mitigate a financial meltdown. Needless to say, this chain of events does not represent a mere anomaly, as the apologists of laissez-faire tend to proclaim, but is endemic in a deregulated market economy.

Conclusion

The intention of this chapter has been to develop rigorous alternative approaches to the study of the process of capitalist accumulation under oligopolistic conditions, based on the seminal theories of Kalecki, Steindl and Baran/Sweezy. The various post-Keynesian strands of thought embodied in the Fisher/Minsky theories of financial instability and debt deflation augment these stagnationist perspectives and also provide an invaluable contribution to our understanding of recurrent financial crises. It is therefore possible to construct a dynamic theory, which elucidates the conditions by which the economy fluctuates between boom and slump. In stark contrast to the prevailing comparative static methodology of neoclassical models, the original Kaleckian theory was essentially based on the short- and long-term consequences of investment and its determination. It can be surmised that under the conditions of oligopolistic competition, the normal tendency of the capitalist economy is toward chronic stagnation rather than full employment equilibrium as suggested by neoclassical theories.

4
Long Cycles of Growth and Stagnation?

Introduction

During the 1970s and 1980s, a revival of interest was experienced over the existence of long waves in economic life. Much of this renewed interest was motivated by the onset of economic stagnation after the postwar phase of rapid growth in the advanced capitalist countries. Debates over the existence of long waves were revitalized, while the seminal research undertaken by Kondratiev (1935) and Schumpeter (1939) were rehabilitated. Many long-wave theorists identified the dynamic of technological revolutions as the propulsion to the phase of upswing in these long waves in economic life. There is considerable evidence of the pervasive effect of these secular waves, especially when one considers the impact of railways in the nineteenth century or the profound changes engendered by "generic" technologies (information technology, biotechnology and new raw materials technology) over the past 20 years. It will be argued that these Schumpeterian waves of "creative destruction" tend to act as powerful countervailing forces to the inherent tendency toward stagnation under the conditions of oligopolistic competition.

1 "Creative destruction"

Schumpeter argued that the shorter business cycles were closely interwoven with the general trajectory of the long wave or "cycle." He identified the shortest of these cycles as the "Kitchin" which is associated with the turnover of inventories over a 2–3-year period. The other visible cycle is the normal business cycle or the "Juglar" which is driven by capital investment over a 6–10-year period. As a general rule, these shorter cycles become more expansive if the underlying momentum of the long wave is in the upswing phase. Conversely, cyclical recoveries tend to become less expansive and recessions more severe during the secular downswing.

The controversy that still surrounds the empirical existence of long waves over a period of 50–60 years can be assigned into two separate critiques. First, the theory is scrutinized on the basis of the available empirical data used by Kondratiev to identify each hypothetical wave or "cycle." Second, there have been perennial debates over the causes of these fluctuations. In the latter case, Schumpeter's business cycle theories rather than Kondratiev's original hypothesis constitute the core rationale for these critiques.

A convincing earlier critique of Kondratiev's original hypothesis disputes the statistical time series and questions the validity of the methodology employed by Kondratiev to interpret the data (Garvey, 1943). The main thrust of Garvey's critique is that Kondratiev relied exclusively on the fluctuation of wholesale prices rather than the physical output of production to identify long-term growth cycles. A similar statistical critique has been developed by Van Ewijk (1981). Both critiques are quite valid, although they provoke more questions than they resolve. Schumpeter himself had attempted to resolve these difficulties but admittedly, he also encountered major empirical obstacles not only because of the lack of available data on earlier waves but also because of the absence of a coherent methodology by which to systemize and interpret the evidence. More recent studies by Mensch and Kleinknecht have proven quite fruitful within the neo-Schumpeterian paradigm but remain at best inconclusive and in many cases, quite arbitrary in their selection of data (Mensch, 1979; Kleinknecht, 1990).

According to the critics of long-wave theory, these waves cease to exist if one analyses the physical series as a whole; the fluctuations merely reflect price movements. However, their attempts to interpret long waves out of existence and to suggest that these visible fluctuations are merely the outcome of stronger classical cycles prove to be unconvincing. The fact that there exists a rhythmical alternation of relative prosperity and stagnation which lasts beyond the normal duration of the business cycle is quite self-evident at only a cursory observation of the evolution of modern capitalism. In this regard, the monumental evidence – published in three volumes of economic history – is provided by Braudel (1984). The central problem, therefore, stems not so much on whether these fluctuations have an empirical foundation, but if an explanation can be discovered for their behavior.

The critical proposition that these disturbances in economic life constitute regular waves or cycles has been augmented by a further set of hypotheses. Schumpeter stressed the role of major technological innovations as the primary source of these trajectories. Furthermore, Schumpeter assumes that phases of prolonged crisis and depression are characterized by a fundamental economic restructuring as a cluster of innovations is introduced. The diffusion of these innovations propels the economy into a new phase of prosperity. However, as these basic innovations reach the end of their life cycle, a renewed phase of overcapacity and investment "overshoot" is experienced in those industries that had formerly grown disproportionately faster in relation to the diminution of demand. The Harrodian distinction between trend and cycle therefore ceases to have any real meaning (Harrod, 1948).[1] "Schumpeter was right that these two fundamental features of historic capitalism are inseparable. Specifically, it is the vigorous boom, which does generate the trend, and it is this leap forward into new levels of output which governs the subsequent slump" (Goodwin, 1982, p. 115).

In the Schumpeterian schema, the dramatis personae are the pioneering entrepreneurs who, either through good fortune or foresight, seize the opportunity and take the necessary risks by introducing revolutionary techniques and product innovations. It is the "animal spirits" of these entrepreneurs who are driven by competition to invest in basic innovations and act as prime movers in the process of *creative destruction*. These entrepreneurial innovations are then followed by a swarm of imitators that eventually ignites the economic boom. However, this irrationalism is equaled, if not exceeded, by the financial profligacy and speculative excesses of the ensuing downturn. In this rather crude simplification of the Schumpeterian dynamic, the role of heroic innovations introduced by pioneering entrepreneurs constitutes the leitmotiv of long waves in economic life.

Most of the recent debates over long-wave theory have focused on the business cycle theories of Schumpeter and the role of innovations in the trajectory of long waves. The critique by Kuznets of the Schumpeterian dynamic is still regarded as the most systematic and convincing (Kuznets, 1940). In order to confirm Schumpeter's thesis, Kuznets suggests two criteria. First, one should establish that a strict periodicity or "symmetry" exists between both the duration and alternating phases of boom and depression. In other words, is it possible to locate an internal dynamic in the same way that one is capable of analyzing the behavior of normal business cycles? Second, it is necessary to establish a causal relationship between possible exogenous forces and the trajectory of the long wave.

From the standpoint of Kuznets's first condition, Mandel (1980) has provided the most persuasive case. Mandel highlights the process of capital accumulation as the underlying determinant of these discontinuities in the secular growth trajectory. As the accumulation of capital reaches a certain point during the upswing, the total mass of capital can no longer realize the previous average rate of profit; there will be a long-term tendency for the rate of profit to fall. This will manifest itself in a crisis of excess capacity. During the phase of downswing, the rate of investment is curtailed. Increased competition between rival enterprises hastens the introduction of new techniques and technology. Capital is substituted for labor and, accompanied by rising unemployment and falling real wages, the costs of production can be lowered in order to restore the rate of profit. Consequently, the phase of depression corresponds with a rise in the capital/labor ratio and the process of economic restructuring.

Mandel's explanation is quite plausible, though it is more applicable to the fluctuations of the normal business cycle. In order to resolve this problem, Mandel contends that since these long waves are propelled by major technological revolutions such as the construction of railways or the introduction of electricity, the long-term cyclical characteristics can be identified with investment cycles for major capital goods. Thus, a possible explanation of the ebbs and flows of these secular movements might be found in the longevity of capital expenditure in the capital goods sector that exceeds the normal duration of the business cycle.

In the long run, investment in capital goods sets in motion associated investment in infrastructure. The multiplier–accelerator mechanism implies that major innovations not only stimulate new industries but also generate capital investment in new infrastructure. The most striking example of this cumulative process can be demonstrated in the postwar "automobile boom" which was augmented by a vast network of urban infrastructure. The economic expansion engendered by this process exceeds the normal duration of the business cycle. One of the earlier theories that explained this behavior of long waves through the dynamics of long-term investment was known as the "echo-principle" (Tinbergen, 1981). Consequently, the behavior of industrial life cycles can be considered as the most plausible explanation for long waves.

Industrial life cycles were originally developed by Kuznets who postulated that they form an S-shaped pattern and are governed by a combination of technological innovation and the presence of expanding markets (Kuznets, 1953). These new industrial sectors require their own infrastructure. As a result, the associated "backward linkages" generate a multiplier effect, which propels a sustained phase of growth and expansion. The original hypothesis developed by Kuznets suggests a normal time span of about 20 years for the period of gestation of the innovation but a much longer period is necessary for the process of diffusion to occur. Therefore one would expect industrial life cycles to last for more than 50 years, a period that tends to coincide with the Kondratiev wave.

Historically these leading sectors have emerged from major innovations or a cluster of related innovations. It is quite evident that textiles, iron and steel, railways, electricity, chemicals, automobiles and electronics have performed this role of catalyst in generating related infrastructure and capital goods investment. Indeed, complementary technologies have provided a major impetus to these phases of accumulation. Revolutions in the technical basis of production frequently originate from the enhanced capacity to transform inanimate energy into mechanical energy (Landes, 1970). This is quite evident when one studies the impact of steam-driven motors in the nineteenth century, the internal combustion engine and the enormous impact of electrification last century. To be sure, each of these technological revolutions has been so pervasive that the material basis of production has been transformed beyond recognition. No sector of the economy escapes its inexorable logic.

The "swarming" of associated innovations is precisely the way Schumpeter described this phenomenon, which can best be conceptualized as a process of technological diffusion in which related and complementary techniques and technological trajectories combine to propel economic expansion. The "bandwagon" effect of these technological breakthroughs can be described in terms of both forward and backward industrial linkages. If the innovation takes the form of a factor input, then the immediate impact is to lower the costs of production. This would tend to induce further innovations in the production chain upstream. Examples would include the impact of the microchip and the innovations in chemicals and the energy sector. Backward linkages are usually associated with infrastructure developments that stimulate the capital goods sector and induce a secondary wave of investment.

A major innovation may be seen as generating a cumulative process in which a Schumpeterian cluster of major innovations is set in motion and replicated by a series of "imitators" who seek to capture temporary surplus profits (Schumpeter, 1939). This sequence is characterized by "growth poles" in the industrial system which consist of the technological leaders (the primary, "autonomous" innovators) and "follower" industries and firms which respond to this primary innovative impulse and both diffuse the innovation and act as a catalyst for secondary induced innovations. Growth pole theories identify the formation of industrial and sectoral linkages rather than the diffusion of innovation as the structural dynamics that drive growth (Pasinetti, 1981). Input–output analyses inform these theories in which technical coefficients are assumed to be fixed. Industrial complexes based on the capital goods sector exhibit forward linkages with the intermediary and consumption goods sector (Leontief, 1963, 1986). The core of this industrial complex can be partly formed by means of an inverted input–output matrix that shows the direct and indirect inputs used for one unit of output in each industry of the industrial system. Large technical coefficients tend to characterize these core industrial linkages in a hierarchical configuration (Halevi, 1996).

It should be stressed, however, that the linkages between industries and sectors revealed by the input–output tables might not necessarily imply a growth pole. It might, in fact, indicate a mature industrial life cycle with routine deliveries and few possibilities of change and development. In other words, these linkages might exhibit *declining* industrial sectors and economic stagnation. The problem with growth pole analyses is to identify the more dynamic sectors and their forward and backward linkages with other industrial sectors. Infrastructure linkages augment these industrial life cycles (Kuznets, 1953). A more detailed exposition of technical progress using Pasinetti's (1981) taxonomy is highlighted in Appendix 4B.

Structural analyses focus on the tensions generated by radical innovations and the intersectoral linkage effects. These exogenous shocks induce a phase of disequilibria that sets in motion a sequence of structural imbalances or tensions and their partial resolution. In other words, the core innovation creates a whole new set of technological trajectories and "lock-in" failures as associated industries and sectors adjust to these new technological opportunities. The issues of technological complementarities and the new learning curves required to adjust to these exogenous shocks inform structural analyses. Figure 4.1 illustrates these sectoral linkages in relation to the engineering industries (including machinery and electronics).

The competitiveness of firms ultimately stems from the long-term strength and efficiency of a national economy's productive structure, its technical infrastructure and other factors determining the externalities from which firms can benefit. Similarly, the crucial role played by generic technologies implies that the competitiveness of most industrial sectors

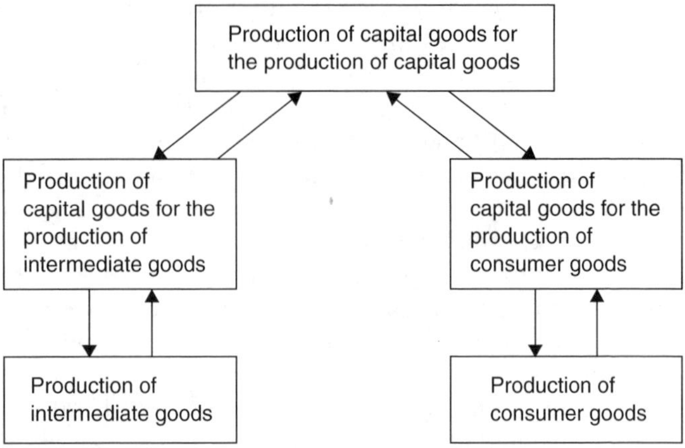

Figure 4.1 Forward and backward linkages within a production system
Source: Andersen (1992, p. 88).

depends on the capacity by which intersectoral and interindustrial transfers of technology can be accommodated. Industrial clustering contributes to the capabilities associated with the rapid commercialization of new products and processes, the ability to make rapid modifications in product design in response to feedback information from users and the flexibility to respond to short lead times in changing demand conditions (Rosenberg, 1992). According to Pavit, the following sectoral taxonomy in the formation of industry clusters can be identified (1984):

1. *Supplier-dominated sectors*: (textiles, clothing, leather, printing and publishing, wool products, etc.). In these sectors, process innovations tend to predominate. Innovative opportunities are generally embodied in new varieties of capital equipment and intermediate inputs that originate from outside these sectors. Thus the process of innovation primarily takes the form of inputs to production.
2. *Scale-intensive sectors*: (transport equipment, electrical consumer durables, metal manufacturing, food products, chemicals, etc.). Both product and process innovation takes place which generally involves mastering complex systems and economies of scale of various types. Firms tend to be large and devote a relatively high proportion of their own resources to innovation through vertical integration with the capital goods sector.
3. *Specialized suppliers*: (mechanical and instruments engineering). Innovative activities relate primarily to product innovations that

enter other sectors as capital inputs. Firms tend to be relatively small, operate in close contact with their users and embody a specialized knowledge in design and the production of equipment.

4. *Information-intensive industries*: (information and communications technology). This sector is closely related to the science-based industries and is based on systems and software design and reverse engineering.
5. *Science-based sectors*: (electronics, chemicals and pharmaceuticals). Innovation is frequently linked to new technological paradigms made possible by scientific advances. Thus technological opportunities are very high and scientific knowledge confers considerable economic returns from patents and other forms of ownership. Most of the innovative activity is formalized in large laboratories controlled by oligopolistic firms that exhibit economies of scale and scope. A high proportion of the product innovations enter a wide number of sectors as capital and intermediate inputs.

Kleinknecht has contributed to Schumpeter's original hypothesis by proposing that during the upswing of the long wave, quality-augmenting improvements and process innovations tend to predominate, while during recessional phases, radical product and process innovations are more frequent (Kleinknecht, 1981). In other words, Kleinknecht supports Schumpeter's thesis of the "swarming" of radical innovations during periods of economic downturn. Closely related to this hypothesis is the concept of "Schumpeterian profits" which individual firms can temporarily obtain by introducing innovations and techniques that temporarily capture a monopoly position in the market. These basic innovations will be accompanied by a swarm of imitators through the bandwagon effect.

The problem of causality has fuelled controversy over the proposition that depressions trigger basic innovations. To put it simply: do the new Schumpeterian industries induce an endogenous recovery, or is the upswing propelled by exogenous factors? Unfortunately, the precise role of innovations in long-wave theory continues to elude empirical investigations. One can only suggest that the dynamic between technological change and long-run growth is dialectical rather than linear. The law of circular and cumulative causation implies that increases in output tend to accelerate the rate of technical diffusion.

Recent studies raise doubts over the causal relationship between the onset of major economic downturns and the clustering of radical innovations during these secular phases (Rosenberg, 1982; Mansfield, 1987; Freeman, 1983). Schumpeter's original proposition that depressions "trigger" the development of innovations encounters considerable empirical difficulties. Although a prolonged economic slump might hasten the process of creative destruction as a consequence of the intensification of competition and rivalry, there is no firm evidence to suggest that the rate of basic innovations should increase. Rosenberg and Frischtak (1984) claim that innovations are essentially random events and are independent of the prevailing economic environment.

> In spite of this long listing of possible influences, we are left without a precise knowledge of what are the necessary and sufficient changes in the environment, which, even conceptually, can bring out a bandwagon-like diffusion of some number of basic innovations. In other words, there is no well-specified set of elements that effectively link and elucidate the direction of causality between the basic innovations, the "general level of profitability and business expectations," and their diffusion in the form of a swarm of new products and processes. (Rosenberg & Frischtak, 1984, p. 11)

Indeed, the contrary proposition might be just as plausible, that is to say, depressions could inhibit the introduction of major innovations. If sales and output are depressed and investment confidence is rather grim, then it is just as likely that funds available for research and development will be curtailed. Major innovations will normally be introduced if the prospects for growth and profitability are perceived as optimistic. Their introduction and commercialization after a prolonged period of gestation and experimentation will hinge critically on the state of business confidence. However, as soon as evidence of a possible recovery appears, the clustering of several innovations contributes to the phase of recovery.

> New technological paradigms might emerge during either depression or prosperity periods simply because – as we tried to show – their rules of generation cannot be defined in terms solely of economic inducements ... the emergence of new technological paradigms activates the expansion of one or – more likely – several vertically integrated sectors which represent, or are linked to, the new technologies and products. In macroeconomic terms, the emergence of new sectors and industrial activities together with radically new technologies for making old things can be seen as an "autonomous expansion of effective demand." (Dosi, 1984, p. 95)

The historical evidence appears to support both propositions. In the light of the present status of research in this area, any firm conclusions can only be regarded as problematic. On theoretical grounds, however, it might be more plausible to surmise that, contrary to the original "depression-trigger" hypothesis propounded by Schumpeter, basic innovations tend to cluster around strategic turning points or the "conjunctures" of long waves. In this sense, the Schumpeterian logic of "creative destruction" corresponds to the downturn. However, it should be stressed that the recovery is not automatic, nor an entirely endogenous process. In this regard, an institutionalist explanation should be identified as a possible source of these secular fluctuations.

> The depression, therefore, does not act "directly" upon the innovative processes; but it does act on the institutional structure, producing innovations in this sphere. These institutional changes affect business expectations, and these act upon the uptake of the new technology, giving rise to associated radical innovations...I would argue that the combination of increased technological opportunities and increased business expectations, conditioned by institutional change, is what may induce an increase in the rate of innovation. It is therefore not the depression which triggers innovation, but the expectation of the boom. (Coombs, 1987, p. 386)

During the recovery phase, the principal economic agents continually exaggerate; they expand the capacity of the capital goods sector too much in the phase of boom and, conversely, underestimate the magnitude of the downturn. It is usually at this crucial turning point that a financial crisis will emerge as the volume of investment exceeds demand in saturated markets, or as Joan Robinson has argued, the volume of investment tends to "overshoot" as a result of the multiplier effect of the previous boom (Robinson, 1979).

In the absence of an internal dynamic that governs the behavior of long waves, it should be conceded that the "cyclical" characteristics are highly doubtful. In order to avoid these semantic ambiguities, it would be more accurate to describe these phases as "trajectories" rather than cycles because of the obvious lack of symmetry between troughs and peaks. However, it cannot be denied that the crucial turning points or "conjunctures" signify the end of one process and the beginning of another by which a new technological basis of production is launched. The culmination of this process is necessarily one of catharsis and reconstruction, or to paraphrase Schumpeter, a process of "creative destruction." Since industrial change is rarely harmonious but moves along a trajectory that is punctuated by sudden spurts and catastrophes, the element of contingency cannot be ignored.

> First, if innovations are the root cause of cyclical fluctuations, these cannot be expected to form a single wave-like movement, because of the periods of gestation and absorption of effects by the economic system will not, in general, be equal for all of the innovations that are undertaken at any time. There will be innovations of relatively long span, and along with them others will be undertaken which run their course, on the back of the wave created by the former, in shorter periods. This at once suggests both multiplicity of fluctuations and the kind of interference between them that we can expect. When a wave of long span is in its prosperity phase, it will be easier for smaller waves – which as a rule, will correspond to less important innovations – to rise, and as long as the underlying prosperity lasts, there will be a cushion ready for them while, say, in the depression phase it might be impossible for them to rise visibly at all, although they might still assert themselves by softening that depression through their prosperities and intensifying it through their depressions. (Schumpeter, 1939, p. 167)

Technological revolutions hasten an increase in the productivity of labor. Capital will be attracted to the more profitable sectors and firms. This will be accompanied by the liquidation of the less profitable firms and industries that are not capable of surviving the chill winds of competition. Technological revolutions also give rise to drastic reductions in the turnover of capital investment, while competition between rival enterprises will accelerate the introduction of new technology as each firm attempts to capture short-term "Schumpeterian" profits. The dynamic of "creative destruction" goes beyond short-term overproduction crises and temporary gluts in the market. Instead, it is necessary to examine the deeper forces at work that originate from long-term structural changes as the older, less competitive industries fall into decline. If technological revolutions are, indeed, the source of long-wave fluctuations, then one should not be too mortified to discover that this primary trajectory is rarely, if ever, a neoclassical notion of equilibrium. The tendency is dominated by the inherent unevenness of capitalist accumulation in which disequilibrium is always the most likely outcome.

2 Oligopoly and technical progress

Schumpeter identified innovation with the "carrying out of new combinations." This implies that innovation in the economic system involves, to a large extent, a recombination of physical materials and innovative research that were previously in existence. In his earlier work, Schumpeter stressed the importance of heroic innovations by pioneering entrepreneurs as the primary catalyst in the "gales of creative destruction" (Schumpeter, 1939). In his later work, the emphasis shifted to the collective work in R&D laboratories and the incremental nature of most innovations (Schumpeter, 1942). Schumpeter recognized that in oligopolistic firms, innovation had become bureaucratized and that specialized research and development departments played an increasingly important role in the innovative process.

Diffusion of innovations in the Schumpeterian schema, however, came under widespread critical scrutiny. Most empirical studies demonstrated that new products and processes are changed considerably during the process of diffusion itself (Freeman, 1994; Lundvall, 1992; Nelson, 1987). It was also revealed that the productivity gains associated with diffusion vary considerably, partly because of the strong systemic features of most innovations. Similarly, comparative international evidence suggested that the country of origin of particular innovations is not necessarily the one that accrues the greatest gains. In most cases, reverse engineering and the appropriation of prototypes, patents and other types of intellectual property provided the catalyst for successful commercial exploitation. Indeed, much of Japan's earlier policies of import substitution and export-led growth had assimilated and improved upon foreign product and process innovations.

In the course of the early postwar years, the evidence suggested that the rate of technical change and of economic growth generally depended more on efficient diffusion than on pioneering radical innovations (Freeman, 1995). To be sure, incremental innovations from the production process itself, from the interface with the market and with related firms were identified as the major source of innovative activities. Formal R&D was still the principal source of radical innovations but it was no longer possible to ignore the many other influences on the process of technical change at the level of the firm and in specific industries. Finally, research on technological diffusion revealed the *systemic* aspects of innovation that contributed to advances in productivity growth. As the three major "generic" technologies (information technology, biotechnology and new raw materials technology) were diffused throughout the world economy in the 1970s and 1980s, these systemic aspects of innovation had acquired a greater degree of importance.

According to Rosenberg (1982), there are two means by which technological knowledge is diffused, often described as *learning curves*. *Learning by doing* is a form of learning that takes place at the manufacturing stage after the product has been designed, that is to say, after the learning in the R&D stages have been completed. On the other hand, *learning by using* generates two very different kinds of useful knowledge, which can be designated as *embodied* and *disembodied*. In the first case, the early experience with a new technology leads to a better understanding of the relationship between specific design characteristics and performance that permit subsequent improvements in design. The result is an appropriate design modification or a *feedback loop* in the development stage. In the second case, *disembodied knowledge* leads to certain alterations that require only minor modifications in hardware design. Prolonged experience with the hardware reveals information about performance and operating characteristics, which over time, lead to new practices that increase the productivity of the hardware, either by lengthening its useful life or by reducing the operating costs.

Technological knowledge can be best conceptualized as a cumulative process with reciprocal feedback loops between invention, innovation and diffusion. The process of innovation is governed by the acquisition and accumulation of knowledge. Some of this knowledge turns out to have useful applications to productive activity. At the basic research end of the spectrum, the learning process involves the acquisition of knowledge concerning the laws of nature. Conversely, the development end of innovation consists of searching out and discovering the optimal design characteristics of the new product or process. An evolutionary explanation of innovation is based on two distinct but related mechanisms. The first mechanism generates economic variety and the second selects between those varieties and changes their relative economic importance over time (Nelson & Winter, 1982). Selection in the economic sphere also influences the generation of variety (Saviotti & Metcalfe, 1991).

Within any "cluster of innovation," technological advance may follow a particular trajectory. These trajectories are governed by the prevailing *techno-economic paradigm*. In terms of the taxonomy of innovations, the following categories can be identified (Freeman & Perez, 1988):

- *Incremental innovations*: These occur more or less continuously in any industry or service activity although at differing rates in different industries. They are the result of minor, discreet and incremental improvements by technicians, engineers and others directly engaged in the production process or by advice and feedback from users (i.e. "learning by doing" and "learning by using"). Although their cumulative effect is extremely important, no single incremental innovation has any profound effects and might simply constitute a form of *tacit* rather than *codified* knowledge.

- *Radical innovations*: These are disparate and discontinuous events governed by systematic research and development activity. They often involve a combined product, process and organizational innovation, which could engender a structural change but are confined to relatively small and localized effects in terms of their aggregate economic impact. However, it is possible that a cluster of radical innovations could give rise to new industries and services such as the synthetic materials industry or the semiconductor industry.
- *Changes of the "technology system"*: These are far-reaching changes in technology affecting several branches of the economy, as well as generating entirely new sectors. The structural changes could impinge on the existing institutional framework or the existing *modes of regulation* which spill over into major organizational and managerial innovations (Boyer, 1988).
- *Changes in the "techno-economic paradigm"*: Often described as technological revolutions, the changes in technology systems are so pervasive that the entire economy is transformed. Schumpeter's long cycles and "creative gales of destruction" represent these recurrent techno-economic paradigms associated with a characteristic institutional framework that emerges after a painful and prolonged process of structural change. New paradigms impart their effects well beyond their source of origin and provide new investment opportunities through input/output flows and technological complementarities. Indeed, the emergence of a new techno-economic paradigm and the diffusion of its effects throughout the economy tend to counteract the secular tendency toward *diminishing returns*. Static and dynamic economies of scale and scope are generated by these new technological trajectories (Pavit, 1984).

Changes to the techno-economic paradigm will provoke correspondingly radical transformations in institutions and the prevailing regime of national regulation. Conversely, the institutional framework will influence the introduction and diffusion of new technologies. Social institutions can be described as sets of habits, routines, customs, laws and norms that regulate the relations between individuals and social groups. Institutions reduce uncertainties, coordinate the use of knowledge, mediate conflicts and provide economic incentives (North, 1990). Organizational and institutional innovations are inextricably linked with technical innovations. Indeed, institutional change often acts as a catalyst for technical innovation (i.e. containerization, self-service). In this sense, rules, regulations and standardization provide coherence and predictability in the face of diversity and instability generated by radical technological change (Freeman, 1995). Institutions determine these transaction costs. Furthermore, the institutional framework will shape the direction of the acquisition of knowledge and skills. It can be argued that some degree of the "creative destruction" of knowledge is necessary in order to allow the diffusion of radical innovations throughout the economy (Lundvall, 1992). The new technological trajectory might encounter "lock-in" failures in terms of the institutional framework. Institutional and organizational innovations are therefore inseparable from changes in the techno-economic paradigm.

Technical progress will generally increase the productivity of labor. In this sense, it will induce an increase in capacity utilization and a corresponding increase in aggregate profits. Innovations and their diffusion therefore act as powerful countervailing forces and tend to mitigate the inherent tendency toward stagnation under the conditions of oligopolistic competition. Just as military spending by the state will tend to increase aggregate profits, so too the technological spin-offs from these investments can impart quite substantial expansionary forces in the long run. The classical exemplars of these secular, stimulating effects can be readily observed in the stream of commercially exploitable innovations emanating from the military technology and research undertaken during the Second World War and the Cold War. Prime examples would encompass the earlier prototypes of the computer embodied in the deciphering machines used to intercept and decode enemy espionage communications; the development of atomic power; advances in aeronautical design made possible by the bombing campaigns; new raw material substitutes; the development of automation; the invention of radar and the deployment of satellite surveillance networks; to mention only a few of the innovations that were nurtured by the postwar military–industrial complex.

> "Monopolistic" (or oligopolistic) firms are generally in control of their markets and able to regulate the rate of introduction of new technology to preserve their profit margins. Assets that would have been wiped out under competition are retained and serve as a protective barrier against new competitors. What Schumpeter called the competitive process of "creative destruction" is slowed down, and so also is the overall rate of new investment. (Magdoff & Sweezy, 1988, p. 32)

On the other hand, it can be argued that technical progress tends to increase the degree of monopoly because it creates "Schumpeterian" profits, which will be defended against new entrants in the market. By designing the standard prototype, other firms and consumers can be effectively "locked in" to the existing technical infrastructure. Although technical progress tends to dampen the general level of prices in the long run, this will be counteracted by an increase in the degree of monopoly, which will keep prices and mark-ups higher than would normally be the case under more competitive conditions. As a general rule, oligopoly will not be conducive to igniting the forces of creative destruction. Indeed, innovations might even be inhibited in order to preserve monopoly profits and rents.

Conclusion

Overaccumulation in the form of semi-permanent excess capacity and recurrent financial crises are endemic under the mature stage of monopoly capital. This predominantly "rentier" phase of capitalist development carries with it the seeds of its own demise as the level of unemployment remains intolerably high and the enormous social benefits derived from technical progress begin to diminish. As Schumpeter quite succinctly observed, the very success of the earlier phases of capitalist evolution, embodied in vigorous competition and the creative impulses of technological and scientific advances, eventually encounter the barriers of the social institutions upon which the system had grown, but which are now threatened by the very same logic of creative destruction. It would be more accurate to modify Schumpeter's dialectic by arguing that rather than its conservative social institutions, the monopoly phase of capitalism itself represents the greatest barrier to social progress and material well-being for the greater majority of the population. In the final analysis, to paraphrase Marx: "The real barrier to capitalist production is capital itself."

Appendix 4A Harrod's theory of the trade cycle

Harrod constructed a dynamic theory, which elucidated the conditions by which the economy fluctuated between boom and slump on the one hand, and between trend and cycle on the other. The inspiration for the Harrodian model was Keynes's *General Theory*. The Keynesian theory was essentially based on the short term and had neglected the long-term consequences of investment and its determination. Harrod attempted to build on the Keynesian foundations by introducing the acceleration principle. The theory makes the critical assumption that the capital stock is proportional to the rate of output growth.

Harrod's analysis begins by introducing the basic growth equation:

$$GC = s \qquad (4A.1)$$

G stands for growth and is the increment of total production in any unit period expressed as a fraction of total production. Hence, if the steady growth path involves an increase in output of 5 percent per annum, G would be 1/20. C (capital) is the increase in the volume of goods and services outstanding at the beginning of each period divided by the increment of production in that same period. The fraction of income saved is denoted by s. Any changes in s should be small by comparison with changes in G.

$$GC = s - k \qquad (4A.2)$$

where k consists of current additions to capital and is therefore the capital outlay in long-term investment in plant and equipment.

$$G_w C_r = s \qquad (4A.3)$$

G_w stands for the warranted rate of growth and expresses the conditions in which producers will be content with the average rate of profit. C_r is the term for capital requirements, defined as the need for new capital divided by the increment of output to sustain the new capital requirements. C_r is therefore the required capital coefficient. It should be noted that this definition implies a *steady state* in that the existing output is only required to sustain additional output. This follows from the assumptions that (1) the capital/output ratio (v) remains constant, that (2) new inventions are neutral, and (3) the rate of interest is constant. C_r is a marginal notion; it is the new capital required to sustain the output that will satisfy the demands for consumption arising out of consumers' marginal addition to income.

From the previous analysis, it can be surmised that the greater the G, the lower the C. If G has a value above G_w, C will have a value below C_r. Furthermore, if C is less than C_r, there will be an undersupply of capital investment relative to the growth of capital requirements. In order to establish the conditions for steady state growth, there are two fundamental conditions:

$$G_n C_r = \text{or} \neq s \qquad (4A.4)$$

G_n (n for natural) denotes the *rate of advance* that the increase in population and technological improvements allow. It has no direct relation with G_w. Hence, it is necessary to consider not only the divergences of G and G_w but also those of G_w from G_n.

Harrod argued that the warranted rate of growth could be expressed as

$$G_w = s/v \tag{4A.5}$$

where v is denoted as the capital/output ratio and s the rate of saving. Since s and v tend to remain constant over the long run, this gives rise to the famous "knife-edge." Whenever G exceeds G_w, there will be a tendency for a boom to develop. Yet if G_n exceeds G_w, there is no reason why G should not exceed G_w for most of the time to produce recurrent booms. In other words, if actual growth exceeds the warranted growth rate, the increase in effective demand outstrips the rate of investment and the rate of capacity utilization. In this case, firms will increase their investment, which will have the effect of inducing a further rise in effective demand via the multiplier/accelerator effect.

On the other hand, if G_w exceeds G_n, then G must lie below G_w for most of the time, since the average value of G over a period cannot exceed that of G_n. In other words, excess capacity is generated, which will induce firms to curtail their investment. The fall in investment feeds into a decline in effective demand via the multiplier effect, which causes an expansion of excess capacity. Therefore, there is a natural tendency acting in the opposite direction toward stagnation. It is the divergences from G_w, not the value of G_w itself, which have a critical influence in producing either a slump or a boom. If G_w is greater than G_n there will be a tendency toward a slump. Since later neoclassical economists assumed full employment equilibrium, this critical distinction has been ignored. Saving is beneficial only as long as G_w is less than G_n. Increased saving therefore increases G_w and allows a steady expansion of output. The "knife-edge" implies that steady state growth is unstable. In order to ensure stable growth, the warranted rate of growth (G_w) must equal s/v in the long run with fluctuations oscillating around this ascending trend line.

The Harrodian dynamics of growth suggest two sets of problems: (1) the divergence of G_w from G_n and (2) the tendency of G to diverge from G_w. While the former is a problem of chronic unemployment, the latter is the trade cycle problem. An important critical question, which has been the source of perennial controversy, is what are the engines of growth that propel the upward trend over the long run? The most likely explanation would be to identify the impact of exogenous factors such as technical change. In this sense, Harrod's distinction between the warranted and the natural rate of growth was inspired by Keynes's distinction between an equilibrium level of unemployment and full-employment equilibrium. In the long run, however, it is difficult to justify this distinction.

Appendix 4B Classification of technical progress

Capital-intensity increasing, when:
Qi > Qki

Capital-intensity neutral, when:
Qi = Qki

Capital-intensity decreasing, when:
Qi < Qki

Always physical-capital using

Physical-capital using when
Qki < Qi + Q*

Physical-capital neutral when
Qki = Qi + Q*

Physical capital-saving when
Qki > Qi + Q*

Always direct labor-saving

Direct labor-saving when
Qi > 0

Direct labor-neutral when
Qi = 0

Direct labor-using when
Qi < 0 (and yet (*dli(t)/dt*) < 0)

Index

Q* = Standard rate of productivity growth in the economy as a whole.
Qi = The rate of technical progress in the production of commodity i.
Qki = The rate of technical progress in the production of capital goods for commodity i.
(*dli(t)/dt*) = The ratio of output to labor over time in the production of commodity i.

Source: Pasinetti (1981, p. 213).

Part II

The Era of Stagnation and Crisis: 1975–2000

5

The Demise of *Pax Americana*

Introduction

By the early 1970s, the "golden era" of postwar prosperity and growth in the advanced capitalist countries had come to an end. Since the mid-1970s most OECD countries have experienced alternating phases of growth and stagnation, punctuated by the outbreak of episodes of severe and debilitating financial instability. In many ways, it appeared that the capitalist world economy had entered into another long era of laissez-faire and globalization, reminiscent of the period preceding the First World War. Globalization set in motion destabilizing forces, as capital was no longer constrained by their respective national markets.

In short, the relatively stable postwar era of Keynesianism and the international regulatory framework established under the Bretton Woods agreements was gradually superseded by a more laissez-faire international economic order. Both the social and public spheres were now subjected to the commodification of the market place. Pre-Keynesian economic doctrines – embellished by the apparent mystique of mathematical and deductive techniques – soon gained the ascendancy. Globalization and neoliberalism reinforced each other; the constant mantra was that there was simply no other alternative. After the collapse of the Soviet Union, this mantra assumed even greater currency.

With the onset of global stagnation and crisis, interimperialist rivalry had intensified between the three major capitalist blocs in the US, the European Union and Japan/East Asia. After the collapse of the Bretton Woods fixed exchange rate system, the US authorities pursued a policy of "benign neglect" and allowed the dollar to depreciate. By doing so, it was assumed that US international competitiveness could be restored. Successive dollar depreciations, however, had generated phases of quite severe financial instability in international financial markets as the holders of dollar-denominated assets and overseas claims on dollar-denominated debts were confronted by enormous losses. The privileges bestowed by *seigniorage* meant that the US authorities could use the dollar as a powerful weapon against their rivals.

After the election of the Reagan administration in 1981, however, a strong dollar policy was pursued to attract a net inflow of capital and by doing so, to reconstitute US global financial hegemony. A strong dollar policy was pursued by aggressive interest rate hikes and by the deregulation and liberalization of capital markets, which attracted an enormous inflow of highly mobile, short-term capital. At the same time, aggregate profits could be increased through fiscal expansion, driven by a massive increase in military expenditure. This was achieved on an ideological level by the escalation of a "new" Cold War with the deployment of cruise missiles and the introduction of the Strategic Defense Initiative (SDI) or the Star Wars programme. This strategy to reestablish US global hegemony soon encountered its limits with the crash of the dollar after the Plaza accords of 1985, which culminated in the stock market crashes of 1987 and 1989. These seminal events led to the prolonged crisis in Japan as the bubble economy burst in the early 1990s and also to the renewed attempts by the Europeans to establish monetary union. In the meantime, the Third World debt crisis threatened the very foundations of the international financial system.

1 The crisis of overaccumulation

Quite contrary to the nostrums of neoliberal ideology, it will be argued that in the absence of countervailing forces, the normal state under the conditions of oligopolistic competition is economic stagnation. In other words, the "golden era" of postwar prosperity and full employment was the exception rather than the rule. The very existence of a socialist alternative made it absolutely imperative that capitalism should be reformed and made to work for the greater good. It was in this context that a new class compromise was forged between capital and labor. Hence, the enormous appeal of Keynesianism. The welfare state, full employment and collective bargaining were the major pillars of this new consensus. Furthermore, it was precisely this institutional framework that provided a certain degree of coherence and stability to the postwar phase of growth. The breakdown of what the French *regulationist* school refers to as the "Fordist" model of accumulation, gave rise to a new finance-led regime in which "shareholder value" and the demands of finance capital now acquired a more potent political expression with the rise of monetarist orthodoxy and the capture of central banks to the doctrine of "sound" money. As a result of these new realignments of political/class forces – driven by the imperatives of globalization and propagated by neoliberal ideology – the foundations of the postwar Keynesian consensus were ultimately destroyed. In this sense, capitalism had simply reverted to its normal, historical logic of recurrent booms and busts. Capitalist accumulation was now, more than ever, motivated by the primacy of the profit motive above all other social considerations. The profound difference, however, was embodied in the infinitely greater historical preeminence of oligopoly and monopoly, a scenario that even Marx could not have foreseen.

Under the conditions of monopoly capital, a rising economic surplus was generated but could not be sustained because the rate of accumulation tended to exceed the capacity of effective demand to absorb this growing surplus. Overcapacity and a profits squeeze intensified the struggle between labor and capital over the distribution of income. Unlike the classical Marxian formulation, however, it was not the upward pressure of wages during the boom that caused a profitability crisis but the problem of the *realization* of surplus value into profit. It should be conceded that Marx had not entirely extricated himself from the classical theory of wages. Since the publication of Keynes's *General Theory*, the issue of effective demand has assumed center stage. An increase in wages will not necessarily induce a fall in profitability as long as investment (and capitalist consumption) remains relatively high. Thus a fall in wages does not automatically lead to a higher rate of profit, unless it is *preceded* by an increase in investment. Investment is therefore the independent variable and wages constitute the dependent variable. In Marxian terminology, surplus value must not only be "produced" but also "realized." The crisis of overaccumulation can be conceptualized in terms of the problem of realizing an increasing proportion of surplus value. These crises become even more endemic under the conditions of monopoly capital. Consequently – in the absence of spontaneous, countervailing expansionary forces (i.e. technical innovation, the expansion of new markets), an increase in government spending and/or an increase in the trade surplus – the natural tendency is economic stagnation.

> As long as the national income rises at a constant rate, or a declining one, the capital stock should also rise at a constant rate, or even at a declining rate, to assure full utilization. But a continuous rise in national income involves a rise in surplus value, and *a fortiori* a rise

> in the rate of investment. Now a rise in the rate of investment, of course, implies that the capital will not grow in a linear fashion, but *at an increasing rate,* which clearly cannot be reconciled with the requirement of full utilization. The argument shows that a discrepancy between consumption and the production capacity must necessarily arise, a discrepancy, which most probably shows itself in under-utilization of capacity. (Steindl, 1976, p. 244)

It would be reasonable to contend that the expansionary forces, which had propelled and sustained the long postwar boom, began to diminish and had exhausted themselves by the early 1970s. The pent-up demand during the war and the phase of postwar reconstruction set in train an expansionary impetus characterized by the dynamic logic of circular and cumulative causation as increases in investment and productive capacity generated higher levels of income, employment and effective demand. This virtuous circle, however, began to encounter the problems of excess capacity and overaccumulation in the late 1960s. Furthermore, the introduction and diffusion of innovations and technologies were gradually absorbed and assimilated, which led to a general slowdown in the rate of productivity growth. Toward the end of the long boom, labor shortages emerged in most OECD countries, which had the effect of accelerating the rate of substitution of labor by capital. However, the falling output/capital ratio imparted a depressive impulse on the level of profits. The profitability crisis curtailed investment in new plant and equipment quite abruptly as the underutilization of capacity reached crisis proportions. It was in this environment that the struggle between capital and labor was waged over the distribution of the national income. In this Kaleckian drama, the "captains of industry" could not tolerate a loss of discipline in the factories. Their innate class consciousness instinctively compelled them to oppose full employment policies even though rising unemployment would inevitably have a negative effect on the level of effective demand and ultimately, on the level of aggregate profits.

Table 5.1 summarizes the profit shares in the advanced capitalist countries (ACCs) between 1960 and 1973.

> Between 1968 and 1973 the share of profits in business output fell by about 15 percent. All of the blocs experienced the squeeze, though with varying intensity. In Europe the profit share fell in the early sixties and again in the early seventies. A sharp decline began in the US after 1966. In Japan, profitability plummeted after 1970. Although

Table 5.1 Profit shares, 1960–73 (%)

	ACC	*USA*	*Europe*	*Japan*
Business				
Peak year	23.5[a]	22.5[b]	25.4[c]	36.1[d]
1973	19.9	16.7	19.5	28.1
1973/peak year	0.85	0.74	0.77	0.78
Manufacturing				
Peak year	23.7[a]	22.8[b]	25.9[c]	40.7[d]
1973	20.6	17.8	17.9	32.9
1973/peak year	0.87	0.787	0.69	0.81

[a] 1968, [b] 1966, [c] 1960, [d] 1970.

Source: Armstrong et al. (1984, p. 257).

> the squeeze on profits occurred during very different time periods, the falls were quite similar: profit shares declined around 75 percent of peak levels almost everywhere. 1969 marks the onset of decline for the ACCs as a whole because that is the first year in which a rising share in Japan no longer outweighed declines elsewhere. (Armstrong et al., 1984, p. 246).

The inability of oligopolistic capital to curtail wages growth in order to shift the burden of adjustment onto labor by decreasing prime costs was the outcome of the increased bargaining power and militancy of organized labor to resist an erosion in their living standards. Under the conditions of oligopoly, therefore, profit margins were defended by increasing prices, which in turn, set off a self-perpetuating series of wage–price spirals. At the same time, most governments had been pursuing traditional Keynesian policies to preserve high levels of employment in order to get reelected. In terms of the classical political business cycle, most governments incurred budget deficits and accommodated the expansion of credit by pursuing relatively loose monetary policies. The end result was a vicious spiral of inflation, accompanied paradoxically, by a sharp slowdown in the rate of economic growth, or what was to become known as the phenomenon of stagflation. Table 5.2 illustrates this slowdown in the rate of growth in the ACCs in the years 1973 to 1982, compared to the high growth era of 1960–73.

By the early 1970s, the historic compromise between capital and labor based on Keynesian full employment policies, the welfare state and other forms of corporatism and state regulation, was beginning to disintegrate and revert to earlier prewar forms of class conflict. Sooner or

Table 5.2 The growth slowdown, 1960–90 (average annual % growth ratios of GDP)

	1960–73	*1973–79*	*1979–90*	*1979–82*	*1982–90*
USA	4.0	2.4	2.6	−0.1	3.6
Europe	4.8	2.6	2.3	0.9	2.8
Japan	9.6	3.6	4.1	3.5	4.3
OECD	4.9	2.7	2.7	0.9	3.4

Source: OECD Main Economic Indicators, 1992.

later, all of the leading capitalist countries entered a long period of stagnation characterized by increasing levels of unemployment and the onset of global overcapacity. The automatic stabilizers performed by the existence of a substantial state sector and the expansion of public and private debt ultimately prevented the emergence of a depressive spiral reminiscent of the Great Depression. Yet it can be argued that the hyper-expansion of credit during this era of stagnation could eventually prove to be the harbinger of even more chronic levels of excess capacity with the possible onset of a phase of debt deflation.

The emergence of stagflation witnessed a radical political transformation as the postwar Keynesian consensus disintegrated. From the early 1980s onward, orthodox monetarist policies gained the ascendancy in most advanced capitalist countries. Anti-inflationary strategies became the norm with the imposition of tight fiscal and monetary policies, accompanied by financial deregulation, privatization of public assets and a push to deregulate labor markets. Neoliberals argued that the purgative forces induced by competition would achieve efficiency gains. At the same time, the role of the state in economic life should be curtailed to allow the market to allocate resources and prevent the "crowding out" of private investment.

> This was the "revenge of the rentiers" after the depredations of the 1970s. Since that time the rhetoric of the macroeconomic debate has focused almost entirely on financial issues, such as the need to cure inflation, the need to balance the government budget, the need to maintain the value of the exchange rate, and so on. In a very real sense, however, the ultimate purpose behind the "conservative" prescriptions in all of these issues is to maintain and increase the real rate of return to financial capital. (Smithin, 1996, p. 5)

In retrospect, it is evident that these policies merely accentuated the stagnationist tendencies and hastened a succession of policy-induced recessions. The social costs of containing inflationary forces proved to be quite severe, especially in terms of unemployment and the loss of potential output. It is also clear that the recoveries from these policy-induced recessions have not been the result of spontaneous market forces but by a political reversal of the original policy objectives. If monetarism had been pursued to its logical extreme, it is more than plausible to contend that an economic depression might have been inadvertently engineered. Yet neoliberalism was never pursued in its purest form in the more advanced capitalist countries because of the political backlash it would have provoked. On the other hand, neoliberal economic fundamentalism could be imposed on poorer Third World countries by the Wall Street–IMF–US Treasury complex with quite disastrous social consequences.

Quite apart from the economic rationality and efficacy of neoliberalism, the policies of "sound money" tend to benefit financial and rentier interests rather than industrial capital and the working class. Hence, over the past two decades, a finance-led regime of accumulation has superseded the former "Fordist" model based on the national imperatives of full employment and corporatist forms of regulation and state intervention. Indeed, the policies of financial deregulation have acted as the deus ex machina in unleashing the forces of globalization. However, the accumulation of "fictitious capital" merely represents an unproductive form of expenditure and will only postpone and temporarily mitigate these stagnationist tendencies. As a means of exchange value, money simply represents a valid claim on the flow of goods and services produced by the real economy. Divorced from the productive circuits of capital, the accumulation of money capital signifies a deepening crisis in the realization of surplus value.

2 The demise of the Bretton Woods accords

> A system of fixed exchange rates such as the Bretton Woods system, with some latitude for independent macroeconomic policies, is incompatible with freedom of capital movement because capital flows could undermine both fixed exchange rates and independent macroeconomic policies. A system of fixed exchange rates and independent macroeconomic policies promotes economic stability and enables a government to deal simultaneously with domestic unemployment. However, such a system sacrifices freedom of capital movement, one of the most important goals of international capitalism. (Gilpin, 2000, p. 123)

The United States emerged as the principal creditor nation after the Second World War. Its status as the reserve currency nation and "central banker" for the international payments system was established with the signing of the Bretton Woods agreements in 1947 which created a fixed, though flexible exchange rate system based on gold/dollar convertibility. Free trade and multilateralism formed the basis of the American vision of the postwar economic order. The whole tenor of this neoliberal strategy asserted itself in the economic doctrines, which informed the institutions and economic agreements of *Pax Americana*; from the IMF Charter, the GATT agreements and most notably in the gold/dollar monetary and exchange rate system.

The expansion of US direct investment abroad was governed by the preeminent role performed by the dollar as the international means of payments and as the principal reserve currency, which provided a coherent vehicle by which the profits of American corporations could be converted and reinvested in global capital markets. Furthermore, as a result of an overvalued US dollar, American corporations could purchase foreign assets more cheaply and could take advantage of relatively lower foreign wages. The security and stability of the gold/dollar regime not only provided a favorable environment for long-term investment but also allowed American firms to borrow on more attractive terms in international capital markets. The preeminent international status of the dollar therefore promoted the expansion of US direct investment abroad (Gilpin, 1975). The Bretton Woods system also promoted the expansion of international trade. In the course of the postwar era, trade had increased from 7 to 21 percent of total world income. The value of world trade has also grown from $US57 billion in 1947 to over $US60 trillion in the 1990s (Gilpin, 2000, p. 20). For over two decades since its inception, the system provided a relatively stable and coherent mechanism in the settlement of international payments and the regulation of international liquidity.

In stark contrast to the dollar shortage of the early postwar years, the US dollar had flooded world markets by the late 1960s. This enormous expansion of international liquidity was accentuated by the permissive financing of the Vietnam War as the US Treasury resorted to the printing press and US governments incurred successive budget deficits (Block, 1977). It was the emergence of US balance of payments deficits, however, which ultimately caused a loss of confidence in the US dollar as an international reserve currency and as a means of payments. This flight from the dollar led to a serious drain on US gold reserves, which shrank from an estimated $23 billion in 1950 to about $12 billion in

1967. At the same time, official and private foreign dollar holdings increased from $15.1 billion in 1957 to $31.5 billion in 1968 (Gilpin, 1979, pp. 369–70). The culmination of the gold drain and the loss of confidence in the US dollar induced an unprecedented rise in the demand and market price for gold, which eventually destroyed gold/dollar convertibility. As long as it had fostered the expansion of international trade, foreign economic agents had accepted seigniorage of the dollar. Seigniorage can be defined as the financial gains accrued to a country that issues an international currency. This can take the form of acquiring foreign assets through a depreciating currency or the gains associated with an inflationary policy, which transfers resources from both residents and nonresidents who possess US dollars to the US government which issues the money. In its strictest definition, seigniorage refers to the ability of a reserve currency nation to perform the role of world central banker (Triffin, 1961).

Under the fixed exchange rate system, only one country can set its monetary and exchange rate policies independently of all other countries. In the monetary literature this is defined as the *nth country* paradox. If one assumes that a group of countries are governed by a fixed exchange rate regime, only *country n* is theoretically able to fix its exchange rate in relation to countries $n-1$. The *nth country* therefore performs an anchor role or reference point in an asymmetrical system to which all of the other countries are compelled to align themselves. Under the former Bretton Woods system, the US economy performed this dominant anchor role (Moon, 1982).

The US economy was therefore capable of exporting capital by accumulating short-term current account deficits since, unlike the rest of the capitalist world, it was relatively unencumbered by the external balance of payments constraint. Similarly, American financial markets could borrow in the short term in order to lend in the long term. Yet the cohesion and stability of the fixed exchange rate system were ultimately dependent on the ability and willingness of the US authorities to act as a world central banker. As soon as their liabilities in the issuing of US dollars were no longer regarded as "good as gold," the "solvency" of the US monetary authorities in their role as world bankers was imperiled (Guerrieri & Padoan, 1986).

In short, the success of the system was too highly dependent upon the capacity and willingness of the US monetary authorities to perform the role of world central banker. With the collapse of the fixed exchange rate system based on gold/dollar convertibility, international confidence in the dollar evaporated which hastened an international exchange rate crisis. The relative decline of American industrial productivity and international competitiveness contributed to the erosion of its role as reserve currency nation. Close analogies with the demise of the gold standard under the aegis of *Pax Britannica* can be drawn. Just as the decline of Britain's relative economic power had hastened the dissolution of the gold standard, so too the relative decline of US economic power undermined its role as international central banker under the Bretton Woods system.

Between 1950 and 1971, US productivity growth had fallen behind the European Economic Community (EEC) by 35 percent and Japan by as much as 60 percent. During the same period, average annual productivity growth in the US was estimated at only 1.7 percent, compared to 4.5 percent in the EEC and 10.6 percent in Japan (Kaldor, 1978, p. 67). After the demise of the Bretton Woods system, successive US governments adhered to a policy of "benign neglect" which allowed the dollar to progressively devalue (Parboni, 1981). In other words, successive dollar devaluations contributed to the restoration of US international competitiveness. Dollar devaluations, however, tended to impart inflationary impulses transmitted through the expansion of international liquidity.

Despite the demise of the fixed exchange rate regime, the US dollar continued to perform the role of international means of payments and reserve currency. Indeed, the US was no longer constrained by its obligations to accumulate trade surpluses in order to defend gold/dollar convertibility. It was now possible for the US monetary authorities to pursue reflationary policies and dollar devaluations in order to restore their international competitiveness (Parboni, 1981). The relatively small tradable sector of the US economy as measured as a share of GDP, implied that successive devaluations of the dollar were more inflationary overseas than within the domestic economy. In this sense, the US economy was capable of "exporting" inflation through an increase in international liquidity. Its major industrial rivals were more vulnerable to the inflationary consequences of US expansionary policies. In Western Europe, these policies had an adverse impact in terms of the inflationary effects and the exchange rate instability generated by speculative financial flows. As the dollar crisis deepened, exchange rate volatility in Europe threatened further progress toward closer economic union. The dollar crisis thus spurred European leaders to construct a zone of monetary stability across the Atlantic (Kruse, 1980).

The exponential growth of the private Eurodollar market was the most visible manifestation of this unregulated expansion of international liquidity and credit creation. After the demise of the gold/dollar regime, demand for liquidity increased as both international firms and central banks resorted to the Eurodollar market as a source of credit. The origins of this market can be traced back to the Kennedy administration in which the Federal Reserve Bank had imposed limits on interest rates to deposits within the domestic economy (Kindleberger, 1984, p. 445). With the restoration of currency convertibility in 1958, financial institutions in Europe could purchase US bonds and securities and engage in foreign exchange transactions. Since investors could earn a higher rate of return by transferring their funds from the US to the Eurodollar market, the growth of the latter was set in motion.

The magnitude of this flight of capital was reflected in the expansion of US banks operating abroad; by 1972 there were 107 banks with total assets exceeding $80 billion. Two years later, this figure had increased to an estimated $140 billion or equivalent to one-fifth of the value of the US national product (Mayer, 1974, p. 437). Most of the transactions of the Eurodollar market occurred in the London branches of US banks, which would issue "certificates of deposits" against the payment of their dollar liabilities in the US. Since US banks retained possession of dollars deposited abroad, the growth of lending in US dollars by international financial agents generated a multiplier effect and increased the volume of international liquidity. The Eurodollar market therefore acted as a catalyst in the expansion of international liquidity and contributed to the inflationary upsurge of the 1970s. Consequently, the entire pyramid of credit was no longer governed by the regime of regulation based on gold/dollar convertibility. A more laissez-faire system had emerged based on what many commentators described as the "paper dollar" standard (Triffin, 1987).

Despite the demise of the Bretton Woods system, the US balance of payments and domestic US interest rates continued to act as the unofficial pivot by which international liquidity was likely to behave. A rise in US interest rates relative to average international rates was more than likely to have a contractionary effect on international liquidity. Conversely, a relative fall in US interest rates would impart an expansionary impetus to international liquidity. This inverse relationship depends quite critically on the continuation of the strategic role performed by the US dollar in international trade and payments. In the absence of the regulatory function performed by a fixed exchange rate regime, both private and public debts have become increasingly monetized. In short, the expansion of international liquidity has mirrored the growth of American international indebtedness.

The cessation of gold/dollar convertibility did not necessarily imply the demise of the strategic international role of the dollar. Indeed, the expansion of international liquidity had more than quadrupled in the decade after the collapse of the Bretton Woods system (Triffin, 1978). US trade deficits were no longer financed by the depletion of US reserves but by the acceptance of central banks of US treasury bonds and debts in the form of international reserves. These international reserves had more than doubled between 1970 and 1972 alone (Triffin, 1978, p. 53). The US dollar continued to reign supreme as the world's foremost reserve currency, as the principal intervention currency by central banks and as the major numeraire in international transactions. The emergence of this free market system, however, bred speculation, exchange rate volatility and interstate rivalry over markets and investment outlets. A relatively stable hegemonic regime was replaced by an oligopolistic system driven by competition and rivalry between the US, Japan and the EEC.

After all attempts to stabilize gold prices had failed, a two-tiered system emerged in which the official price of gold was preserved at $35 per ounce between central banks but the market price was allowed to fluctuate. This system merely bred further speculation. In the meantime, multilateral negotiations had been convened by the Group of Ten industrial countries, to devise a new means of issuing international reserves. An agreement was reached to create Special Drawing Rights (SDRs) issued by the International Monetary Fund and managed jointly by the Group of Ten (Spero, 1977, p. 48). However, these proposals ultimately failed to prevent the collapse of the international monetary system.

The Group of Ten were eventually able to reach a tentative accord in their negotiating stance during the Smithsonian Agreements in December 1971. The outcome of these negotiations involved the official renunciation of gold/dollar convertibility and the unilateral devaluation of the US dollar by 9 percent. The Group of Ten also agreed to a modified version of fixed exchange rates, which would allow managed, adjustable parities. Parity bands would be increased from the Bretton Woods margin of 1.5 percent to 2.25 percent in order to ease speculative propensities. At the same time, confidence in the dollar had not been restored as the US current account deficit exceeded $US10 billion in early 1973. After a series of meetings between the Finance Ministers of the Group of Ten, the US dollar was devalued by 10 percent in February 1973. The second dollar devaluation signaled the demise of the Smithsonian accords and the international postwar system of fixed exchange rates.

The US economy was no longer encumbered by the problem of generating a current account surplus with which to finance its capital account deficit. The US trade and budget deficits could be financed by the issuing of bonds and securities, which would be purchased by the rest of the world. In other words, US interest rates would act as the sole means of regulating international liquidity, while market forces would govern exchange rates. American policy-makers could now pursue an unfettered strategy of restoring their international export competitiveness through successive dollar devaluations (Parboni, 1981, pp. 89–90). The dollar crisis therefore not only imparted an inflationary impulse which had forced governments throughout the OECD to impose quite severe deflationary policies, but successive dollar devaluations also threatened to erode the competitiveness of America's major rivals in Europe and Japan.

3 The dollar and its rivals

The US dollar had been subjected to chronic instability in the course of 1977. The prospect of a prolonged deficit in the US current account and the inability of the government to dampen inflationary forces had hastened a renewed dollar crisis. In response to the slide in the US dollar, the Carter administration was persuaded to abandon their policy of "benign neglect" and actively pursued a more interventionist strategy. With the onset of recession in the late 1970s, the Americans propounded the "locomotive theory" in which they attempted to persuade the major surplus countries of Japan and Germany to pump prime their economies, arguing that a concerted fiscal stimulus would redress the widening trade imbalances and generate a sustained recovery.

Both the German and Japanese authorities, however, were quite reluctant to pursue more expansionary policies because of the inflationary risks involved. In 1977 and 1978, the US economy experienced a current account deficit of $15.2 billion and $13.2 billion respectively. At the same time, official claims on the US Treasury increased by around $35 billion and $32 billion respectively (Thygessen, 1981, p. 502). In other words, the US Treasury was forced to replenish its reserves by borrowings in foreign capital markets. Table 5.3 illustrates these growing trade imbalances between the three major capitalist economies.

Carter's neo-Keynesianism was soon replaced by a more orthodox monetarist strategy with the Presidential victory of Reagan in 1981 and the ascendancy of Paul Volcker as the incumbent Governor of the Federal Reserve Board. With the onset of the second oil price shocks in 1979, the OECD countries were forced to enact restrictive fiscal and

Table 5.3 (1) Balance of trade and (2) current account for the US, Germany and Japan, 1977–80 ($US billions)

	1977	*1978*	*1979*	*1980*
USA (1)	−30.9	−33.8	−29.5	−25.0
(2)	−15.2	−13.5	−0.3	0.1
Germany (1)	19.3	15.5	17.7	10.0
(2)	4.3	8.9	−5.8	−15.5
Japan (1)	17.3	24.6	1.8	0
(2)	10.9	16.5	−8.6	−10.8

Source: OECD Main Economic Indicators, 1982.

monetary policies, which had the effect of dampening the level of effective demand and contributed to the international recession of 1980–82. At the same time, a strong dollar policy was adopted by the Reagan administration. US nominal interest rates also rose sharply, attracting a considerable inflow of capital.

However, the fall in oil prices after the recession and the rapid expansion of the US economy provided an engine of growth for the OECD countries as a whole. In retrospect, the contradictory US strategy of tight monetary policies accompanied by expansionary fiscal policies, which were partly driven by increased military expenditure, could not be sustained as long as the US continued to accumulate a trade deficit. The relative strength of the dollar was not induced by a substantial improvement in the American trade deficit, nor by a recovery of its industrial export competitiveness. Instead, the massive inflow of capital was governed almost entirely by the inducement of high nominal interest rates. Figure 5.1 illustrates short- and long-term interest rate trends between 1975 and 1985 in the United States.

The strong dollar policy in the first term of the Reagan administration generated two contradictory outcomes. Although the strong dollar and high nominal interest rates contributed to a curtailment of domestic inflation, it also had a negative impact on US export competitiveness, which was reflected in the deterioration of the balance of payments. The US trade deficit had increased from an average of $US27 billion in 1978–80 to $US148 billion in 1985, while the current account deficit deteriorated from $US4 billion to about $US128 billion over the same period (Parboni, 1986). By March 1985, the dollar was estimated to have appreciated by more than 30 percent on a trade-weighted average since the beginning of 1981.

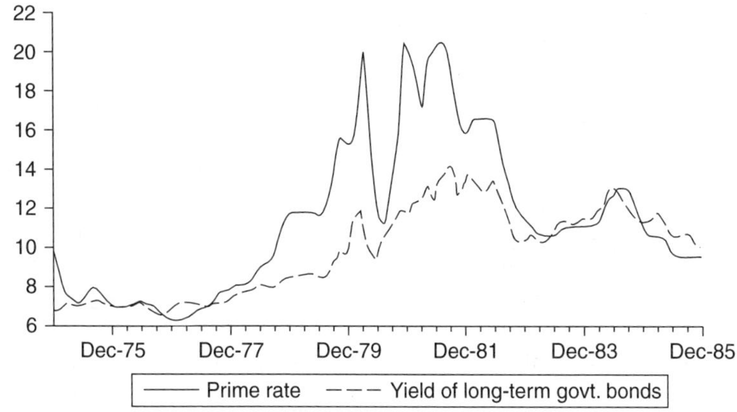

Figure 5.1 United States: interest rates, 1975–85 (percentage, pa)

Source: OECD Main Economic Indicators, 1999.

International pressure began to mount for a series of sustained dollar depreciations, especially after the realization that the US economy had become a net debtor for the first time since the turn of the century. This was accompanied by a growing protectionist sentiment in the US Congress. The Reagan administration could either succumb to these protectionist demands or divert them through dollar depreciations. In the light of these events, a more interventionist policy emerged in contrast to the prevailing neoliberal paradigm that had informed US exchange rate policies. During their second term, the Reagan administration pursued a strategy not too dissimilar to that of the Carter years by attempting to persuade Germany and Japan to adopt more expansionary policies.

Predictably enough, the German and Japanese governments were reluctant to accommodate these demands. With the breakdown of macroeconomic policy coordination between the major industrial countries (the G-5), the central bankers of these countries launched a series of concerted interventions in order to avert a crash landing of the US dollar. An estimated $US12 billion was mobilized in March 1985 to engineer a soft landing. Within a year, the dollar had depreciated by 35 percent on a trade-weighted average; the dollar/mark rate had fallen from 3.47 to 2.25 and its yen value from 260 to 175. After the Plaza accords of September 1985, another concerted central bank intervention was orchestrated to counter the mounting speculation in global currency markets. The failure of Germany and Japan to stimulate their economies as the US had requested during the Plaza summit only provoked US officials to "talk down" the dollar in what soon developed into a dangerous game of monetary brinkmanship (Funabashi, 1986). Although this American strategy eventually persuaded the Japanese to pursue a more expansionary policy after the stock market crash of October 1987, the German authorities remained intransigent.

Quite simply, German exports were not as dependent on the US domestic market as those of Japan. Whereas only about 10 percent of German exports were destined for the American market, the EEC had accounted for about a third of total German exports. Consequently, the maintenance of a stable exchange rate regime in Europe, embodied by the European Monetary System (EMS), represented the primary German concern and had informed their negotiating stance during the Plaza and Louvre summit meetings. As the dollar rapidly fell from 1985 onwards, a vicious circle developed with the onset of interstate rivalries over markets and investment outlets (Parboni, 1986). It was in this volatile environment that international summits were convened to engineer a "soft landing" of the US dollar and to coordinate macroeconomic policies. The ultimate failure of these summits to resolve the basic core of the problem – US deficits and dollar instability – hastened widespread financial panic in world financial markets which culminated in the stock market crashes of 1987 and 1989.

> When Reagan entered the White House in 1981 the federal budget deficit stood at $74 billion and the total national debt at $1 trillion. By 1991 the budget deficit had quadrupled to more than $300 billion a year and the national debt had quadrupled to nearly $4 trillion. As a result, in 1992 net federal interest payments amounted to $195 billion a year and represented 15 percent of the total budget, up from $17 billion and 7 percent in 1973. (Arrighi, 1994, p. 317)

4 Third World debt and delusion

It was in the wake of the oil price shocks and the severe international recession of the early 1980s that Third World and Eastern European debt reached truly critical levels and threatened some of the largest banks in the world. The nonoil-producing less developed countries (LDCs) had to pay $US260 billion more for oil imports, between 1974 and 1982 as a result of the OPEC price rises, which accounted for over half of the total indebtedness of these countries (Cline, 1986, p. 19). When viewed in terms of other related commodity price indices, oil prices had surged ahead by a factor of six (Strange, 1986, p. 19). With the onset of recession, the terms of trade of these nonoil-producing LDCs and Eastern Europe had collapsed. In order to finance their respective balance of payments deficits, most of these countries resorted to foreign borrowings made possible, in many cases, by the infusion of funds from petrodollar recycling. However, as soon as their external indebtedness increased, international interest rates also rose quite sharply. The conditions were therefore established for the emergence of a severe debt crisis.

Despite the collapse of nonoil commodity prices, international banks continued to increase their lending to LDCs. The average debt-servicing ratio (ratio of interest and principal payments to export income) increased from 17.4 percent in 1980 to 24.4 percent in 1982 (Korner et al., 1986, p. 8). Since most loans were denominated in US dollars, their plight was further exacerbated by the sharp rise in the US dollar in the early 1980s. A crucial aspect of this mounting Third World indebtedness was the role performed by the London Inter-Bank Offer Rate (LIBOR), which was deployed by international banks as the official benchmark in the determination of interest repayments. The LIBOR was based on the rate offered by the Eurocurrency market but the US prime rate continued to act as the official anchor. By adopting a variable rate in the negotiation of loan agreements, banks sought to avoid the risk involved. The borrowers effectively incurred the risk premium.

> The floating interest rate system adopted in Eurocurrency lending meant that it was the borrowers' liability which immediately increased if there was a tightening of credit in world capital markets, so that the burden of servicing became heavier just as new borrowing became more difficult and more expensive. (Strange, 1986, p. 49)

Between 1972 and 1981, the LIBOR rose relentlessly, from about 5.5 percent to around 17 percent. With each single-digit rise in the rate of interest, the debt service burden of the Third World increased by over $US4 billion (Wood, 1985, p. 20). In the meantime, the share of world trade by these countries fell sharply, while the terms of trade were estimated to have declined by 16 percent between 1978 and 1983.

> While the LDCs held 28 per cent of world trade in 1980, by 1986 their share had dropped to 19 per cent. The developed countries increased their trade share from 63 per cent to 70 per cent during the same period. In 1980 the rich countries bought 29 per cent of their imports from the poor ones and 66 percent from each other. In 1986 they

> bought only 19 per cent of their imports from Third World countries and 77 per cent from each other. (George, 1988, p. 73)

Despite this visible deterioration of the balance of payments, terms of trade and economic growth of the nonoil-producing LDCs, international banks continued to increase their lending. This lending binge was fuelled to a large extent by the explosive growth of the Eurodollar market, which in turn had absorbed the rising OPEC surpluses made possible by the oil price shocks of 1978–79. Total gross lending to the nonoil-producing LDCs had increased from $US190.8 billion in 1975 to $US612.4 billion in 1982 (Table 5.4).

Needless to say, this situation became increasingly untenable. The severe recession of the early 1980s caused a curtailment in LDC exports as commodity prices collapsed. This was accompanied by rising interest rates and an increase in oil prices. All of these events conspired to hasten the Third World debt crisis of the 1980s. It was the Mexican debt moratorium in late 1982, which became the catalyst that galvanized an international rescue operation. Between 1981 and 1983, there were four major rescue operations in Mexico, Brazil, Argentina and Yugoslavia. The ultimate trigger came from Mexico; it was the declaration that the government would suspend further payments on their debt that set in train an immediate response from the US Federal Reserve. Mexico was encumbered by more than $US80 billion in total debts, which translated

Table 5.4 Indicators of external debt in the nonoil LDCs, 1975–82 (billions of $US and percentages)

	1975	*1976*	*1977*	*1978*	*1979*	*1980*	*1981*	*1982*
External debt, total	190.8	228.0	278.5	336.3	396.9	474.0	550.0	612.4
External debt, long-term	163.5	194.9	235.9	286.6	338.1	388.5	452.8	499.6
Debt/exports (%)	122.4	125.5	126.4	130.2	119.2	121.9	124.9	143.3
Debt service/ exports (%)[a]	16.1	15.3	15.4	19.0	19.0	17.6	20.4	23.9
Debt/GDP (%)	23.8	25.7	27.4	28.5	27.5	27.6	31.0	23.7
Oil as a % of imports[b]	13.3	15.6	15.1	13.9	16.2	20.4	21.0	19.0

Note: Exports of goods and services: [a] includes interest but not amortization on short-term debt; [b] net oil importers only.

Source: IMF *World Economic Outlook*, 1982, 1983.

into an exposure by US banks that threatened to bring down the very structure of the US banking system. For instance, the nine largest banks had 44 percent of their total capital exposed in Mexico alone. To declare that these loans were "nonperforming" would have been tantamount to a declaration of bankruptcy; a scenario which would have sparked off a global financial panic. As is often the case in these dire circumstances, the only resort was to plead for state support. The architect of the rescue operation was Paul Volcker who had no real ideological scruples – in the light of his rhetorical adherence to the virtues of neoliberalism – than to mobilize over a billion American dollars in short-term credit and a similar amount in prepayment for Mexican crude oil, in a desperate bid to avert a global financial meltdown. The rescue operation was soon supported by the central banks of the major Western countries through the Bank for International Settlements (BIS), who designated the IMF as the sole arbiter in preserving the interests of the international banks. Over the next few years, similar rescue operations were orchestrated with the Brazilian and Argentinean authorities to broker a deal which would rescue Western banks from their own duplicity.

> In Mexico, all public debt due in 1982 after August and through 1984 was rescheduled. This amount reached approximately $US20 b, much of which was short-term debt. In Argentina, arrears on short and long-term debt had reached $US2.8 b by early 1983, and all public debt in arrears as well as that due in 1983 was rescheduled. In Brazil, only the public long-term debt due in 1983 was rescheduled, because Brazil made an extreme effort to distance itself from being classed as a standard rescheduling case – for fear of injury to its credit standing in the longer run. (Cline, 1983, p. 43)

The real burden of these IMF "structural adjustment" programs was imposed on the ordinary workers and peasants of Latin America in the form of economic austerity, the cutback of state expenditure on social programs and food subsidies and an assault on real wages. This allowed the oligarchs of Latin America to continue to service their debts. Per capita income declined in real terms throughout the 1980s as a pervasive economic depression gripped the continent.

> And so, the countries of the Third World pay, come what may. The poorer they become, and the more they owe, the more they pay. The logic of the Shylocks of the world market is implacable: a dollar costs a pound of flesh. Between 1980 and 1983, per capita income fell by

> 6.6 per cent in the Third World as a whole. It fell by one third in western Asia, by 10 per cent in Africa and Latin America, but in East Asia it rose by 10 per cent. (Liepietz, 1987, p. 174)

The emergence of what many authors described as "Faustian" finance gave rise to an entirely new form of neocolonialism, driven by the imperatives of the Wall Street–IMF–US Treasury complex, which increasingly exported and imposed its harsh version of neoliberalism (Gowan, 1999). After the Mexican fiasco, banks doubtless became more reluctant to roll over existing loans, let alone extend further loans. In order to prevent the very real possibility of a global financial meltdown, further interventions by the IMF and the central banks of the industrial countries were hastily undertaken. In late 1982, the Group of Ten industrial countries agreed to inject more funds into the IMF statutory reserves, from $US62 billion to $US93 billion (*New York Times*, 14/12/1982). The emergency fund of the IMF was also increased from $US6 billion to $US19 billion (Cline, 1983, pp. 105–6).

By October 1985, a blueprint for reform was proposed with the release of the Baker Plan. The debtor countries were forced to implement "structural reforms," which was the official euphemism for the imposition of neoliberal policies. Further private loans would be conditional on the progress of implementing these "reforms." In order to avert further defaults, the Baker Plan would provide an additional $US20 billion over three years, which would be augmented by official multilateral funds from the World Bank and the Inter-American Development Bank. The private banks themselves escaped any obligation or responsibility for the financial malaise, while most of the burden was placed entirely on the shoulders of the debtor countries. The losses faced by the banks were simply written off. In a frank admission to the *New York Times* in 1983, Paul Volcker stated:

> Bankers say there is no likelihood that the total amount of credit extended to developing countries will ever be repaid, anymore than there is a chance that the US government will ever retire its $US1.1 trillion debt, or that the total $US1.1 trillion in home mortgages outstanding in the US will ever be paid off. As old loans are retired, new ones will be extended. (*New York Times*, 9/7/1983)

The role of the IMF as the world's financial policeman was expanded considerably in the wake of the Third World debt crisis. Its power to impose and preside over neoliberal policies was extended throughout the Third World. Indeed, the IMF not only acted in close concert with and on the behalf of international finance, but also became a powerful leverage for US foreign policy objectives. In an influential report to the Reagan administration, entitled *US Participation in the Multilateral Development Banks in the 1980s*, the IMF–World Bank network was recast in terms of a strategic extension of US foreign policy (*Washington Post*, 7/8/1983). The legacy of the Third World debt crisis still resonates after two decades and has left a trail of human and social devastation in its aftermath.

5 A tripolar world system?

In the study of international political economy, the concept of "hegemony" has acquired a strategic meaning. Whether implicitly or explicitly, the term applies to one country or a group of nation-states, which form a dominant power bloc within a definite hierarchy of nation-states. In the "world system" literature this configuration is viewed as a zero-sum game between the dominant core, satellite and peripheral states (Wallerstein, 1976; Arrighi, 1978). A tripolar system of Japan, the European Community and the United States has emerged as the dominant, core group of states. The demise of the postwar system of *Pax Americana* could witness the emergence of trading blocs and exclusive currency zones gravitating around these hegemonic core regions. This redivision of the world market was accompanied by the disintegration of the Soviet bloc in 1989. One of the most important agents of this process of globalization and rationalization is the multinational corporation (MNC). As the modern bearer of the process of economic concentration and centralization, the MNC is a powerful agency through which uneven development is fostered. According to one of the seminal studies by the late Stephen Hymer,

> Through its propensity to nestle everywhere, settle everywhere and establish connections everywhere, the multinational corporation destroys the possibility of national seclusion and self-sufficiency and creates a universal interdependence. But the multinational corporation is still a private institution with a partial outlook and represents only an imperfect solution to the problem of international co-operation. It creates hierarchy rather than equality and spreads its benefits unequally. (Hymer, 1975, p. 60)

The emergence of the MNC has circumvented traditional state mercantilist policies as intra-MNC trade has increased its share of the total volume of world trade. Similarly, the export of capital in the form of foreign direct investment (FDI) has increasingly superseded traditional trade flows through the export of goods and services. By 1994, for instance, intrafirm trade between US parent firms and their transplants abroad had accounted for between one-third and two-fifths of total US imported goods and services (Gilpin, 2000, p. 169). Transnational corporations have demanded the abolition of state regulations and trade barriers, which impede the movement of capital and trade across national borders. At the same time, it can be argued that instead of constituting an institutional obstacle to the globalization of capital, the modern state has facilitated this process. This is reflected in the ascendancy of the neoliberal paradigm in which the nation-state has provided a framework for the rise of the "informal empire of free enterprise" (Arrighi, 1978). A powerful trade-off has therefore developed between the imperatives of national macroeconomic stability, on the one hand, and the maintenance of an external balance, on the other hand. This external constraint has eroded traditional Keynesian countercyclical policies. The postwar trend toward the growing globalization of capital has had profound consequences for the existing hierarchy of nation-states and interstate economic relations. In other words, how will the nation-state adapt and respond to the overwhelming demands of international capital? Indeed, will the nation-state continue to survive in its present form?

Despite the increased propensity toward the globalization of production, MNCs still require the traditional state functions to defend and legitimize property rights and provide a coherent regulatory framework. In other words, MNCs not only demand the dismantling of national barriers to the free movement of capital and technology, but also the conditions of social and political stability. However, the neoliberal strategies favored by MNCs inevitably erode national sovereignty and impose external constraints on the ability of national governments to pursue economic policies, which promote employment and social cohesion. The problem of "territorial non-coincidence" will ultimately assert itself. The rise of monopoly capital in the late nineteenth century coincided with the ascendancy of nationalism and interimperialist rivalry. Yet the demise of the nation-state over the past three decades as a sphere of accumulation through the development of a domestic market (i.e. "Fordism") has not been replaced and superseded by supranational forms of capitalist expansion and regulation. The present phase of globalization represents a shift in the capitalist mode of accumulation from a predominantly national-based, "Fordist" model to a post-Fordist regime in which capital accumulation is increasingly governed by the imperatives of international finance.

In the *Communist Manifesto*, Karl Marx and Engels were two of the first philosophers to foresee the momentous changes unleashed by the emergence of a global market:

> Constant revolutionising of production, uninterrupted disturbance of social conditions, everlasting uncertainty and agitation ... all fixed, fast frozen relations, with their train of ancient and venerable prejudices and opinions, are swept away. All new-formed ones become antiquated before they can ossify. All that is solid melts into air.... The need for a constantly expanding market for its products chases the bourgeoisie over the whole surface of the globe. It must nestle everywhere, settle everywhere, establish connections everywhere. (Marx & Engels, 1998, pp. 38–9)

The greatest divide is between the developed "North" and the underdeveloped "South." Although some countries – most notably East Asia – have successfully integrated into the global economy, most of the poorest countries have been excluded. This is reflected in international trade and investment flows. For instance, between 1850 and 1950 trade between North and South was about 30 percent of world trade but by the early 1980s the figure was below 20 percent. Investment flows followed a similar pattern with the corresponding decline from 50 to 20 percent. If present trends continue, the share of global trade by the South will be only 4 percent by the year 2020. This means that more than 40 percent of the world's population could be excluded from the benefits of trade (Mann, 2001). In other words, globalization has become synonymous with "northernization."

After the collapse of the Soviet Union, American global hegemony became unrivalled. The 1990s can be described as the era of American triumphalism. The collapse of the Soviet Union heralded the end of the Cold War. This seminal event has sparked a heated controversy over the assertion by American academic, Francis Fukuyama, that the fall of socialism represents the "end of history." By the term, "the end of history," Fukuyama means that the enlightenment ideals of liberal democracy constitute the "end point of mankind's ideological evolution" and the "final form of human government." The liberal revolution over rival ideologies such as hereditary monarchy, fascism and communism will eventually triumph throughout the world. Fukuyama supports his thesis by highlighting the evidence that the number of democratic regimes has grown substantially over the past three decades and that liberal democracy will eventually encompass most of the world's population. By implication, Fukuyama also subscribes to the superiority of the market and neoliberalism as the "natural" order in economic life.

Many critics argued that Fukuyama had tapped into the wellsprings of American triumphalism, which became a raging whirlpool in the course of the 1990s economic boom. In this sense, Fukuyama was portrayed as a leading apologist of globalization and Americanization. The more recent debates over globalization and corporatism suggest that rather than the "end of history," history is about to be reinvented. At the very hegemonic core of the process of globalization is the role performed by US military power, which has been deployed as a "world policeman" in order to invoke United Nations resolutions. Indeed, the US now spends as much on defense as the next 12 countries combined. Despite this enormous military power, the rise of ethnic and religious nationalism represents the most difficult and protracted conflicts that the "new world order" has to contend with.

Although the forces of globalization have undermined national sovereignty, the nation-state continues to act as the basic form of political organization and representation. However, globalization will tend to reinforce the process of regionalism and supranationalism, embodied in the emergence of the European Union and trade blocs such as ASEAN and NAFTA. The dynamics of globalization will intensify competitive forces and hasten the rationalization and concentration of economic power. It is precisely this dialectic between globalization, on the one hand, and regionalism, on the other hand, that constitutes the rationalizing dynamic in the formation of regional trading and currency blocs. The objective historical conditions by which these economic blocs evolve will determine whether they assume either an exclusive/protectionist form that excludes outsiders or a more open and liberal arrangement that complements the existing multilateral system.

> Economic regionalism has become a means to increase the international competitiveness of firms within the regions. Various forms of trade agreements (customs unions, free trade areas and single markets) to some extent provide such advantages of free trade as economies of scale in production while at the same time denying these advantages to outsiders unless they invest in the internal market and meet membership country demands for technological transfers and job creation. Regionalism also facilitates pooling of economic resources and formation of regional corporate alliances;

> therefore it has become an important strategy used by groups of states to increase their economic and political power. (Gilpin, 2000, p. 337)

The liberalization of trade and investment has fostered the emergence of a new international division of labor, in which production in each country or region has become more specialized. This new hierarchy is beginning to emerge as MNCs restructure and rationalize their operations in order to take advantage of greater economies of scale across national borders. An organizational logic is also at work involving a high degree of centralization in the decision-making process. There is a growing tendency to concentrate their key operational bases and research and development facilities in the more advanced economic regions and relegate their less skilled, assembly operations in the less developed regions. Uneven development is thus not only the natural consequence of capitalist accumulation, but also acquires an internal corporate dynamic of integration, which implies a highly centralized structure of control and organization. Yet at the same time, the purgative forces generated by this neoliberal strategy will merely accentuate the process of uneven development. As the rate of concentration and centralization of capital gains even greater momentum, whole industries and regions might no longer be competitive in global markets. The whole vortex of uneven development therefore asserts itself both from within and from without these economic blocs through the agency of the multinational corporation.

Conclusion

In the early postwar years, the Americans had laid the foundations for a more liberal international economic architecture under the aegis of *Pax Americana*. The institutions of the IMF/World Bank and the GATT agreements enshrined this new order, while the US dollar would perform the international role of reserve currency and a means of payments under the postwar Bretton Woods accords. It was in this liberal international environment, which ultimately provided the necessary conditions for the postwar phase of growth. However, as the long boom came to an end in the early 1970s, the onset of a profitability crisis in the advanced capitalist countries and the emergence of chronic global overcapacity undermined the relatively stable system of *Pax Americana*.

The demise of *Pax Americana* hastened an era of hegemonic crisis in which the capitalist world economy gravitated toward a tripolar system of competing blocs with the formation of European Union and the launching of the single currency. Meanwhile, the rise of East Asia created the other major sphere of capital accumulation. In order to restore their international export competitiveness, the US authorities pursued successive dollar depreciations and exploited their international privileges of *seigniorage*. In effect, the US had written off a considerable proportion in the overseas value of their debt at the expense of their major rivals, most notably Japan, which had denominated most of their foreign exchange reserves in US dollars (Brett, 1985, p. 117). However, between 1980 and 1985, the Reagan administration pursued a strong dollar policy to attract an inflow of capital, which had disastrous consequences for the global economy. The precipitous fall of the US dollar after the Plaza accords of 1985 induced a severe international financial crisis and led directly to the stock market crashes of 1987 and 1989. The era of stagnation and crisis was inextricably entwined with the demise of US economic and financial hegemony and the ever more desperate and unilateralist attempts by US monopoly capital to recapture markets and investment outlets. As a result, international finance and the volatile dollar have become the most vulnerable and unstable aspects of the global capitalist economy.

6
The Onset of "Eurosclerosis"

Introduction

The end of the long boom coincided with the demise of the postwar Bretton Woods system of fixed exchange rates. With the onset of the dollar crisis in 1968–73, the international financial markets were thrown into turmoil. The relatively stable hegemonic system of *Pax Americana* was gradually replaced by an oligopolistic system of competing centers of capitalist accumulation based in the US, Europe and later from Japan/East Asia. The struggle over markets, investment outlets and access to strategic raw materials between the three major capitalist blocs has characterized the entire era of stagnation from the mid-1970s to the present.

Economic rivalry with Europe was triggered by the onset of the dollar crisis and the unprecedented outflow of US direct investment during the 1960s. At the same time, the demise of the postwar system of fixed exchange rates had provoked a series of exchange rate crises, which threatened to undermine the international postwar system of *Pax Americana*. International exchange rate volatility continued unabated after the formal abandonment of the Bretton Woods system in 1973. It was now possible for the US monetary authorities to pursue a policy of "benign neglect" and allow the dollar to progressively depreciate. By doing so, the US economy could recover its loss of export competitiveness in international markets. This strategy, however, generated widespread financial volatility and provoked exchange rate crises in world markets, which ultimately threatened to sabotage the process of European integration.

The European Community responded by attempting to construct a zone of monetary stability with the ill-fated fixed exchange rate regime of the "snake in the tunnel." The first experiment toward European monetary union, however, was short-lived and eventually failed. Indeed, the neoliberal path to the single currency in Europe over the past 30 years has left an indelible legacy of stagnation and high rates of unemployment, or what many economists refer to as the onset of "Eurosclerosis." With the demise of *Pax Americana*, the international economic order therefore evolved into a tripolar system of competing blocs centered in the United States, Europe and Japan/East Asia. In short, does the demise of *Pax Americana* herald the disintegration of trade liberalization and multilateralism and the rise of competing regional economic blocs?

1 European Monetary Union: the first experiment

The gulf between the European Economic Community (EEC) and the United States widened in the wake of the dollar crisis, the onset of the severe recession of 1972–75 and the oil price shocks. It was in this volatile environment of exchange rate instability, an inflationary upsurge and the outbreak of financial speculation that hastened European attempts to establish a zone of monetary stability. The postwar international payments system under the Bretton Woods system had furnished a high degree of exchange rate stability. As the American economy expanded, it provided an engine of growth and an expanding export market for the OECD countries. In only 18 months between 1967 and 1968, however, the international economy was thrown into turmoil by three major exchange rate crises: the liquidation of the pound/sterling regime in November 1967, the dollar crisis of March 1968 and the speculative attack on the French franc and German mark in November 1968. At the very epicenter of this financial meltdown was the demise of the fixed exchange rate system based on gold/dollar convertibility. The failure to manage the crisis provided the political rationale for the Europeans to devise their own fixed exchange rate system.

Convened by the European Heads of State, The Hague Summit in December 1969 established a Committee, chaired by Pierre Werner of Luxembourg, to formulate a strategy for European Monetary Union (EMU). Released in October 1970, the Werner Report recommended that monetary union should be accomplished over a ten-year time frame involving three progressive stages. In its final form, monetary union would exhibit: (1) a single currency achieved through the elimination of margins of fluctuation and the irrevocable fixing of exchange rates, (2) the pooling of national reserves and the creation of a federal system of central banks, and (3) the centralization of economic policies under the auspices of supranational institutions attached to the European Parliament and the Commission. Economic and monetary union would thus prefigure political federation.

Most of the earlier debates over monetary union were informed by the theories of optimal currency areas (OCAs). The seminal theory of OCAs has been attributed to the analysis formulated by R.A. Mundell (1961). The theory is based on a simple two-country/region model. It is assumed that countries A and B possess separate national currencies which operate under a fixed exchange rate regime and that both are in a state of balance of payments equilibrium and full employment. If a shift in demand occurs from country B to country A, then B will experience unemployment and A will tend to experience an increase in inflation. Insofar as prices are allowed to rise in country A, the shift in the terms of trade will enable country B to adjust through an exchange rate devaluation and by doing so, avoid incurring the main burden of adjustment in terms of employment and output.

However, if country A pursues an anti-inflationary policy, the whole burden of adjustment will be borne by country B which will tend to experience a higher level of unemployment and a fall in output. Mundell's argument in this regard is quite pertinent to the role performed by Germany under a fixed exchange rate regime in Europe. Since Germany constitutes the principal surplus country, the willingness of the German monetary authorities to reflate and provide an increase in demand for the Community as a whole will play a pivotal role. In the event of a supply shock or a recession, the behavior of the Bundesbank will be critical in terms of which countries incur the greatest burden of structural adjustment. It was precisely the problem of structural adjustment, which had informed debates in Europe over the issue of monetary union. In other words, if an OCA were to be established, which countries or regions would experience the greatest burden of structural adjustment? Would the greatest burden of adjustment be imposed upon the deficit countries, or would the surplus countries provide the necessary liquidity and agree to reflate? This problem was never fully resolved until the introduction of the European Monetary System in the 1980s.

Before the official abandonment of the Bretton Woods agreements in 1972–73, the Community found itself disunited and unable to formulate a common approach to the impact of exchange rate volatility and the speculative flights of capital. These discordant and disparate responses to the dollar crisis merely increased the scope for speculation. The Six were eventually able to reach a tentative accord in their negotiating stance during the Smithsonian Agreements in December 1971 (Spero, 1977). During the Paris Summit convened by the Heads of Government in February 1972, it was agreed to foster exchange rate cohesion between Community Member States by implementing the Smithsonian parities. Quite clearly, the magnitude of these exchange rate divergences was too high and threatened to sabotage further progress towards economic union. The Basle Agreement by the Community central banks in March 1972 reduced intra-EEC exchange rate fluctuations to 2.25 percent, which was equivalent to the central dollar margin. It was from this agreement that the "snake in the tunnel" was born. The parameters of the "tunnel" were set at 4.5 percent, while the "snake" was confined to a margin of 2.25 percent within the "tunnel." The six original members of the currency bloc were soon accompanied by Ireland, the UK, Denmark and Norway (Tsoukalis, 1977).

Despite the Smithsonian accords, further speculative waves engulfed international currency markets in February–March and June–July, 1972. In June a speculative attack was launched against the British pound in the wake of the worsening UK balance of payments. The premature exit of the pound, after only three months, had exposed the institutional weakness and limited resources devoted to defend the fixed parity regime. Encouraged by the capitulation of the European monetary authorities, speculators now targeted the Italian lira, which eventually forced the Italian authorities to exit the "snake-in-the tunnel."

However, the singularly most important event, which overshadowed all attempts to foster exchange rate cohesion, occurred with the sudden quadrupling of oil prices by the OPEC cartel in mid-1973. The oil price shocks coincided with the onset of the most severe international recession since the Second World War. Although it did not cause the recession, the oil crisis accentuated its severity. A net transfer of about 2 percent of income from the OECD countries to the OPEC cartel was estimated to have occurred as a result. The most visible impact of these oil price shocks, however, was experienced in the deterioration of the balance of payments of the most oil-dependent countries and the subsequent adjustments required to offset the inflationary cost-push effects.

Quite severe deflationary policies were imposed which had an adverse effect on employment. Within the Community, the oil price shocks had intensified existing tensions between high inflation, deficit countries and the low inflation, surplus countries. The oil price shocks therefore acted as a profound catalyst in revealing the conflicting economic policies and diverging trends within the Community. Given these divergent economic trends, further progress toward monetary union was postponed.

The French government in late 1973 eventually delivered the *coup de grâce* to the EMU experiment. The onset of a balance of payments crisis set in motion a speculative attack on the franc, which forced the French authorities to withdraw from the EMU. Consequently, the EMU experiment had become nothing more than an exclusive deutsche mark zone. Conceived in an environment of extreme exchange rate volatility after the collapse of the Bretton Woods system, the "snake in the tunnel" lacked both the financial resources and the political cohesion to defend intra-Community exchange rate parities.

2 The neoliberal ascendancy in Europe

The neoliberal ascendancy in Europe was reflected in a general shift to political right within the European Community during the 1980s, regardless of the ideological persuasion of the respective political parties in power. This was most evident in France after the abandonment of "Keynesianism in one country" by the socialist government in 1983. Similarly, the Spanish socialists pursued free market policies after their election in 1981. Given this political configuration, the Thatcher government in the UK found it quite opportunistic to support the single market proposals despite opposition to institutional and procedural reforms embodied by the principle of majority voting in the Council of Ministers and the European Social Charter. The governments in power in the northern industrial "core" countries of France, Germany and the UK therefore dominated the politics of the Community. This favorable political configuration made it possible for a recasting of the European bargain toward a neoliberal direction (Grahl & Teague, 1989).

The crisis of overcapacity and economic stagnation had exposed the limits of prevailing national strategies, which had been governed by the "social market" policies of both the Christian Democrats and Social Democratic coalitions. Even before the official ratification of the Single European Act (SEA), European big business had been mobilizing support in the European Commission to adopt a neoliberal solution to the lack of economic dynamism and growth. These demands coalesced in the Roundtable of European Industrialists, an organization represented by Europe's most powerful corporations, including Philips, Siemens, Olivetti, Fiat, GEC, Daimler Benz, Volvo, ASEA, Bosch and Ciba-Geigy. An elite alliance soon emerged between transnational business interests and the European Commission, which culminated in the election of Delors to the Presidency of the Commission in early 1985 (Moravcsik, 1991).

The process of interstate bargaining over the proposals of the SEA was launched during the European Council Summit at Fontainebleau in June 1984. From this Summit, the Doogue Committee was established and the final SEA White Paper entitled "The Completion of the Internal Market" was presented to the Council at the Luxembourg Summit in March 1985 (George, 1991, p. 160). A few months later in Brussels, the Council agreed to a timetable for the 279 proposals to be implemented by December 1992. By the end of the year, the SEA was officially ratified by the Council and signed by the 12 member states in February 1986. The legislation eventually came into legal force in July 1987 after referenda were held in Denmark and Ireland (Tsoukalis, 1993, p. 61). The SEA defines the single market as "an area without internal barriers in which the free movement of goods, persons, services and capital is ensured" (Article 8a).

The SEA was also accompanied by a set of policy-led initiatives, which would encompass a European "organized space" between the nation-state and the global market. In other words, Europe would become the organizing center of a regional regulatory bloc to counter the destabilizing forces of globalization (Ross, 1992, p. 62). The basic theoretical contention was that market liberalization would generate an increase in the level of productive investment and induce the process of economic restructuring. Moreover, market liberalization would ostensibly foster a rapid upsurge in the rate of corporate mergers and promote greater economies of scale and increased returns to scale as oligopolistic firms integrated their operations across national borders. The whole strategy hinged on the dismantling of national forms of capitalist regulation and state support for "national champions." The fatal flaw of the neoliberal programme, however, was the absence of corresponding regimes of regulation on the supranational level. This was especially evident in the relatively minor role performed by the EC budget as a redistributive mechanism and the very limited development of coherent Community state structures and apparatuses.

The Single Market Programme also reflected dramatic changes in international geopolitical alignments. With the relative demise of the postwar system of *Pax Americana*, the single market emerged as a regional organizing center of the emergent tripolar system of economic blocs. This redivision of the world market coincided with the disintegration of the Soviet bloc. As a result of these dramatic post-Cold War realignments, the Community's international relations have been transformed beyond recognition. In contrast to its former role as a strategic bulwark against the Soviet Union, the Community became the new focus or "center" toward which the newly emergent capitalist countries of Eastern Europe gravitated. After the collapse of the Soviet bloc in 1989, the US defense umbrella of NATO had lost its *raison d'être*. A more independent defense/foreign policy was now possible.

After German reunification, support for closer European cooperation was perceived as a necessary corollary in order to assimilate the former East German socialist state. At the same time, the prospect of potential export markets and investment in Eastern Europe had rekindled Germany's traditional economic dominance of this region (Spaulding, 1991). In this sense, the former socialist countries could now emerge as possible candidates for EC membership. The existing EC-12 have thus evolved as the core of a system of concentric circles with the former European Free Trade Agreement (EFTA) countries and the former socialist countries gravitating as satellite states around this "core." The EFTA countries have signed agreements to establish a European Economic Area, which requires them to adhere to EC rules and procedures even though formal membership is still in its transitional phase. At the Edinburgh European Council in December 1992 it was agreed to proceed with enlargement negotiations with Austria, Norway and Sweden (Artis & Lee, 1994, p. 29). The former socialist countries, on the other hand, have negotiated association agreements with the Community in 1991 (Ross, 1992). These were designed to align Eastern Europe with the Community's economic and institutional procedures and norms.

In May 1989 the Commission produced the first draft of a Social Charter as part of the Internal Market Programme, which had identified three main areas in the creation of a European "social space": (1) a charter of social rights, (2) statutory obligations for workers' participation in management and (3) fostering a dialogue between capital and labor on a European level (Tsoukalis, 1993, p. 156). This progressive vision encountered hostile British Tory opposition. The eventual outcome witnessed an unprecedented scenario in which the other 11 member states signed a separate social protocol at the Strasbourg Summit in December 1989. The Social Charter formed the basis of the Social Chapter of the Maastricht Treaty signed in December 1991 and ratified by all of the member states, with the exception of Britain, in 1993. Under Article 118 of this Treaty, the Community can legislate by a qualified majority vote on issues of health and safety, employment conditions and equal employment opportunity principles. Unanimity, however, is required for legislation covering worker participation, social security and the social protection of workers (Tsoukalis, 1993, p. 172).

European trade unions, represented by the European Trade Union Confederation (ETUC), had quite legitimate reservations about the social consequences of the neoliberal strategy. Their greatest concern was the possible emergence of "social dumping" in the event of the removal of barriers on intra-European investment and competition. There was an explicit danger that firms would exploit lower wages and working conditions in the less developed regions in order to undermine established wages, conditions and fundamental labor rights in the Community as a whole. It was in this context that the first draft of the Social Charter had sought to harmonize wages and social security provisions across the EC. Confronted by hostile British opposition, however, the proposals were diluted and became a mere statement of intent, devoid of any real legislative imperatives (George, 1991, p. 207).

As a result of British opposition, the Social Charter was largely symbolic. Articles 100a and 118a of the SEA enshrine legislation to improve and harmonize national standards of health and safety, environmental laws and consumer protection. The need to compensate those regions and social groups that would be adversely affected by economic restructuring was enshrined in Articles 130a and 130b of the SEA, which commits the EC to strengthen social cohesion through the regional and structural funds, including the Social Fund. Beyond these measures, it is evident that neoliberal ideology has prevailed by confining the social dimension of the Internal Market Programme to the issues of labor mobility and minimal regulation on a European level. The final draft of the Social Charter was devoid of any legal force and had become nothing more than an act of symbolism.

3 The European Monetary System: 1979–87

The renewed dollar crisis of 1978 provided a catalyst to launch a second experiment toward European monetary union in March 1979. The American policy of "benign neglect" had allowed the dollar to slide, which in turn, generated a renewed phase of international volatility in financial and currency markets. The obvious threat posed by these realignments convinced the newly elected Social Democratic government of Chancellor Schmidt that a new fixed exchange rate regime was required within the Community. This became even more evident after the failure of German–US measures to stabilize the dollar. With the recent election of President Giscard d'Estaing of France, Schmidt had found an accommodating ally in reviving the EMU project.

The European Council in Brussels finally adopted the legal and institutional structure of the European Monetary System (EMS) on December 1978. The Greek and British representatives chose to postpone their membership of the EMS. The EMS was, like its predecessor, essentially a Franco-German initiative. A similar logic governed the new accord: while the French sought German support for their exchange rate which had come under renewed speculative attack, Germany demanded support for closer coordination of national economic policies. Although the political rationale in relaunching the EMU project was paramount, the underlying economic conditions were also favorable. Between 1978 and 1982 there appeared overwhelming evidence of a convergence of critical economic indicators after the tensions generated by the oil price shocks.

Both the critical mass of the German economy and its close trading relations with other EU countries placed it in a unique position to impose its economic preferences on the final blueprint for monetary union. In this sense, the EMS can be portrayed as a hierarchical regime with Germany at the very apex. The problem of asymmetry was thus closely related to Germany's strategic trade relations within the EMS.

> To mix a metaphor: Germany is at the heart of the European economy, while all the other economies are peripheral. Economically, Europe may be defined as a German zone. This zone includes all countries that send a significant share of their exports (15 percent or more) to Germany and at least half of their total exports to the German economic zone, including Germany itself. Germany in turn sends half of its exports to the periphery of its economic zone, but no individual country absorbs more than 5–6 per cent of its exports (except Holland and France, each of which account for almost 10 per cent of German exports). This configuration of trade makes economic relations asymmetrical. (Parboni, 1981, p. 91)

Rather than sharing the burden of adjustment, the main burden was imposed on the weaker, deficit countries. The Bundesbank preserved its staunch independence, while Germany was able to pursue relatively autonomous monetary policies within the EMS but was constrained by its relationship with the US dollar and US monetary policies. In short, the dollar/DM relationship ultimately dictated intra-EMS exchange rate alignments. The continued volatility of the dollar and the inflationary consequences of US domestic policies impelled the EMS countries to peg their currencies to the German mark. As a result, German interest rates acted as the unofficial anchor or benchmark within the EMS as Figure 6.1 demonstrates. While the German monetary authorities were able to determine their exchange rate policies through interest rate adjustments, the deficit countries of France and Italy increasingly resorted to

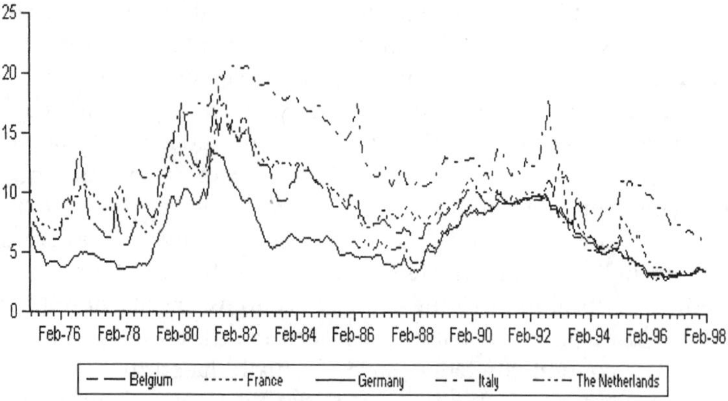

Figure 6.1 Short-term interest rates in the EMS, 1975–98 (three months, % per annum)

Source: OECD Main Economic Indicators, 1998.

the imposition of exchange rate and capital controls. These empirical observations of the internal dynamics of the EMS support the proposition that there was an inherent asymmetry with Germany acting as the de facto *n*th country and providing an exchange rate anchor for the system as a whole.

The problem of asymmetry, however, is not in itself a major obstacle to the maintenance of exchange rate stability. The real problem lies with the role performed by the *n*th country. Under the fixed but adjustable exchange rate system of Bretton Woods, the *n*th country – the United States – provided an expansionary impetus for the system as a whole, while the US financial system was willing and structurally capable of financing the export of capital. By incurring successive current account deficits, the American financial system was acting as a financial intermediary by borrowing in the short term in order to lend in the long term. In stark contrast, the German economy had imparted a deflationary tendency within the EMS and its financial sector was unwilling to act as a financial intermediary for the system as a whole. These constraints have been the product of the DM/dollar relationship and the German structural propensity to accumulate trade surpluses.

The inherently anti-Keynesian stance of the Bundesbank enshrined the objective of price stability as the cornerstone of German macroeconomic policy. By doing so, however, a disinflationary impulse was transmitted throughout the EMS zone (Guerrieri et al., 1989). While the German authorities pursued a trade-off between economic growth and low inflation in order to promote monetary stability, the other deficit member countries were forced to trade off economic growth and exchange rate stability (Ferri, 1990, p. 6). Consequently, most of the EMS countries adopted a "strong currency" option by aligning themselves with the anti-inflationary strategy of the Bundesbank. Although this strategy had fostered greater exchange rate cohesion and discipline within the EMS, evident by the gradual convergence of national inflation rates, the ultimate cost had been the legacy of relatively low levels of economic growth and high rates of cyclical unemployment.

Disinflationary policies thus contributed to the onset of "Eurosclerosis" during the 1980s (Boltho, 1993). By 1986, the average unemployment rate in the Community had increased from 4.7 percent in 1975–80 to around 11 percent. On the other hand, the rate of inflation had fallen from an average of 12 percent to 3.7 percent over the same period (Guerrieri, 1989, p. 2). In order to counteract an appreciating exchange rate in relation to markets outside the Community, the German authorities pursued a rigorous anti-inflationary strategy, which offset any short-term loss of export competitiveness caused by a rise in the nominal exchange rate. In order to maintain their dominant share of these markets, intra-Community exchange rate cohesion was necessary.

The EMS had thus provided a relatively stable monetary zone to which a significant share of their exports was destined, while fortifying the German economy from the destabilizing impact of a volatile US dollar. At the same time, the threat of competition from Germany's European trade rivals was effectively countered through the Exchange Rate Mechanism (ERM), which prevented sudden, sharp devaluations of intra-ERM exchange rates. The basic contradiction between growing German trade surpluses and the trade deficits of France and Italy, however, threatened the cohesion and stability of the EMS. Germany's trade surplus with its EMS partners increased more than fourfold between 1979 and 1988. At the same time, France's trade deficit increased more than threefold (Table 6.1).

The refusal of the German authorities to stimulate the level of effective demand imparted a disinflationary impulse in the EMS zone (Holland, 1983). The cumulative process of competitive disinflation therefore characterized the dynamics of the European economy in the 1980s (Fitoussi, 1993). The survival of the EMS inevitably depended upon the ability of member countries to coordinate their macroeconomic policies and to pursue a convergence of national inflation rates. Germany's low inflation provided an anchor for the other ERM countries while its domestic savings had financed investment in the deficit countries. Conversely, the

Table 6.1 Trade balance of the EMS countries, 1979–88, $US billions/ (percentage of GDP)

Country	*1979*	*1983*	*1986*	*1987*	*1988*
Belgium	−0.8 (0.7)	−0.8	−0.6	−0.7 (0.5)	−3.4
Denmark	−2.2 (3.4)	−1.1	−3.4	−2.8 (2.9)	−1.8
France	−7.0 (1.2)	−12.4	−17.00	−20.7 (2.3)	−21.9
Germany	5.7 (0.7)	4.1	15.4	22.3 (2.0)	26.5
Ireland	0.3 (8.1)	0.9	1.8	3.0 (24.9)	3.4
Italy	−0.9 (0.3)	−1.3	−3.4	−6.1 (0.8)	−8.6
Netherlands	4.9 (3.1)	10.6	7.3	5.0 (2.3)	5.7

Source: OECD Main Indicators, 1990.

nominal appreciation of the German mark had increased Germany's purchasing power over European assets. During the 1970s, this virtuous circle was based on the configuration of low growth and disinflation in Germany, on the one hand, and high growth and rampant inflation in France and Italy, on the other hand. Consequently, Italy and France became more dependent on German investment. The continuation of this virtuous circle could only be sustained if the deficit countries continued to accommodate German investment. In order to do so, however, the deficit countries were required to make a downward adjustment of their respective exchange rates.

During the 1980s, membership of the ERM had imposed limits on this exchange rate adjustment. The emphasis was now placed on internal adjustment through a programme of disinflation. By independently targeting its monetary growth, Germany established the inflationary threshold to which its ERM partners aligned themselves. Average inflation in the EMS fell from about 11 percent in 1980 to around 2 percent in 1986, while the differentials between the highest and lowest national inflation rates had narrowed from 16 percent to about 6 percent (Padua-Schioppa, 1988, p. 371) (Figure 6.2). With the signing of the Single European Act (SEA) in 1986, capital controls were scheduled to be abolished in 1992. Consequently, one of the main pillars of the EMS, which contributed to the stabilization of intra-Community exchange rates, had disappeared. The liberalization of capital movements, however, became difficult to reconcile with the continued existence of national exchange rate regimes. This glaring dichotomy became evident during the speculative turmoil that engulfed the EMS in mid-1992. Monetary union implies a symmetrical regime of exchange rate convergence. Asymmetrical exchange rate relations, however, had characterized the EMS, with Germany acting as the nominal exchange rate anchor for the system as a whole.

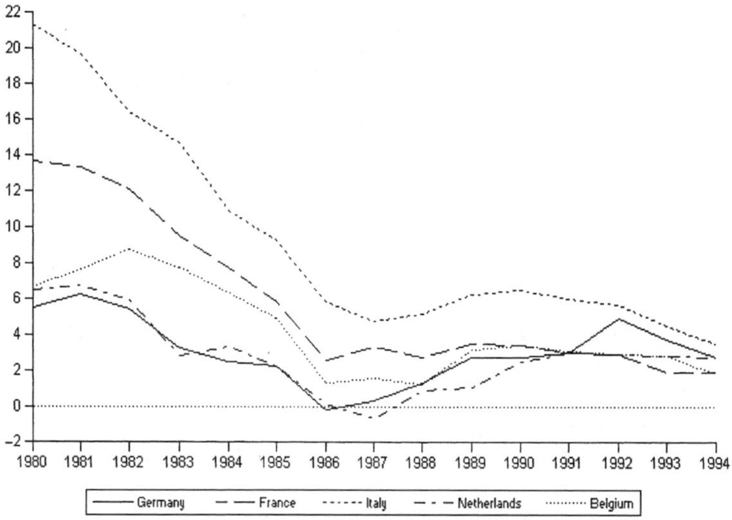

Figure 6.2 Consumer price index (inflation rate) in selected EMS countries (percentage per annum)

Source: IMF World Tables, 1998.

4 The Maastricht blueprint for EMU

With the ratification of the Maastricht Treaty in 1992, European member states had effectively surrendered their traditional fiscal and monetary policy powers to a new and distant, though quite nebulous supranational "sovereignty." It will be argued that the neoliberal economic paradigm – having failed to convince the vast majority of Europeans of its legitimacy and efficacy – was to bypass the nation-state and eventually hijack the economic agenda on the supranational level. Paradoxically, the triumph of neoliberalism was precisely the outcome of national governments *voluntarily* surrendering their core economic policy prerogatives to a supranational agency in order to justify the imposition of an excessively harsh set of economic prescriptions embodied in the Maastricht Treaty. In other words, the nation-state provided the framework for the rise of neoliberalism on a supranational level. In the process of constructing this monetary edifice, Germany would emerge as Europe's economic hegemon. At the same time, however, the European working class would be forced to pay the social costs of disinflation in terms of high levels of unemployment and the imposition of fiscal austerity.

In June 1988 the European Council meeting in Hanover established the Committee for the Study of Economic and Monetary Union under the chairmanship of Delors. The Delors Report, submitted in April 1989 and ratified by the Member States at the Rome Summit in October 1990, provided the blueprint for monetary union. The Delors Plan viewed the existing EMS architecture as the institutional foundation for the completion of the monetary edifice. The Maastricht Treaty established a formal timetable for the progressive stages set out by the Delors Report toward EMU. The Treaty also identified and elaborated on the convergence criteria required to qualify for membership of the final phase and the Charter for a European Central Bank (ECB). Monetary union would be accomplished through three progressive stages.

During the first stage, which officially began on July 1, 1990, the EMS member states were scheduled to abolish all existing capital controls on the movement of capital across national borders. In December 1991 an agreement to establish the ECB was ratified even though exchange rate realignments were still permitted. The second stage was launched on January 1, 1994 with the creation of the European Monetary Institute (EMI), which prepared the groundwork for a more cohesive regime of central bank coordination and monitored progress on meeting the convergence criteria. The final phase would depend on progress achieved by the member states in conforming to the convergence criteria. If these conditions were satisfied, the final stage was scheduled to begin at the end of 1996. The famous convergence criteria can be summarized as follows:

1. The national inflation rate not to exceed 1.5 percent of the best performing member.
2. Budget deficits to be reduced to 3 percent of GDP and the public debt not to exceed 60 percent of GDP.
3. The exchange rate to remain within the narrow band of 2.25 percent for two years before admission to the final stage.
4. Interest rate differentials to be narrowed within 2 percent of the lowest national rates.

The abolition of capital controls raised quite profound implications for the high deficit countries. Capital market liberalization implied a loss of public control over national interest rates, which undermined the ability of ERM countries to maintain exchange rate parities. The choice was between the imposition of highly restrictive fiscal policies to compensate for the loss of monetary policy instruments or the acceptance of higher margins of exchange rate movements as a means of external adjustment. As soon as exchange rates were irrevocably fixed, however, there was a very real likelihood that speculative capital flights could be provoked.

The Maastricht Treaty proposed that the ECB should be governed by two fundamental principles. First, the statutes of the ECB should declare price stability as its overriding objective (Article 103 of the Treaty and Article 2 of the ECB Charter). Second, the ECB Charter should be inscribed with political and institutional independence. Doubtless these protocols exhibit a striking resemblance with the Charter of the Bundesbank. After the final stage of monetary union, the ECB would be conferred with the authority to issue a single currency. The euro will compete against the US dollar and the Japanese yen as an international vehicular currency. Yet, in order to challenge US dollar supremacy, the euro requires a sovereign political entity and coherent military instruments of power to support its international role as a means of payments and as a reserve asset. The EU, however, lacks these attributes of a sovereign power.

Possibly the most contentious and politically sensitive aspect of the Maastricht accord involves the technical prohibition of the financing of public deficits by the ECB (Article 21.1 of the ECB statute). Moreover, the ECB is also prohibited from acting as a "lender of last resort" to a financially bankrupt government. Even though the ECB will assume monetary control, the national central banks would continue to perform a supervisory role. "In the event of a banking crisis, these two roles overlap: the national bank, acting as the lender of last resort, would wish to inject liquidity into the financial system; however, it would be constrained given that money supply falls under the remit of the ECB" (Arestis et al., 2001, p. 125). In order to prevent the monetization of public debts, national governments are obliged to maintain low public debt/GDP ratios. This provision of the Treaty has important implications for the high deficit members of Italy, Spain, Greece and Portugal, all of which rely quite extensively on revenue derived through seigniorage (Emerson, 1992, p. 123). Given the constraints imposed on the level of public debt in order to acquire credibility in the eyes of financial markets, the scope for fiscal expansion to promote employment has been severely limited.

The speculative turmoil in mid-1992 after the British entry into the ERM exposed these glaring contradictions. In retrospect, capital liberalization became incompatible with the existing regime of fixed exchange rates. At the same time, German reunification had induced a rise in domestic interest rates and the appreciation of the German mark. As the DM appreciated, pressure mounted on the British pound and the Italian lira, which culminated in their withdrawal in scenes reminiscent of the earlier "snake" debacle. Market perceptions about the inability of the high inflation/deficit countries to maintain their respective nominal exchange rates in the event of capital market liberalization triggered the crisis. Figure 6.3 illustrates the magnitude of the decoupling of exchange rates after these speculative attacks.

A series of devaluations were inevitable either because of the self-fulfilling speculative propensities generated by large capital outflows, or by the exhaustion of foreign exchange reserves to defend their respective exchange rates. In the course of the speculative crisis, the Italian lira and the British pound had experienced a nominal, effective depreciation of 16 and 15 percent respectively. Over the next year, however, most of the ERM currencies with the exception of the German mark, Dutch guilder and Irish pound, had fallen below their respective divergence threshold which culminated in an increase in the permitted band of exchange rate movement to 15 percent either side of parity within the ERM in August 1993 (Blanden-Hovell, 1994, p. 342). The reverberations of the speculative turmoil of 1992–93 had postponed the EMU timetable for the final stage. The removal of capital controls and the liberalization of capital markets within a regime of fixed exchange rates therefore

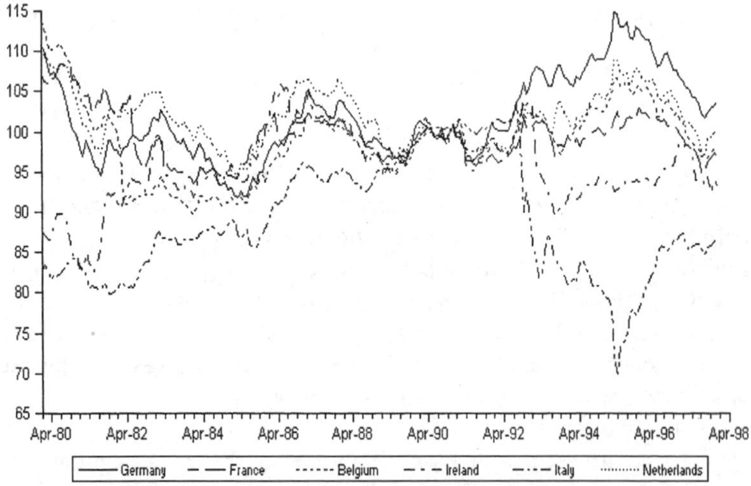

Figure 6.3 Real effective exchange rates in selected EMS countries (1990 = 100)
Source: OECD Main Economic Indicators 1998.

incurred quite considerable risks for the high inflation/deficit countries as the debacle of 1992–93 had already starkly demonstrated.

In the aftermath of German reunification, the specter of greater German economic and political power led to a traditional response by the other member states to contain German power by accelerating the process of European integration. In this geopolitical context, the Maastricht Treaty represented a European attempt, led by France, to curb German economic and political power (Anderson, 1997, p. 132). Yet, at the same time, Germany was able to consolidate its economic hegemony through the EMU. The social costs of the EMU, however, would be borne by the European working class in terms of high levels of unemployment and fiscal austerity (Carchedi, 2001, p. 134).

> But the EMU rests also on fiscal policies which lead to austerity measures and thus to redistribution of surplus value from labour to capital. *The more the EU countries are tied to Germany, the greater the expropriation of value from labour.... The euro, and thus German leadership, is accepted because the bill is paid by labour.... At the same time, these policies appear as if they were dictated by "Europe" in the interest of the "common good".* (Carchedi, 1997, pp. 100–1)

The Stability Pact became the means by which to enforce this excessive regime of economic austerity. Endorsed by the Dublin Summit of December 1996, the "Stability and Growth Pact" enshrined the very strict fiscal criteria which were to be imposed on the member states in the final stage of EMU. However, the new Socialist government of France was able to inscribe a separate title on the "Resolution on Growth and Employment," which was eventually included in the Amsterdam Treaty, or what later became known as "Maastricht 2," signed in October 1997 (Artis & Winkler, 1997, p. 1). Despite the French insistence on promoting employment as a principal objective of the Stability Pact, the general ideological tenor of the Treaty continued to support restrictive policies, which prevented each member state from pursuing expansionary policies to mitigate the effects of recession and stagnation (Pasinetti, 1998a, p. 112). Indeed, the public debt and budget deficit thresholds became the very cornerstone of the Stability Pact to the extent that fines could be imposed by the Council if member states violated these targets (Arestis et al., 2001, p. 117). Quite apart from the weakening of the automatic stabilizers performed by the state sector and the unnecessary burden of high unemployment, the Maastricht Treaty does not specify any real formula over the notion of public finance "sustainability," but simply states in a rather dogmatic and arbitrary manner, the "two reference values" of the public debt and fiscal deficit that should be achieved by member states (Pasinetti, 1998, pp. 17–18).[1]

The anti-Keynesian bias of the Stability Pact has contributed to high levels of unemployment and the curtailment of both private and public investment. It is more than mere coincidence that the countries of the euro-zone have experienced substantially higher levels of unemployment than both those European countries outside the euro-zone (e.g., Norway, Switzerland and the UK) and the other major industrial countries of Japan and the United States (Modigliani et al., 1998). The dampening of the level of aggregate demand has inhibited the self-reinforcing effects of the investment multiplier and has caused serious problems of excess productive capacity. The fiscal constraint imposed by the Maastricht Treaty therefore failed to be entirely convincing. In this sense, the fiscal criteria of the Delors Plan were difficult to justify on conventional Keynesian grounds unless there was a corresponding fiscal regime on a supranational level. The Community budget would perform the redistributive and stabilization functions now performed by national governments. Quite apart from the enormous political obstacles involved over national sovereignty with the sensitive issue of fiscal federalism, the existing EU budget, estimated at about 1.2 percent of the combined EU GDP, is simply inadequate to perform this function (Giovannini & Spaventa, 1991, p. 101).

> Because Euro-zone members are not allowed to use independent monetary policies and pull themselves out of a shock-induced recession, they would normally utilize such a fiscal policy as tax cuts or public works to stimulate demand. The EU itself could have a fiscal policy to distribute financial resources to a depressed area to stimulate demand. However, the role of fiscal policy in Euroland has not been determined. Although it is unclear whether or not members will retain some fiscal powers, the Stability Pact demanded by Germany suggests those members' fiscal powers will be greatly restricted. (Gilpin, 2000, p. 208)

As a result of the imposition of quite harsh monetary and fiscal policies, all of the 15 member countries, with the exception of Greece, had qualified for membership of the final phase of EMU. On the eve of the single currency, both Belgium and Italy with 118.1 percent and Greece with 107.7 percent had failed to meet their respective public debt/GDP ratios of 60 percent, while for the budget deficit criteria, all of the 15 countries achieved the target of 3 percent of GDP. Indeed, progress on budget deficits was quite exceptional; the overall EU budget deficit fell from 6.1 percent of GDP in 1993 to 2.7 percent in 1997. The European Summit in early May 1998 endorsed 11 of the 15 member states to join the final stage of EMU, which will involve the creation of the ECB and the issuing of the euro. Britain, Denmark, Sweden and Norway will temporarily postpone their membership until they hold national referenda. While Norway's referendum rejected membership in 2001, Greece was officially admitted in the same year. The official launch of the euro was on schedule in January 1, 1999. After that date, there will be a three-year transition period during which national currencies will continue to exist as a subdivision of the euro. By January 1, 2002 euro rates and coins will be issued and by July 1 of the same year, all national currencies will cease to have legal tender status.

Conclusion

The most significant development over the past two decades in Europe has been the emergence of German economic dominance (Halevi, 1995). Although the Franco-German axis still constitutes the pivot around which the process of European integration revolves, the German economy occupies the very core of Europe. German economic dominance is reflected in the politics of monetary union. The German mark emerged as the nominal exchange rate anchor for the EMS, while German disinflationary policies have prevailed in the creation of a European Central Bank, which has been modeled on the Bundesbank. Competitive disinflation set in motion a vicious circle as each country's pursuit of lower inflation in order to qualify for the euro-zone, led to a severe dampening the level of effective demand. It was precisely this process of cumulative disinflation, which had contributed to the onset of Eurosclerosis in the 1980s and the 1990s (Fitoussi, 1993). The broad outlines of this stagnationist phase were evident by chronic unemployment and a decline in productive investment. An analysis of the Maastricht blueprint for EMU reveals that the "convergence criteria" had institutionalized this German ideological preference. With the birth of the euro, a tripolar system of international economic blocs has emerged with the US and Japan/East Asia constituting the other two poles.

7
The US–Japanese Axis: Unity or Rivalry?

Introduction

In the wake of the East Asian economic turmoil, the international financial system has experienced a severe crisis. The aim of this chapter is to articulate several hypotheses about the dynamics and historical causes of this phase of instability in the world capitalist system and highlight some of the more critical developments, which could hasten a global economic slump. Since the outbreak of the Asian economic crisis in early 1997, Russia and Latin America have succumbed to the "contagion" effect. Despite the impending threat to trade and investment as a result of the slump that is now engulfing these emerging markets, Wall Street has continued its irrational exuberance. Yet the evidence suggests that the problem of global excess capacity has not been resolved, while commodity prices have not fully recovered from their historic lows.

The critical question proposed is whether the global financial crisis is now poised to enter into a second phase. At the very epicenter of this emerging crisis is the growing trade imbalance between Japan and the United States. A looming trade war across the Pacific would prefigure the onset of economic rivalry between the three major economic blocs in the European Union, Japan/East Asia and the United States over markets, investment outlets and access to raw materials.

It will be argued that the dynamics of East Asia's recent phase of growth and crisis have been governed, to a large extent, by the evolving US–Japanese axis. Over the past two decades, this trans-Pacific relationship has been characterized by a seemingly symbiotic and self-reinforcing logic. Competition and rivalry between the two great economic powers has been tempered by a confluence of interests. It is evident that this mutual, if not entirely perilous embrace, has been based upon the twin pillars of markets and investment outlets. While Japan emerged as East Asia's major source of investment, the United States domestic economy has provided the most important market for East Asia's phase of export-led growth.

Yet this virtuous circle is only possible as long as the US economy continues to perform the role of "market of last resort" for East Asian and more specifically, Japanese exports. With the sudden outbreak of the recent financial panic, however, the foundations of this regime of accumulation have been severely shaken. The end of the 1990s economic boom and the possible onset of recession in the United States could witness the breakdown of this virtuous circle and hasten an intensified phase of interimperialist rivalry in the region between Japan and the United States. At the same time, Japan's economic stagnation over the past decade has led to a severe curtailment of their investment in the region. From this standpoint, East Asia represents the most critical and vulnerable intersection of the US–Japanese axis. In short, the recent East Asian financial crisis might be viewed as a dress rehearsal for a more profound historical drama over the region's markets and investment outlets.

1 The historical context

On a very general stylized level, manufacturing acted as the engine that propelled Japan's postwar economic development. From the mid-1960s onward, Japan had shifted from a strategy of "forced" industrialization through import-substitution designed to safeguard the balance of payments and protect the domestic market, to a strategy of export-led growth based on the development of a dynamic comparative advantage in several lines of manufacturing production. The Ministry of International Trade and Industry (MITI) could therefore relax their import-substitution program and concentrate on an export-expansion strategy of growth. This was accomplished by devoting scarce resources to stimulate growth and exports in selected heavy industry sectors such as steel, petrochemicals, automobiles, industrial machinery and electrical machinery. However, in the initial stages, wages growth lagged behind economic growth, which increased the share of profits for future investment. At the same time, public investment in infrastructure was largely devoted to the provision of public goods for the private sector (e.g. transport, R&D, training) rather than in the funding of a social wage and public services (e.g. housing, welfare, recreation) (Sheridan, 1998). This "skewed" development toward the capital-goods sector and exports at the expense of the consumption-goods sector still characterizes Japan's economic development. Moreover, the lack of an adequate social infrastructure has merely accentuated these structural distortions.

As a late starter, it can be surmised that Japan exhibited a product-cycle type of development that consciously sought to catch up with the more advanced industrial countries. According to Yamazawa (1990), the sequence of this product cycle development has followed three stages since the Meiji restoration:

1. Export of primary products and import of light industrial goods.
2. Export of light industrial goods and import of heavy industrial goods and raw materials.
3. Export of heavy industrial goods and import of raw materials.

Most of the development in the postwar period up until the 1970s was therefore driven by investment in heavy industries. These sectors exhibited large sunk costs and economies of scale, which acted as effective barriers to entry. Consequently, a highly oligopolistic industrial structure emerged in the shipbuilding, iron and steel and general machinery sectors dominated by a few large *keiretsu*, most notably Mitsui, Mitsubishi and Sumitomo. These large conglomerates were vertically integrated in a very hierarchical pattern through a subcontracting system with the small to medium-sized enterprises (SMEs) or the *chusho-kigyo*. This structure still survives today and the SMEs account for about 80 percent of the total labor force. However, their contribution to overall productivity is quite low, estimated at less than half of the levels of the larger firms (Kunio, 1994). Japan's industrial anatomy thus exhibits dualistic features in which the large conglomerates dominate the economy, while the growth of effective demand has been stunted by the relative neglect of the consumption-goods sector.

Much of Japan's postwar development has been guided by the state. Indeed, one can legitimately trace this preeminent role of the state back to the modernization drive of the Meiji restoration in 1868 (Chowdhury & Islam, 1993, p. 18). However, Japan's present-day regime of planning and regulation has its lineage from the system of central planning presided over by the Planning Board to mobilize resources for the war effort during the Sino-Japanese and Pacific wars (Tipton, 1998). During the war years, this "plan-rational" state was governed by the bureaucracy, which would implement their economic plans by using the corporate groupings (*zaibatsu*) as their executing agencies (Okazaki et al.,

1999). According to Chalmers Johnson, the "plan-rational" or "developmental" state is governed by the imperatives of industrialization:

> In the plan-rational state, the government will give greatest precedence to industrial policy, that is, to a concern with the structure of domestic industry and with promoting the structure that enhances the nation's international competitiveness. The very existence of an industrial policy implies a strategic, or goal-oriented approach to the economy. On the other hand, the market-rational state usually will not even have an industrial policy (or, at any rate, will not recognise it as such). Instead, both its domestic and foreign economic policy, including its trading policy, will stress the rules and reciprocal concessions (although perhaps influenced by some goals that are not industrially specific, goals such as price stability or full employment). (Johnson, 1982, pp. 19–20)

Although the system of planning became more indicative after the war, the state continued to guide the economy through both direct and indirect methods. *Dirigisme* would be exercised most effectively by the state through the channeling of finance to selected sectors and industries. State control over the banking system gave the authorities enormous leverage over investment. At the same time, restrictions were imposed on Japanese firms from raising capital by stock floatation or from foreign sources (Henderson, 1993, p. 98). This type of credit rationing was accomplished through both the state-owned banks and the state-regulated financial institutions (Wade, 1990). The engine room of this "convoy system" of state-directed investment has been performed by the Ministry of Finance (MoF) and the Bank of Japan (BoJ). Competition was effectively regulated through administrative guidance in which the convoy system encouraged the cross-ownership of shares between the big banks and the large *keiretsu*. Consequently, the flow and circulation of funds were usually through indirect finance supplied by the banks affiliated to each respective industrial grouping. The MoF has long guided the convoy system and has underwritten the financial viability of the major banks. However, this system of bureaucratic guidance has perpetuated what many economists refer to as "moral hazard" risks in the guise of cronyism and patronage. A bureaucratic web of tacit "credit rights" has evolved regardless of the profitability of the large firms (Taggart-Murphy, 2000).

The "relative autonomy" of the state in Japan and most of East Asia was largely the product of American military and political intervention in the region during the cold war. This high level of structural autonomy of the state from civil society was developed in the geopolitical context of the cold war in which the Americans supported authoritarian and semiauthoritarian regimes as strategic "bulwarks" in their struggle against the perceived threat of communism (Stubbs, 1994). Indeed, it can be argued that the Korean War boom and the Vietnam War promoted the rise of Japanese economic and regional power. At the same time, Japan enjoyed the benefits of the US military umbrella by diverting potential military spending into the investment of productive capacity. The Americans also lifted the barriers to the transfer of technology after the war. Japan could now take advantage of the dynamic economies of scale and assimilate both the codified and tacit knowledge embodied with the absorption of foreign technologies and techniques. Indeed, Japan soon acquired the reputation as a successful imitator of new technologies. New inventions and innovations were not only assimilated but were also improved upon which translated into a source of strategic, international competitive advantage.

Politically and militarily, the US continues to exercise hegemony in East Asia, but unlike its strategic preeminence during the formative postwar years, US political power has become more nuanced and less emphatic. Although the Japanese state remains subordinate to US geopolitical imperatives in the region, it no longer performs the subaltern role to which it was assigned and was quite willing to perform during the cold war. Japan's phoenix-like rise from the ashes of war has once again catapulted the country as the economic powerhouse of the region. Indeed, it can be argued that the East Asian economic "miracle" was propelled, to a large degree, by Japan's unprecedented postwar growth. The Asian newly industrialized countries (NICs), to a larger or lesser extent, had successfully emulated and replicated Japan's state-guided, developmental model. At the same time, the success of East Asia's phase of export-led growth continued to be highly dependent upon the US market. By the early 1980s, US economic and political influence began to wane. Japan emerged as the region's preeminent economic power as their share of investment and trade soon eclipsed their American rivals.

The significance of this shift in the balance of economic power was that the Japanese state could now pursue a greater degree of autonomy in the promotion of trade and investment in the region. Yet despite the end of the cold war and China's historic opening to the West, US political and military power continued to dictate the geopolitical alignments within the region. In this sense, the Japanese bourgeoisie were quite willing to support US hegemony as long as they could share in the economic spoils. To be sure, regional suspicions of Japan's hegemonic ambitions – which still resonated after more than half a century since Japan's ill-fated drive to establish an Asian "co-prosperity" sphere – could be allayed by the US military presence. Hence, with the relative demise of the postwar system of *Pax Americana*, and the rise of East Asia as the most dynamic growth pole in the global economy, the US–Japanese axis provided a coherent and relatively stable political framework for the region.

However, the outbreak of the financial crisis in 1997–98 revealed the simmering contradictions that had been previously concealed beneath the thin veneer of regional stability and harmony. The crisis signified that the twin pillars of markets and investment were ultimately based on very shaky foundations and had the potential to generate both intended and unintended damaging consequences. First and foremost, from the standpoint of markets, the whole dynamic of export-led growth could only be sustained as long as the US domestic market continued to absorb East Asian exports, which implied an ever-growing, cumulative increase in the US trade deficit. Second, from the standpoint of investment, Japan's "lost" decade of stagnation during the 1990s had led to the curtailment of their long-term investment in the region. Indeed, it was already evident before the East Asian crisis that the Japanese bubble economy had been "exported" to the region in the early 1990s, which had induced a speculative wave of excess liquidity. Quite severe problems of excess capacity had also emerged in the region, which had imparted a series of balances of payments deficits, exceeding 6 percent of GDP in Malaysia, Thailand and South Korea in 1996–97 (Lucarelli, 2002).

A third weakness in this distinctive East Asian regime of accumulation was also exposed by the crisis. Most East Asian currencies had been pegged to the US dollar. As long as the US dollar continued to depreciate against the yen after the Plaza accords of 1985, the East Asian tiger economies could improve their export competitiveness. With the sharp dollar appreciation against the yen after mid-1995, however, this favorable trend was reversed and the tigers encountered an erosion of their international competitiveness, which was accompanied by a sharp export slump. Under these circumstances it was not too surprising to witness the wholly destructive and predatory behavior of hedge funds, who had sensed that the central banks were vulnerable in their ever more desperate attempts to maintain the dollar peg. A series of speculative attacks were launched on their respective currencies, which led to the collapse of the dollar peg (with the exception of Hong Kong). The existence of unhedged, dollar-denominated borrowings only further accentuated the financial crisis as one country after another was confronted with an avalanche of private sector indebtedness.

The subsequent IMF bailout packages provided the final nail in the coffin. If one ignores for a moment the debates that have since raged over the efficacy of these IMF programs, it is quite evident that the IMF has always acted as the lender of last resort on the behalf of international finance capital. A cursory analysis of IMF policies in the Third World over the past two decades would tend to support this claim. As usual, the creditors were rescued and the costs were socialized in terms of the imposition of economic austerity programmes. As Gowan (2001) has quite succinctly argued, the role of the IMF is more ideological than it is technical. It forms part of the "Washington consensus" and is imbued with the most virulent strain of neoliberal ideology. Indeed, as even Joseph Stiglitz – a recent Nobel laureate and former Washington insider – has conceded, the whole aim of propagating neoliberal ideology is to bring about capital market liberalization in order to allow international financial institutions (mostly US-based) to engage in speculative operations (Stiglitz, 2002). This does not necessarily imply a conspiracy theory but rather reflects an ideological affinity between IMF/US Treasury officials and Wall Street bankers (Wade & Veneroso, 1998). In this context it is possible to examine the propagation of neoliberal ideology in terms of the political forces that have coalesced around and have legitimized the interests of international financiers and rentiers. To paraphrase Marx: "the ideas of the ruling class of an epoch are also the ruling ideas of that epoch."

2 From virtuous circle to vicious circle

The causes of the recent economic crisis have been the subject of an ongoing debate over the structural dynamics of East Asia's phase of growth. The debate was originally sparked by MIT Professor, Paul Krugman, who had raised doubts about the sustainability of East Asia's growth potential (1994). His basic contention was that the major source of this rapid expansion had been spurred by high rates of capital accumulation, which have been based on increasing inputs of labor and capital rather than improvements in efficiency and increases in productivity per unit of input. As a result, capital/output ratios will tend to increase which will induce a fall in profitability and marginal output per unit. In other words, the law of diminishing returns will tend to manifest itself. Although recent evidence might lend credence to the Krugman thesis, it would be too premature to confirm the evidence of a long-term structural decline and a similar erosion in international competitiveness. Quite contrary to this thesis, the recent steep currency depreciations will improve East Asia's export competitiveness. The real danger now lies with the specter of competitive devaluations as these countries compete against each other for export markets. The evidence appears to suggest that the crisis was preceded by a sharp export slump in the region as early as 1996. Figure 7.1 illustrates the magnitude of this decline in the volume of exports.

Extenuating short-term and cyclical factors could just as easily explain the recent crisis. For instance, the recent appreciation of the US dollar in relation to the yen can be identified as an important factor. Since most of the East Asian currencies were pegged to the US dollar, the nominal appreciation of the dollar had a profound impact on the competitiveness of East Asian exports. Similarly, the collapse of the semiconductor markets contributed to the fall in the value of exports. The sluggish demand in the European Union and Japan had also imparted a depressive impact on exports. In stark contrast to the Krugman thesis, which implies an endogenous process of entropy, this chapter will focus on the

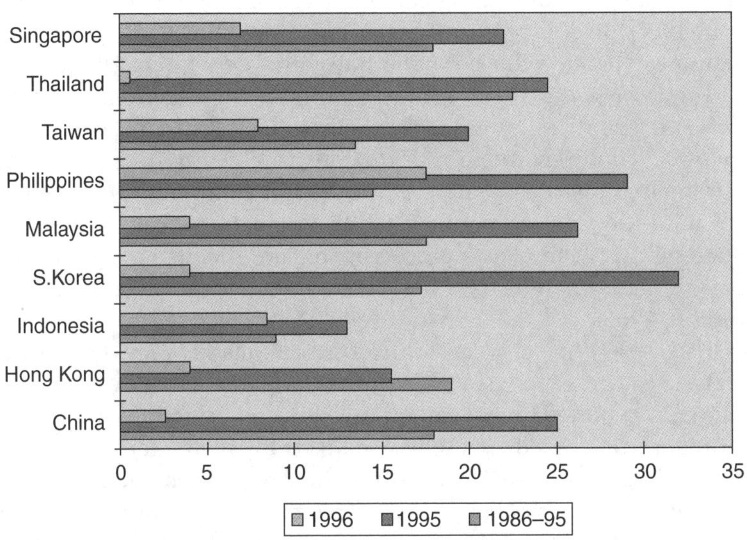

Figure 7.1 East Asia's export slump (average annual percentage increase)
Source: Asian Development Bank, 1996.

exogenous factors (i.e. export markets and international investment) as the most important elements in the East Asian regime of accumulation. The basic contention is that the sustainability of East Asia's growth trajectory depends on a complex trade and investment configuration, which is driven by the law of comparative advantage in terms of lower labor costs (Vernon, 1966).

One of the most distinctive characteristics of the East Asian regime of accumulation has been embodied in their ability to take advantage of the international product cycle by shifting their comparative advantage in terms of labor costs in specific industries and sectors. This has become known as the "flying geese" paradigm which provides a description of the life cycles of various industries and their relocation from one country or region to another (Cumings, 1984). The industrial life cycle in certain sectors – textiles, steel, automobiles, electronics, etc. – of origin, rise and decline, appears to follow a specific trajectory governed by shifts in international competitiveness.[1] In each individual life cycle there emerges a phase of decline in which production is no longer profitable because of rising costs of production in terms of labor costs or the appreciation of the exchange rate. These industries are relocated to cheaper labor zones through either trade or foreign direct investment. Taiwan and South Korea, for instance, have been receptacles for declining Japanese industries in chemicals, steel, shipbuilding and textiles (Itoh, 1990). In this process, foreign direct investment (FDI) has been the most dynamic vehicle for the transfer of new products and technologies to less developed regions/countries. Imports from the more advanced countries allow new products to be introduced into the "follower" countries. These countries are now in a position to exploit their international comparative advantages by exporting to other countries until they also encounter a fall in international competitiveness. As a result, this cumulative process assimilates the life cycle of a particular product or industry with the logic of comparative advantage (Vernon, 1966).

The relatively liberal access to the American market provided a major catalyst for the East Asian phase of export-led growth. The original four tigers imported capital and intermediate goods from Japan in order to produce final goods for the US market. By 1990 almost two-fifths of Japan's exports were destined for the American market. Japanese manufactured imports constitute the largest penetration of the American market, while Taiwan ranks fourth, South Korea fifth, Hong Kong ninth and Singapore eleventh. In 1994, the trade of the US with the East Asian NICs (about $272 billion) was greater than its trade with either the EU

($218 billion) or Japan ($176 billion). Similarly, the trade of both the EU and Japan with the East Asian NICs (about $229 billion and $283 billion, respectively) exceeded by a large margin, trade between themselves ($94 billion) (UNCTAD, 1996). On the other hand, the East Asian absorption of US exports has been much lower, accentuating their chronic trade surpluses. With the sharp rise of the Japanese yen against the US dollar between 1985 and 1995, however, this triangular trade flow has shifted East Asia's exports to the Japanese market and accelerated the process of intraregional trade. In order to counter a fall in their international competitiveness, Japanese corporations increased their investment in East Asia as export platforms.

The shifting dynamic of comparative advantage is reflected in the changing composition of East Asia's exports. In the course of industrialization, countries naturally progress from lower to higher value-added products (Boltho, 1975). From a historical standpoint, the rate at which this structural shift has occurred in East Asia is quite astounding. In the period from 1956–61 to 1966–71, the share of capital goods exports (including electrical machinery and transport equipment) increased from about 4 percent to about 23 percent in Taiwan and from 5 percent to about 20 percent in South Korea. In Japan, this shift was even more profound, increasing its share of capital goods exports from about 14 percent in the early 1950s to about 39 percent ten years later (Wade, 1990). This structural shift reflected record levels of capital formation. Taiwan averaged 28.4 percent of GNP and South Korea 26.5 percent between 1965 and 1980 (World Bank Development Report, 1985).

Although the "flying geese" paradigm provides a useful description of this changing process of dynamic comparative advantage within the East Asian region, it should be stressed that international markets, especially the US market, were and continue to be critical in the success of this trade and investment configuration. In short, the American market has provided the major impetus for East Asia's trade expansion. At the same time, since these currencies were pegged to the US dollar, the nominal exchange rate of the dollar has played a crucial role. A nominal appreciation of the dollar has imparted a recessive impact on East Asian exports for those countries with currencies pegged to the dollar, while conversely, a nominal depreciation has provided an expansionary impetus. US–Japanese exchange rate relations also have a powerful effect on trade and investment flows in the region. Japanese trade surpluses generate a strong yen in relation to the dollar, which has had a favorable effect on East Asian exports to the US market and increased the level of Japanese investment in the region. Conversely, a strong dollar in relation to the yen tends to have a detrimental effect on East Asia's exports and has curtailed the outflow of Japanese investment in the region.

Over the past ten years there has been a rapid increase in the rate of intraregional trade. Trade among the countries of East Asia (excluding Japan) has been expanding much faster than trade with the outside world, accounting for about one third of their total imports and exports. Although Japan has accumulated a large trade surplus with the rest of East Asia, the latter countries now import more manufactures from each other than they import from Japan. Japan still dominates in the export of capital goods and vehicles but has been eclipsed in the more labor-intensive manufactures in chemicals, electronic equipment and office machinery in which intra-East Asian trade now exceeds their trade with Japan. Since Japan buys a comparatively small proportion from East Asia, an asymmetrical trade relationship has developed. This means that the Japanese market is more important for the East Asian countries than East Asia is for Japan. The East Asian countries have enjoyed a relatively large trade surplus with the EU and the US in labor-intensive products while, until very recently, have accumulated a large deficit with Japan. Industrial conglomerates in Taiwan and South Korea are already beginning to invest on a large scale in Europe and the US. Although some of this investment might initially stimulate exports of intermediate and capital goods from their home countries, a more important effect is likely to be an overall loss of exports. Table 7.1 highlights exports of manufactures from selected East Asian countries in terms of their major destination between 1985 and 1994.

A similar logic appears to govern Japan; the outward flow of FDI will gradually replace exports. In 1985, the outstanding stock (cumulative value) of Japan's global FDI was around $84 billion, equivalent to about a half of the country's total exports in that year. Despite a slowdown in the outflow of capital in the early 1990s, the share of Japanese FDI remained quite high, estimated at 12 percent of the world stock of FDI in 1994, compared to 4 percent in 1980 (UNCTAD, 1996). Indeed, Japan emerged as the largest source of international investment in the less developed countries to which an overwhelming proportion of these outflows were destined for Asia. Japan's earlier direct investment in the ASEAN-4 countries was associated primarily with resource extraction (Halliday & McCormack, 1973). However, the sharp appreciation of the yen after the Plaza Accords of 1985 increased the incentives for shifting a substantial share of Japan's manufacturing capacity offshore, especially in the more labor-intensive industries. The North East Asian tigers, on the other hand, tend to act as intermediate countries in that they are themselves significant recipients of FDI but also invest in the poorer countries of Asia.

Table 7.1 Exports of manufactures from selected East Asian countries, by major destination, 1985 and 1994 (billions of dollars)

Exports from		*Total*	*First-tier NICs*	*ASEAN -4*	*China*	*Japan*
To						
World	1985	102.2	82.7	10.2	9.3	169.4
	1994	483.8	281.7	102.5	99.6	377.8
Developing	1985	19.1	13.1	2.9	3.1	39.7
East Asia	1994	173.2	101.9	34.3	37.0	142.3
First-tier NICs	1985	11.9	6.6	2.4	2.9	20.9
	1994	114.8	51.9	28.4	34.5	86.0
ASEAN-4	1985	5.1	4.5	0.4	0.2	6.9
	1994	42.9	36.2	4.2	2.5	38.8
China	1985	2.0	1.9	0.1	–	11.9
	1994	15.5	13.8	1.7	–	17.5
Japan	1985	7.8	5.9	0.8	1.1	–
	1994	50.3	23.9	11.7	14.7	–
Other OECD	1985	61.7	53.1	5.7	2.9	100.5
	1994	105.8	122.0	46.3	37.5	196.4
Rest of the	1985	13.5	10.5	0.8	2.2	29.2
world	1994	54.5	33.9	10.2	10.4	39.1

Source: UNCTAD (1996).

East Asia attracted the largest inflows of investment in the developing countries as a whole. An estimated $65 billion of inflows in 1995 accounted for about two thirds of all developing country FDI. China has emerged as the largest recipient since 1992 accounting for 58 percent of the region's total capital inflows (UNCTAD, 1996). Japanese capital exports have displaced US investment in the region. In order to recover from a loss of international competitiveness caused by the appreciating exchange rate, Japanese corporations have undergone a process of industrial restructuring and technological upgrading. An important element of this strategy had been the relocation of production in cheap labor zones in South East Asia as a result of the more than 25 percent increase in the effective exchange rate of the yen between 1993 and 1995. Most Japanese FDI is aimed at establishing regional and global networks or supplying the local market (Kosai & Ogino, 1984). As a result, Japanese firms are establishing "second generation" affiliates abroad. For example, 47 percent of Japan's subsidiaries in Hong Kong and 43 percent in Singapore have already established their own affiliates. Thus, in terms of sequencing FDI among sectors and countries, the intraregional pattern is consistent with the "flying geese" paradigm. Japan was the first major regional investor, initially in the primary sectors and then in manufacturing. Japan's FDI in manufacturing gradually moved from the more to the less industrialized countries of the region. The sectoral pattern of FDI seems to have continued when the first wave of East Asian NICs also emerged as regional and international investors.

This analysis of the dynamics of growth in East Asia reveals a complex trade and investment configuration. Since much of this phase of rapid growth was driven by exports, it is not possible to treat the success of one national policy regime in isolation from the East Asian experience as a whole. A quite distinct East Asian regime of accumulation can be identified. The political and institutional means by which this process of rapid industrialization was undertaken appears to conform to Japan's earlier policies of import substitution and also export subsidization (Johnson, 1982). To a lesser or greater degree, the original East Asian tigers have sought to emulate the Japanese model. In stark contrast, the newly emergent ASEAN-4 countries have adopted a strategy, which is essentially based on attracting foreign investment and the creation of export platforms. These countries have only partially, if at all, embarked on a program of second-stage industrialization, which would involve a shift toward heavy industries and the production of capital goods (Lall, 1996).

Although the "flying geese" paradigm provides critical insights into the dynamics of East Asia's development and the shifting regional division of labor, US–Japanese economic relations will continue to play a decisive role in the future evolution of the East Asian economies. The enormous inflow of capital before the outbreak of the crisis had induced a speculative boom, which was reflected in asset price inflation and financial speculation. In retrospect, the boom could not be sustained. As the financial and property bubble burst, a speculative attack was launched on their respective currencies. Since most of the accumulated debt was denominated in US dollars, the sharp depreciation of most East Asian currencies only accentuated the debt burden and was responsible for an inflationary upsurge as import prices soared. An ensuing severe credit crunch drastically curtailed growth, increased the rate of bankruptcies and swelled the ranks of the unemployed.

The foundations of the "flying geese" pattern of trade and investment have been severely shaken by the recent financial and currency turmoil. The onset of competitive devaluations could have a devastating effect on this virtuous circle of export-led growth and intra-regional investment in East Asia and imperil the impressive economic gains achieved over the past 20 years. East Asia has accounted for about a third of global economic growth over the past decade. The imposition of IMF-inspired restrictive fiscal and monetary policies has dampened the level of effective demand and curtailed the pace of economic growth in the region (Thurow, 1997). If export markets outside the region diminish, either as a result of protectionism or the outbreak of an international recession, this virtuous circle could turn into a vicious circle.

The immediate causes of the Asian financial meltdown can be attributed to a convergence of three factors:

1. The weak export demand in the EU and Japan as these economies struggled to recover from recession and sluggish growth. The export slump, which preceded the financial crisis, caused chronic problems of excess productive capacity.
2. The appreciation of the US dollar, which had risen by 50 percent against the yen from its low point in April 1995 to June 1997 (or from 80 to 120 yen). Since most Asian currencies were pegged to the exchange rate of the US dollar, their export competitiveness was eroded in world markets. Conversely, the rapid depreciation of the US dollar after the Plaza accords of 1985 was a major factor in the export boom of these economies.
3. The slump in the semiconductor market has had an adverse impact on South Korea, Singapore, Thailand and Malaysia. Electronics exports as a percentage of their total exports account for about 70 percent in Singapore, 50 percent in Malaysia, 36 percent in South Korea and 33 percent in the Philippines. In the course of 1996, the price of memory chips had fallen by about 70–80 percent.

Many analysts have identified the emergence of private sector debt as a major factor. Since most of this debt was unhedged and denominated in US dollars, the rapid depreciation of currencies multiplied the debt and caused widespread bankruptcies and financial stress. This argument, however, appears to be tautological. It remains unclear how domestic credit expansion could have been prevented in the event of the massive inflow of capital, much of it purely speculative. Indeed, the whole aim of financial deregulation before the crisis was to attract inflows of capital. In the absence of central bank sterilization policies and the imposition of high interest rates, the expansionary impetus of foreign capital flows on domestic liquidity was inevitable. The expansion of credit creation induced a speculative boom in the equity and property markets, most notably in Indonesia, Thailand and Malaysia. The boom became self-fulfilling. As asset prices rose, overpriced collateral values financed further borrowing (Akyus, 1998). Furthermore, as the investment boom gained momentum, problems of surplus capacity emerged which imparted a negative impact on the balance of payments.

Current account deficits exceeded the IMF danger zone of 6 percent of GDP in Malaysia, Thailand and South Korea in 1996–97. In order to prevent the outbreak of inflationary forces, central banks increased interest rates. Higher domestic interest rates, however, only had the opposite effect of attracting further inflows of capital. This whole dynamic could not be sustained. The financial bubble eventually burst as an avalanche of nonperforming loans and indebtedness hastened a general economic slump (Wade & Veneroso, 1998). The level of corporate profitability in several East Asian countries fell sharply during the currency crises and imparted a depressive impact on stock market prices with the emergence of financial indebtedness. East Asia's major vulnerability is its sensitivity to foreign trade and continuing close dependence on the American market. Exports to the US market account for more than 10 percent of GDP in several countries including Singapore, Hong Kong, Taiwan and Malaysia.

Between July 1 1997 and January 26 1998, the cumulative, nominal declines of the ASEAN-4 currencies against the dollar exceeded 80 percent for Indonesia, 54 percent for Thailand, 44 percent for Malaysia and 38 percent for the Philippines. The South Korean won fell by 36 percent over the same period (OECD, 1998). The epicenter of the eruption began in Thailand as early as May 1997 and then spread to Malaysia, South Korea and Indonesia. The failure to dampen their overheating economies in the wake of massive capital inflows in Thailand, Malaysia and Indonesia induced a speculative spiral in the property and equity markets. At the same time, the maintenance of pegged exchange rate regimes merely encouraged further external borrowing and led to excessive exposure of foreign exchange risk in the private sector. The lack of transparency in terms of prudential rules and moral hazard risks associated with government guarantees for private loans contributed to concealing the true magnitude of the risks involved (Sachs, 1997).

3 A trans-Pacific trade war?

The cycle of maturity in Japan has been characterized by the outflow of capital. Persistent trade surpluses have led to the accumulation of foreign exchange reserves. Under a flexible exchange rate regime, the accumulation of surpluses has inevitably induced a secular appreciation of the exchange rate. In the long run, however, the outflow of FDI can only provide a temporary respite to the process of economic maturity. Sooner or later, foreign assets generate income in the form of repatriated profits and dividends, which will be spent in the domestic market. Japan will inevitably encounter a "wealth trap" (Rowthorn & Wells, 1987). In other words, it will cease to be a net capital exporter and become a "rentier" nation. This evolution has its antecedents in the decline of *Pax Britannica* last century and the relative demise of *Pax Americana* after the collapse of the Bretton Woods system in the early 1970s. In the case of the UK, industrial maturity was characterized by the outflow of capital, which promoted the industrialization of foreign rivals and eventually led to the UK's industrial decline. The same general process contributed to relative US decline in the period leading up to Nixon's abandonment of the dollar's convertibility into gold in 1971.

A similar process could imperil Japan's regional dominance with the rise of the Asian NICs. At present, however, the Asian NICs still run trade deficits with Japan and rely on the importation of "knowledge"-intensive industrial goods from Japan, most notably in sophisticated capital goods (Jarjoura, 2000). Indeed, the whole composition of Japan's FDI is concentrated in the transfer of mature technologies, while most of the scientific and technological know-how is undertaken within Japan. Unlike the United States, Japan has been very reluctant to relocate strategic high technology and knowledge-intensive industries to their competitors in East Asia (Morris-Suzuki, 1991). Nor has it been willing to export its technical know-how and scientific knowledge. Japan's major international competitive advantage lies in its sophisticated machinery and equipment sectors. The exports of electronics, integrated circuits, computers and mechatronics (industrial robots) have become the most dynamic growth poles over the past decade. In short, Japan has successfully shifted its emphasis onto the high value-added, low energy-using industries (Kunio, 1994, p. 24).

From the standpoint of its role as an international net creditor country, the Japanese authorities have so far prevented the yen from becoming an international vehicular currency. In contrast to the Bretton Woods regime in which the American financial system performed the role of world "central banker" with the issuing of international reserves, the Japanese financial system has remained firmly anchored to the imperatives of industrial accumulation. Whereas the US ran successive current account deficits and presided over the export of capital, Japan has accumulated substantial trade surpluses. The inability of Japanese finance capital to become the center of payments for East Asia as a whole appears to be linked to the close triumvirate between the MoF, finance capital and the large industrial *keiretsu* (the so-called "convoy" system). These links which express themselves in the form of cross-ownership and government guidance, prevent the internationalization of Japanese finance capital. In other words, the financial sector does not exhibit the degree of autonomy that one associates with the London and New York capital markets. The Japanese financial system is therefore governed by the imperatives of industrial capital and neomercantilist state policies, which ensure the maintenance of export competitiveness.

Japan's current economic malaise has its roots in the chain of events that led to the expansionary monetary policies enacted after the September 1985 Plaza accords. The sharp appreciation of the Japanese yen failed to restore a balance of payments equilibrium with the US. Quite contrary to the theoretical expectations of the Mundell–Fleming model, the trade imbalance became even more acute. The period of *endaka*, or the skyrocketing increase in the value of the yen, soon began to undermine the profitability of Japan's exports. By shifting a substantial proportion of their labor-intensive manufacturing offshore to the cheap labor zones of South East Asia, Japanese transnational corporations were able to restore their export competitiveness (Kriesler & Halevi, 1996). In order to mitigate the effects of an appreciating yen, the Japanese government embarked upon a program of monetary accommodation by reducing interest rates. Yet by pursuing relatively loose monetary policies, the government set in motion an unprecedented expansion of excess liquidity in the capital markets, most of which was channeled into what became known as *zaitech* operations, or speculative financial engineering (Yoshikawa, 2001). In retrospect, a financial mania was triggered in the real estate and equity markets.[2] The boom became self-fulfilling. As asset prices rose sharply, further borrowing only served to fuel the asset price spiral.

These events set in train the biggest build-up of excess liquidity in modern history. When the speculative bubble eventually burst in the early 1990s, the Japanese economy was effectively caught in a liquidity trap from which it has yet to recover. The current slump should also be viewed as the product of a severe crisis of excess capacity and over-accumulation. At the very core of this problem is the lack of effective demand. The structural propensity to build up productive capacity while experiencing a concomitant and relative diminution of effective demand has led to a severe slump not witnessed since the 1930s. The only components of effective demand keeping the Japanese economy afloat are government spending and net exports. In the absence of a recovery of domestic consumption, both of these components will ultimately reach their economic and political limits.

Consequently, a considerable share of investment was also channeled into net capital formation, which in turn had induced a severe phase of industrial overcapacity (Itoh, 2000). Indeed, by the late 1980s, most of the large *keiretsu* began to generate internal funds for investment and curtailed their traditional reliance on the BoJ and the big banks. In the early 1970s the large oligopolies relied on about 40 percent of their loans from the big banks. By the late 1980s, after the deregulation and liberalization of capital markets, this dependence had fallen to only 6 percent (Yoshikawa, 2001, p. 57). Deprived of their traditional sources of investment, the banks began to engage in reckless speculation in real estate and the stock market. Japan's financial institutions injected about $US220 billion in new loans to the property sector alone between 1985 and 1990 (Whittaker & Kurosawa, 1998). In the aftermath of financial liberalization in the mid-1980s, speculation reached truly astounding proportions. The large *keiretsu* who had invested in extra capacity to meet the demand by the 1980s boom soon found that they were burdened with massive excess capacity. In 1989–90, the BoJ increased interest rates from 3.8 to 8.2 percent, which triggered the bursting of the financial bubble. Stock market prices tumbled by more than 60 percent from their peaks (Halcvi & Lucarelli, 2002).

By the early 1990s, the Japanese economy was engulfed in a debilitating crisis of overaccumulation.

> The rate of capacity utilization in Japanese manufacturing in 1993 had declined by 17 percent from its peak of 1990, and it fell again after a feeble recovery in 1994. Continuing excess capacity certainly depresses investment in plant and equipment (p. 27)... With huge excess productive capacity, Japanese firms sharpened their competitive pressure in the market. Thus a vicious circle leading to a spiral of depression set in in the Japanese economy, comprising falling prices of shares and land, falls in workers' income, and depressant prices in the markets for products and services. (Itoh, 2000, p. 91)

To be sure, increases in productivity had outstripped wages growth by a large margin. The lack of effective demand in the domestic market only further encouraged outflows of capital, mostly destined to the East Asian region. By the early 1990s, East Asia had been transformed into a formidable export zone. Whereas in 1985, East Asia (excluding China) had only accounted for 12 percent of world exports, by 1993 this figure was

19 percent and reached as high as 23 percent before the outbreak of the financial crisis in 1997 (Hatch & Yamamura, 1996, p. 189).

The high yen made Japanese wages simultaneously too high and too low. In terms of costs, wages were too high to compete against East Asian exports and sustain previous levels of manufacturing employment. From the standpoint of effective demand, however, wages were too low to absorb the excess capacity. Consequently, Japanese corporations accelerated their export strategies in order to resolve their problem of domestic surplus capacity and counteract a falling profitability. The high yen after 1985 therefore had a perverse effect in that capital could appropriate higher profits through a strategy of exporting capital to East Asia in order to export goods from these production zones to Europe and the United States. The domestic market could not act as the engine of growth as long as real wages lagged behind productivity growth in order to increase the level of oligopolistic profitability. FDI provided low cost production sites in East Asia that enabled Japanese corporations to export to the high wage markets in Europe and the United States (Steven, 1991, p. 59). In essence, Japan sought "to maintain its export-led growth by 'regionalizing' it" (Gilpin, 2000, p. 270).

As a large, industrialized capitalist economy with a relatively high level of per capita income, the role of effective demand in the dynamics of growth is critical. The investment of the large, oligopolistic *keiretsu* who dominate the Japanese economy will depend on the level of effective demand, which determines the degree of utilization of their productive capacity and their level of profits. In Japan, the phase of postwar development has encountered the limits to its growth in terms of reaching what Joan Robinson has described as the "golden age" of the full employment condition of effective demand (Robinson, 1962, p. 52). As soon as this state of "maturity" is reached, the main problem that confronts the process of capital accumulation is the lack of effective demand (Halevi, 1992, p. 468).

It can be argued, with considerable justification, that Japan had, in effect, generated a speculative mania in the East Asian region after the collapse of its own asset price bubble in 1990. This claim can be supported by the fact that Japan's commercial loans to the region had increased from only $US40 billion in 1984 to over $US265 billion in 1996 (Yoshikawa, 2001, p. 9). The sharp fall in the volume of exports from East Asia just before the crisis had induced a series of balance of payments deficits, which were financed by short-term capital inflows, predominantly from Japan. At the same time, the collapse of Japan's speculative bubble led to a curtailment of FDI in the region from 1995 onwards. This process of retrenchment was also amplified by the sharp depreciation of the yen at about the same time. Between June 1995 and June 1997, Japanese claims in the Asian NICs fell from $US301 billion to $US180 billion (Hughes, 2000, p. 229). Hence, it can be surmised that the crisis of overaccumulation in Japan had been regionalized before the onset of the financial meltdown of 1997–98. As soon as the East Asian countries encountered balance of payments deficits, spurred by problems of overcapacity, Japanese FDI was sharply curtailed, which would then act as one of the catalysts for the ensuing currency crises.

The perverse effects of the collapse of the "bubble" economy since the early 1990s have yet to be resolved. Private consumption – which accounts for 60 percent of GDP – is still quite subdued, while deflationary forces have threatened to spill over into a liquidity trap (Krugman, 2000). Similarly, imports have been severely curtailed and unemployment remains at record high levels, reflecting the slump in domestic demand. Problems of excess capacity have made Japanese corporations even more reliant on external markets and investment outlets. The Japanese government is continuing to bail out overleveraged banks. Despite successive stimulus packages, Japan has experienced a postwar record in the number of bankruptcies. The MoF estimates that Japanese financial institutions are burdened by $US388 billion in debt which represents about 16 percent of GDP. Some reports suggest that the level of nonperforming loans could be as high as 30 percent of GDP.

Despite these domestic problems of deflation and a credit squeeze, Japan continues to accumulate balance of payments surpluses. A large proportion of these trade surpluses have been accomplished by falling imports as a result of the stagnation of domestic demand. It is precisely this problem of excess capacity that will compel Japanese corporations to expand their exports in order to counteract a falling profitability on the domestic market. The emergence of a growing trade deficit in the US, however, could provoke retaliatory protectionist measures. The conditions are therefore quite favorable for the outbreak of a classical Keynesian trade war as each country pursues "a desperate expedient to maintain employment at home by forcing sales on foreign markets and restricting purchases, which, if successful, will merely shift the problem of unemployment to the neighbor" (Keynes, 1936, pp. 382–3).

Over the past two decades, this trans-Pacific trade imbalance has been based on a tacit agreement between the Japanese and American monetary authorities that Japan would continue to recycle their trade surpluses by purchasing US government bonds and securities. In return, Japan would have access to the US domestic market, which would provide an expansionary impetus for Japanese export-led growth.[3] Successive yen appreciations have been effectively countered with the export of capital through the agency of FDI. The MoF has also been able to limit the extent of a yen appreciation either through open market operations in concert with the BoJ or by a tacit agreement with the US monetary authorities. Japan has emerged as the principal foreign holder of claims on the US government. Consequently, it has financed successive US current account deficits either directly by purchasing US bonds and securities, or indirectly by denominating its trade and overseas claims in the US dollar rather than the yen (Taggart-Murphy, 2000). This tacit reciprocity imparts considerable leverage to the Japanese monetary authorities over their American counterparts and has been deployed as a bargaining weapon in trade negotiations. The recent birth of the euro, however, could pose a profound dilemma for the Japanese monetary authorities. Unlike the US Treasury, the European Central Bank is not obliged to accommodate Japanese demands for a depreciation of the yen (Lucarelli, 1999).

Despite this convergence of interests, American–Japanese trade frictions have flared recently. The US authorities have demanded that Japan liberalize their domestic markets and provide a stimulus to their economy in order to generate demand for East Asian exports. Japan accounts for about 70 percent of East Asia's GNP and possesses the largest foreign exchange reserves in the world. A major stimulus to the Japanese economy would thus have a favorable effect and reverberate throughout the region. The Japanese authorities, however, have been quite reluctant to act as a locomotive for East Asia as a whole. The postwar dynamism of the Japanese economy has been driven by exports, most notably in the capital goods sector (Yamamura, 1986). While East Asia has been an expanding market for Japanese exports and investment, the American market remains its major export outlet and sphere of investment. In this sense, trade relations with East Asia are essentially asymmetrical. Given this inherent asymmetry in the trade relations between Japan and the rest of East Asia, Japan has been quite reluctant to provide an expansionary impetus for the region as a whole. Most of its exports are destined to the industrialized countries of Europe and the United States. East Asia is perceived as an important sphere of investment rather than a market for Japanese exports (Kunio, 1988). Indeed, under the conditions of unused capacity, exports to the East Asian region can be increased by means of credit and commercial loans, which will only accentuate these asymmetrical relations (Kriesler & Halevi, 1996).

Japan is therefore expected to run a trade surplus with the United States and Europe in order to resolve its problem of domestic excess capacity.

In order to sustain an economic recovery, Japanese corporations are highly dependent on the US market for their exports. The lack of effective demand in Japan means that an export-led recovery is the only viable short-term option. This also implies a relatively weak yen against the US dollar. An inflow of capital into Japan, however, would tend to militate against a yen depreciation. Indeed, one would expect the yen to strengthen against the US dollar and the euro as international financial agents and institutions switch their portfolio preferences away from US dollar-denominated assets during the course of a Japanese recovery. Much of the recent expansion of the US economy has been fuelled by the perverse "wealth effect" induced by the inflow of short-term capital into equity markets. A sustained fall in US share prices could act as a profound catalyst for a sustained phase of asset price deflation. In this sense, there are close parallels with the collapse of Japan's asset price bubble more than a decade earlier.

Recovery in Japan is thus closely interwoven with the future prospects of the US economy. The implications of a prolonged recession in Japan could be quite serious for international financial markets. If the financial crisis in Japan persists, the US equity and capital markets will continue to provide a relatively safe haven for international investors. On the other hand, if the Japanese economy recovers, investors could resort to recalling their funds invested in US equities, bonds and securities. This action will inevitably reverberate in global financial markets and could trigger further financial panics. A sudden reverse flow of capital from US dollar-denominated assets to yen and euro-denominated assets would unwind the irrational "wealth effect" in the US economy. This possible scenario could act as the harbinger to the eventual bursting of the "bubble" economy in the United States.

Over the past few years there has developed a powerful asymmetry between the United States and the rest of the world. Indeed, it can be argued that the Asian economic crisis represents the reverse side of the coin to US prosperity. The unprecedented surge in equity prices in Wall Street can be partly attributed to the enormous inflow of capital from the Asian markets. For instance, the US invested about $45 billion in Asia during the first half of 1997 but in the second half, Asian investors pumped about $21 billion into US equity markets (Omae, 1998). The fact that most of these capital flows were denominated in US dollars means that the US will continue to enjoy the privileges of seigniorage.

In other words, US consumers can continue to purchase foreign goods with domestically printed dollars. The emergence of negative real savings in the US, however, suggests that the absorption of foreign savings, denominated in US dollars, has had a negative effect on world investment.

The maintenance of a strong dollar policy since April 1995 imparted a beneficial effect on US domestic consumption. US consumers have indulged in a credit binge, spurred by cheap imports, which have contributed to the maintenance of low inflation. Accompanied by historically low interest rates and an unprecedented "wealth" effect through an upsurge in property values and equity prices, domestic consumption has provided the catalyst for robust domestic growth. At the same time, high profits and stock prices have attracted a further inflow of foreign investment. According to the Commerce Department, private foreign investors purchased $US265 billion worth of US stocks, bonds and other securities in 1998. This excessive overaccumulation of capital, increasingly skewed toward the hyperindulgent consumer sector and financed by the proliferation of credit, has had the effect of blowing out the current account deficit and encouraging a severe misallocation of resources away from the productive sector to the consumption-goods sector of the economy. In other words, the US economy has been impaired by endemic structural distortions, which have favored luxury consumption over investment in industrial capacity.

Conclusion

The stage is therefore set for a possible trade war between Japan and the United States, which could prefigure a global economic slump. Although one should be wary of historical analogies, the present configuration of forces suggests that a classical phase of interstate rivalry could emerge in the absence of policies, which redress the critical issue of international markets. Even though the problem of effective demand has been internationalized, nation-states continue to pursue neomercantilist policies, which seek to "export" unemployment. Accompanied by the problem of global excess capacity, the process of trade liberalization will be imperiled.

The US equity markets are experiencing a bubble economy that is reminiscent of the Japanese experience in the late 1980s. The bursting of the financial bubble will inevitably provoke a flight of capital from the United States, which would act as a catalyst to a sharp dollar depreciation. Stability of the dollar depends on its acceptance as the only credible currency in the denomination of international payments and as a store of value in international reserves. A general loss of confidence in the US dollar, however, would prefigure the loss of financial privileges conferred through seigniorage. The United States would at this critical moment no longer be capable of financing its current account deficit through its capital account surplus. The US current account deficit reached a historic high level of $430 billion in 2000, equivalent to 4.3 percent of GDP. By the end of 1999 US foreign liabilities had exceeded overseas assets by as much as $1.5 trillion (Kwan, 2001, p. 186). If the US foreign debt and current account deficit were no longer denominated in the US dollar, the US Treasury would lose its ability to monetize the process of money and credit creation. In other words, US corporations, private agents and the public sector would be compelled to repay their debts in foreign-denominated currencies, most notably in the euro and the yen.

By stark contrast, Japan is the world's largest creditor nation with net assets estimated at $819 billion in 2000. Indeed, Japan owned about $336 billion of US Treasury securities in the same year, equivalent to 12 percent of the total held outside the Federal Reserve and the US Federal government, which represented more than 28 percent of total claims held by foreigners (Kwan, 2001, p. 187). This made Japan the largest foreign holder of US securities. If Japanese corporations withdrew their equity holdings denominated in US dollars and Japanese financial institutions also switched their portfolio holdings out of US bonds and securities as a result of a loss of earnings and the decline in the exchange rate of the US dollar, a phase of quite severe financial instability would be set in motion. Similarly, a sell-off of dollar securities would trigger sharp falls in US bond prices and induce an upsurge in interest rates. The US bubble economy would burst and find itself burdened with an avalanche of nonperforming loans which could take years to resolve. In this scenario, a phase of intensified interimperialist rivalry over the East Asian markets would inevitably be waged between the US and Japan.

Conclusion: the Coming Crisis

Introduction

Since the onset of the East Asian crisis, the world economy has lurched toward chronic stagnation. Over the past decade, the US economy has effectively acted as the market of last resort for the rest of the capitalist countries, especially for East Asian exports. With the recent curtailment of effective demand in the United States, however, the final pillar of support has crumbled. For the first time in over two decades, the world economy is now at the threshold of a synchronized downturn, which will engulf the three major poles of accumulation in East Asia, the EU and the US. The only question that remains is over the severity of the emerging slump. Indeed, we have shown that this crisis of chronic stagnation has already engulfed Japan over the past decade. The question that will be posed in this final chapter is whether the crisis of overaccumulation will ultimately assume global proportions. In other words, will a similar dynamic of debt deflation and excess capacity characterize the core economies of Europe and the United States? Furthermore, is there a real likelihood that the world economy could relapse into another phase of depression?

1 The privileges of US financial hegemony

> In modern complex economies, a large and growing part of money capital (i.e., money invested with a view to earning more money) is not directly transformed into productive capital serving as a means by which surplus value is extracted from the productive utilization of labour power. Instead it is used to buy interest-bearing or dividend-yielding financial instruments.... Many capitalists are being offered

> an enormous variety of financial instruments to choose from – stocks and bonds, certificates of deposit, money-market funds, titles to all sorts of assets, options to buy and sell, futures contracts, and so on. There is no presumption, let alone assurance, that money invested in any of these instruments will find its way, directly or indirectly, into real capital formation. It may just as well remain in the form of money capital circulating around in the financial sector, fuelling the growth of financial markets which increasingly take on a life of their own (Magdoff & Sweezy, 1987, pp. 96–7).

Since the emergence of floating exchange rates and deregulated financial markets over the past two decades, most OECD countries have experienced the development of a finance-led regime of accumulation, which has gradually superseded the former national-based Fordist system. Historically, finance for investment has originated either from banks and credit institutions or from the internal sources generated by large, oligopolistic firms. The logic of deregulation and globalization has led to the ascendancy of shareholder value over the previous Fordist model in which the managers, or the "technostructure" to paraphrase Galbraith (1976), played a strategic role in investment decisions. Shareholder value reinforces the tendency toward deregulation, privatization, restructuring and the internationalization of dollar finance. This process appears to be more advanced in the English-speaking countries than in East Asia and Europe.

> The imposition of financial norms, such as shareholder value, requires a new and coherent architecture for the mode of governance of firms, the form of competition, the wage/labour nexus and the objectives of monetary policy, public budget and tax system.... The stability of an equity-based regime depends on monetary policy which controls financial bubbles and thus the diffusion of finance may push the economy into a zone of structural instability. The next major financial crisis may originate in the USA whose economy approximates most closely to the model. (Boyer, 2000, p. 111)

Shareholder value presupposes a more rigorous form of market discipline imposed on private corporations in which the overriding imperative is to maximize returns on investment. Financial returns therefore increasingly assume potent hegemonic forces in the dynamics of capital accumulation. In this sense, Pigou's wealth effect, which transforms millions of ordinary workers into investors, acts as a powerful transmission mechanism in the maintenance of the purchasing power of consumers.

In 1987, 25 percent of US households had a stake in the stock market. By the late 1990s, over half of all US households owned shares, either directly or indirectly through mutual funds (Harmes, 2001). Indeed, the financial assets of mutual and pension funds had grown by almost tenfold since 1980, estimated at about $20 trillion in the mid-1990s (Gilpin, 2000, p. 32). Yet despite the growth of a mass investment culture, the distribution of wealth is still extremely skewed toward the top 10 percent of households in the US and this disparity is becoming even more extreme. In 1995, for instance, the wealthiest 1 percent of US households accounted for 42 percent of stocks owned by individuals and 56 percent of bonds; while the top 10 percent accounted for about 90 percent. "Since households own about half of all corporate stock, the posh 1% owns a quarter of the productive capital and future profits of corporate America; the top 10%, nearly half" (Henwood, 1998, pp. 66–7).

Between 1993 and 1999, equity prices increased by more than 13.9 percent above the growth of real output (Pollin, 2000, p. 33). In the decade 1991 to 2000, this excessive "wealth effect" represented more than $8 trillion. If one assumes that a one-dollar increase in net financial wealth increases consumption by 3 cents, the wealth effect has therefore increased private consumption by an estimated $240 billion over the same period. According to Pollin (2000), this excess consumption was equivalent to the 4.5 percent decline in national savings in the US. It has been estimated that for every dollar decline in the market value of their wealth, American consumers would curtail their spending by 4–5 cents, which would be large enough to induce a recession (Strange, 1998, p. 79). At the same time, wages in the US have remained relatively stagnant and have lagged behind productivity growth.

> With wages held down as output and productivity rise, profits inevitably increase. Under Clinton they have reached a 30-year peak. In 1997 the share of total corporate income accruing to profits was 21.6 per cent, as opposed to the cyclical highs under Nixon (1973) of 18 per cent, Carter (1979) of 17.4 per cent, and even Reagan (1984) of 18.4 per cent. (Pollin, 2000, p. 32)

As passive savers are converted into active investors, this finance-driven logic of accumulation merely reinforces the tendencies toward neoliberal economic policies in the sense that millions of investors now have a vested interest in these very same policies. Neoliberal ideology alone could not have mobilized this enormous constituency. Yet the most perverse characteristic of this financial mania is that it resembles a casino. Between 1986 and 1996, bond issues tripled, securities issues increased by more than tenfold and foreign exchange transactions quadrupled to over $1 trillion (Strange, 1998, pp. 17–18). Furthermore, the value of outstanding derivatives contracts in the OECD was estimated at $77.5 trillion in March 1995, which represented twice the value of world GNP. By far the greatest share of this market was in the foreign exchange and interest rate contracts (Strange, 1998, p. 30). The volume of foreign exchange trading in the late 1990s has been estimated at about $1.5 trillion per day, an eightfold increase since 1986 (Gilpin, 2000, p. 22). Hedge funds, which speculate in foreign exchange markets, are capable of mobilizing between $600 billion and $1 trillion to bet against currencies in well-organized, speculative attacks (Gowan, 1999, p. 98). The real vulnerability of this finance-led regime of accumulation is that it has been based upon the greatest equity boom in modern history. The 1990s speculative boom in the United States has already reached its zenith. The bursting of the financial bubble will reverberate on a global scale.

In short, the US economy is very prone to financial crises. The business cycle is almost entirely dependent upon asset price bubbles. For instance, the Dow Jones Industrial Average stood at about 3600 in 1994. By 1999 it had exceeded 11000, or more than tripling in five years. Price/earnings ratios reached a historic record of 44.3 in January 2000, compared to 32.6 in September 1929. Conversely dividend yields reached record lows. The historical average dividend yield has been estimated at 4.7 percent. In January 2000, the dividend yield was estimated at only 1.2 percent of asset prices (Shiller, 2000, p. 8). The US economy has been very dependent on the inflow of short-term, highly liquid funds, which are quite prone to reversal if Wall Street ceases to generate high rates of return. Indeed, this process of chronic financial retrenchment had already been set in motion even before the events of September 11, 2001. According to Eatwell and Taylor (1999), the US economy is caught in a debt trap: "The jaws of the trap are the growing imbalances between outstanding *stocks* (or volumes) of financial claims, on the one hand, and *flows* of interest payments, imports and exports, and consumer spending, on the other hand. Critical stock-flow ratios are dangerously high" (Eatwell & Taylor, 1999, p. 34).

Most of the recent speculative activity has been concentrated in the telco and Internet stocks. Excessive market valuation in the latter is reflected in the unrealistic price/earnings ratio, estimated at an average of 300 to 1 in March 2000. Most of these "virtual" companies have yet to realize a profit. To be sure, America's estimated 371 publicly traded

Internet companies were collectively valued at about $US1.3 trillion in March 2000 which was equivalent to about 8 percent of the entire US stock market. Given the fact that the vast majority of these stocks continue to be unprofitable, there has been an inevitable shakeout of the market as the Schumpeterian forces of creative destruction have been set in motion. The consequences for the US bubble economy would appear to be quite dire. The recent collapse of market valuations in this "new" economy sector could prefigure a major stock market correction and reverse the irrational wealth effect.

> The Internet stocks that have headlined the mania over the last year (1999) are without known precedent in US financial history. At its highs in early April, the market capitalization of Priceline.com, which sells airline tickets on the web and has microscopic revenues, was twice that of United Airlines.... America Online (AOL) was worth nearly twice as much as Disney and Time Warner combined, and more than GM and Ford combined.... At its peak, AOL sported a price/earnings ratio of 720, Yahoo! of 1468 and eBay of 9571. (Henwood, 1999, p. 129)

A classical phase of debt deflation could emerge in this process of financial retrenchment (Fisher, 1933; Minsky, 1982). Between 1976 and 1999, the level of personal debt as a proportion of disposable household income had increased from 64.3 percent to over 94.2 percent in the United States (Pollin, 2000, p. 33). By 2000, outstanding private debt was two and a quarter times GDP, while total outstanding debt – private and public – reached three times that of GDP (Ed., *Monthly Review*, April, 2002). Indeed, since the early 1980s Americans have borrowed from the rest of the world's savings, most notably from Japan, in order to finance their domestic consumption and investment. In the event of a loss of confidence in the US dollar, these debts would have to be validated in foreign currencies, especially in the euro and the yen.

2 A hegemonic crisis?

> Undoubtedly the fact of hegemony presupposes that account be taken of the interests and the tendencies of the groups over which hegemony is to be exercised and that a certain compromise equilibrium should be formed – in other words, that the leading group should make sacrifices of an economic-corporate kind. But there is no

> doubt that such sacrifices and such a compromise cannot touch the essential; for though hegemony is ethical-political, it must be economic, must necessarily be based on the decisive function exercised by the leading group in the decisive nucleus of economic activity. (Gramsci, 1971, p. 161)

Just as the interwar crisis witnessed a global transition from one hegemonic power to another – or from the free trade imperialism of *Pax Britannica* to the rise of *Pax Americana* under the aegis of the postwar Bretton Woods system – so too the present systemic crisis carries with it the clash between the three great hegemonic powers of the EU, Japan/East Asia and the US. In the absence of a stable hegemonic system, the world economy could enter into a prolonged period of chronic instability and interstate anarchy. Viewed from the standpoint of these secular phases of hegemonic transition, the financial explosion over the past two decades represents the demise or the "autumn" phase of the present regime of *Pax Americana* (Arrighi, 1994).

The crisis of overaccumulation means that markets have become saturated and in order to reinvest profitably, financial markets become the channels through which a growing proportion of capital is held and reinvested in its liquid form, while an ever-growing volume is devoted almost entirely to short-term speculation. The financial expansion, in turn, sets in train a more intense struggle over the capture of mobile capital by competing oligopolies and nation-states. Hence, there is a paradoxical tendency to inflate the power of the dominant hegemonic state as it attracts a disproportionate share of mobile capital. The fact that most of these financial flows are denominated in the American dollar tends to increase US global financial preeminence. In other words, over the past two decades, the US has been reaping the fruits of its privileged access to financial markets and has enjoyed the benefits derived through its powers of seigniorage over the dollar. Throughout the 1990s, this enormous financial leverage has been exploited through the agency of the Wall Street–IMF–US Treasury complex and the export of neoliberal ideology (Gowan, 1999). These enormous advantages have, in a sense, postponed the impending and inevitable decline of US global hegemony.

In this context, the greatest interimperialist fault-line lies across the Pacific as the new dynamic centres of accumulation in East Asia inevitably collide with US geostrategic imperatives in the region. An apt historical analogy might be the rivalry between ancient Rome and Carthage over the trading routes of the Mediterranean.

> In past hegemonic transitions, the crises that ushered in the demise of the old financial centre were felt earliest and most severely in the *rising* financial centres (London in 1772 and New York in 1929). It follows that the Asian financial crises of the 1990s cannot be taken as proof of long-term weakness. Indeed, no matter how much US power may have been reflated, it is unlikely to have been reflated enough to stop the rotation of the global economy's centre of gravity back to where it was in pre-modern times .... Just as victory in the First World War destroyed Britain's status as the leading creditor nation, so victory in the Second Cold War turned the United States into the largest debtor nation. (Arrighi & Silver, 1999, pp. 275–6)

In a broader geopolitical context, the basic contradiction lies in the fact that the US has emerged as the unrivalled, global military hegemon since the collapse of the Soviet Union in 1989. Yet at the same time, Japan and the East Asian archipelago have emerged as the largest streams of surplus value and sources of world investment and liquidity. Politically and militarily, however, East Asia is still subordinate to the geopolitical imperatives of US imperialism. Their global power has been circumscribed and emasculated, while historical enmities and political rivalries within the region continue to prevent the creation of a cohesive trade and currency bloc.

If the European experience is any guide, economic and monetary union is first and foremost a *political* process. It should be borne in mind that the European experiment was consummated amidst the ruins of war and evolved into a peculiar creature of the Cold War. Monetary union was the culmination of a long, protracted political engagement in the construction of an economic edifice and a supranational framework that has its origins in Franco-German rapprochement after the war. In this sense, the making of Europe was the answer to Germany's own making. The political dimension could ultimately prove to be the Achilles' heel of Asian economic and monetary integration. Unlike Europe, Asia has not developed, to any great degree, deep-seated institutions and the political machine required to propel the rationalizing dynamic of regional integration. History might unwittingly be recast as Asia's ultimate enemy. Regional suspicions of Japan's hegemonic ambitions still resonate after more than half a century has elapsed since Japan's imperialist wars.

The creation of a possible yen zone will inevitably encounter strident American opposition. This was recently highlighted by the IMF/US rejection of Japan's proposal to establish an Asian monetary fund in the wake of the speculative turmoil of 1997/98. It is highly doubtful if the Americans would tolerate the prospect of a loss of markets, investment outlets and the curtailment of their military presence in the region. If the Americans were to surrender their privileges of seigniorage, the subsequent adjustment would be intolerably painful in terms of the loss of purchasing power afforded by a relatively strong dollar and the swelling ranks of the unemployed that a collapse in effective demand would entail.

> If it had to pay these debts in other currencies, it would quickly find itself in very serious difficulties. Short of being able to use its military-industrial muscle to insist upon the continued dominance of the dollar, it would have to undergo a radical social reorganisation internally and cope with the disruptive consequences. Such a challenge to the dollar could, of course, come from a rise of the euro or some East Asian regional currency. (Gowan, 2002, p. 143)

The sudden collapse of the dollar would impart quite profound ramifications for the global economy as the events after the 1985 Plaza accords have already starkly demonstrated. Indeed, what is ultimately at stake is the very existence of the postwar system of *Pax Americana*. In Gramscian terminology, the American–Japanese axis is one of *catastrophic equilibrium*. In the event of a crash of the dollar, Japanese investors in US bonds and equities would stand to make considerable losses, which could trigger a sudden withdrawal of their funds from the US. At the same time, the US would no longer be able to finance its current account deficit by attracting an inflow of capital. It might not be too implausible to evoke the specter of an intensified phase of interimperialist rivalry across the Pacific and the mobilization of US military power to reassert their hegemonic power in the East Asian region.

An alternative scenario would be a gradual US withdrawal and retreat into its own trade and currency bloc analogous to the experience of the United Kingdom during the interwar crisis as it retreated behind the sterling bloc area. In other words, the US could eventually sever its imperialist ties with the "informal" empire and reconstitute its formal links. The formal spheres would include most of the English-speaking countries as well as the traditional neocolonial countries of Latin America. In this sense, the creation of the North American Free Trade Agreement (NAFTA) between the US, Canada and Mexico in 1994 signaled a radical shift away from multilateralism and towards the formation of a regional trading bloc. The NAFTA was, in this critical perspective, a US reaction against the EU and East Asia's flying geese formation. It was an attempt to increase their leverage in international trade negotiations and exploit a regional division of labor to improve their international competitiveness. Indeed, these tendencies toward regionalism were already evident as early as 1988 with the signing of the US–Canada Free Trade Agreement (FTA). This process of integration had also been well advanced over the previous decades as the Canadian economy gravitated closer to the US.

> Beginning with the auto pact and the linking of the American and Canadian dollars in the 1980s, economic integration of the two economies accelerated rapidly. Canadian FDI in the US economy grew significantly. By 1985, over 70 percent of Canada's exports went to the US, and over 70 percent of its imports came from the US. Furthermore, nearly 50 percent of these exports and imports have involved intra-firm transfers by US and Canadian MNCs. Thus, both trade and FDI have linked the American and Canadian economies closely together. (Gilpin, 2000, p. 240)

In the meantime, the process of negative integration between the US and Mexico has also accelerated. This took the form of increased US FDI in Mexico as US manufacturers restructured and began to relocate their plants in Mexico in order to improve their international competitiveness by taking advantage of lower Mexican wages, less stringent environmental laws and by the lure of tax incentives. By 1994, over 60 percent of FDI in Mexico originated in the US, while 70 percent of Mexico's trade was destined to the US (Gilpin, 2000, p. 242). Hence, the formal signing of the NAFTA accelerated the process of trade and investment liberalization. The major accent of the treaty was on the phasing out of most trade barriers in manufactured goods, especially in the auto sector and in textiles. However, tariff barriers on most agricultural commodities will be phased out over a 15-year period.

The extension of the NAFTA to include all of Latin America was proposed by the Clinton administration but has encountered widespread skepticism by other Latin American countries. Many of them were quite wary of US political motives in the region, given the long history of US political and military intervention. The willingness of the Americans to open up their agricultural markets was also met with considerable skepticism. Indeed, the creation of the Mercosur trade pact in 1991 between Brazil, Argentina, Paraguay and Uruguay can be viewed as a political counter to the NAFTA.

Conclusion

The rise of neoliberal economic doctrines and the unleashing of the forces of globalization since the mid-1970s have led to the demise of the postwar Keynesian consensus. We can surmise that globalization is a complex, hybrid process that integrates as well as disintegrates. This era has been characterized by stagnation and crisis. One of the unintended consequences that accompanied the neoliberal ascendancy has been a widespread myopia and historical amnesia over the bitter lessons of the great depression. The critical question, therefore, is whether the world economy is on the brink of another prolonged crisis. If so, then the lessons of the 1930s acquire greater resonance. History would vindicate the economic theories of Keynes and Kalecki and bestow them with the intellectual authority that has been denied to them by the latter-day "vulgar" economists. Yet despite the demise of neo-Keynesianism, which was born out of the neoclassical synthesis of the 1950s, the institutions and policy instruments that one normally attributes to the Keynesian revolution, still remain relatively intact. The question therefore arises that, given this institutional framework, is another great depression possible? After all, one could quite easily contend that, unlike the great depression, the automatic stabilizers performed by the state sector are still in place despite being considerably weakened by the neoliberal counter-revolution. Similarly, the onset of a recession could be mitigated to some extent by expansionary fiscal and monetary policies, despite the penalties imposed by deregulated financial markets. Furthermore, with the demise of *Pax Americana*, will the global economy evolve into competing trade and currency blocs reminiscent of the interwar crisis? These issues still remain open to debate and will be tested by the severity of the coming crisis.

Notes

Introduction

1. A highly recommended recent study is Peter Gowan's *The Global Gamble* (1999).
2. The disastrous consequences of these types of economic policies were most evident in Russia in the early 1990s. Yeltsin and his economic chief, Gaidar, responding to advice from the IMF and Western economists, introduced "shock therapy" which involved price liberalization and the removal of subsidies to industries, which in turn, triggered wholesale bankruptcies and a growing army of unemployed. The end result was mass unemployment and a collapse in the standard of living. At the same time, the privatization of public enterprises gave rise to a small class of overnight billionaires who emerged from the ranks of the old nomenclature. An upsurge in hyperinflation wiped out personal savings and reduced purchasing power by a half. While income rose by 600 percent in the first half of 1992, consumer prices increased by almost twice that rate. Indeed, the period of "shock therapy" represented a phase of unprecedented economic collapse from which Russia has yet to recover. Global market pressures – made explicit by the tough IMF program – have threatened to reduce most of the country to a Third World status based primarily on extractive and agrarian industries. By the mid-1990s, the Russian GDP was slightly larger than that of Belgium.
3. The onset of a deflationary spiral was particularly evident in Japan in the 1990s.

1 Accumulation and Crisis: Marxian Controversies

1. The simplified two-sector Lewis model was developed in the 1950s in which surplus labor in the traditional agricultural sector migrates to the higher wage, higher productivity industrial sector. The rate at which this process occurs is determined by the rate of industrial development and capital accumulation in the modern sector. Lewis assumes that all profits in the modern sector are reinvested and that wages in this sector are generally higher due to higher productivity growth (Lewis, 1956).
2. The law of increasing returns is explored in more detail in Chapter 2.
3. The Marxian concept of equilibrium is quite different from the Walrasian version of general equilibrium. It refers to the *interrelatedness* of the different sectors of a closed economy and has its intellectual roots in the classical economists (Smith and Ricardo) as well as in the original Physiocratic treatment of Quesnay's *Tableau Economique* (Junankar, 1982, p. 9).

2 Circular and Cumulative Causation

1. Appendix 2A provides a very simple elaboration of the Solow/Swan growth accounting model.

2. The original general equilibrium models were grounded on the mathematical principles of Newtonian mechanics.
3. Endogenous growth theories, unlike the Keynesian schema, generally support the neoclassical linear, causal relation between saving and investment. The causation runs from saving to investment.
4. The theoretical difficulties associated with the existence of heterogeneous capital goods have been a serious issue of contention in the very construct of an aggregate production function. The "capital controversies" of the 1950s and 1960s highlighted some of these logical inconsistencies (Pasinetti & Scazzieri, 1990). The limited scope of this study precludes a more detailed treatment of these issues.
5. The Kaleckian concept of the "degree of monopoly" will be explored in more detail in Chapter 3.
6. A more detailed treatment of innovation and technical change is elaborated in Chapter 4.
7. Some excellent studies of the Institutionalist and Evolutionary strands of economic thought are provided by Hodgson (1999, 2001).
8. Harrod's original formula was that assuming exports (E) of a particular country are given exogenously and imports are a simple linear function of income ($M = mY$, with $0 < m < 1$), and there are no other "leakages" from income (Y), so that

   $$Y = \frac{1}{1-r}E \text{ (the general multiplier formula)}$$

   where $1 - r = m$, so that $E = mY$, or $E = M$.
9. Thirwall developed a "dynamized version" of the Harrod multiplier:

   $$\alpha y = \alpha e / \beta$$

   where αy and αe are the logarithmic growth rates of income and exports respectively, and β represents the income elasticity of demand for imports.

3 Overaccumulation and Crisis

1. According to Kalecki, capitalists earn what they spend and workers spend what they earn.

4 Long Cycles of Growth and Stagnation?

1. Appendix 4A provides a more detailed elaboration of Harrod's trade cycle theory.

6 The Onset of "Eurosclerosis"

1. An excellent critique of the Maastricht fiscal criteria is elaborated by Pasinetti (1998, 1998a).

7 The US–Japanese Axis: Unity or Rivalry?

1. The product-cycle type of development was first formulated by Japanese economist Akamatsu in the early 1940*s* and has become known as the "flying geese" pattern of industrialization (Yamazawa, 1990).
2. During the 1980s, the price of real estate rose by a factor of 5. At their respective peaks, the total estimated value of Japanese land was 60 percent of world property values, while Japanese equities accounted for almost 40 percent of world stock market values (Linge, 1997, p. 62).
3. These coordinated central bank operations triggered the most recent financial crisis in October 1998 with the collapse of the "yen-carry" trade. Hedge funds had borrowed at the low Japanese interest rate in order to make a profit through arbitrage by lending at the higher interest rates in Europe and the United States. However, after the Russian default in August 1998, most of these hedge funds were caught short and were forced to cover their exposure in Russia by deleveraging their accumulated yen borrowings. In October 1998, the yen soared from 135 to 115 to the dollar, which wiped out most of the profits in the yen-carry trade and precipitated the near collapse of the Long-Term Capital Management hedge fund. These events led to a massive rescue operation by the US Federal Reserve in concert with private investors in order to avoid a global credit crunch.

Bibliography

Aglietta M. (1979), *A Theory of Capitalist Regulation*, New Left Books, London.

——(2000), "Shareholder Value and Corporate Governance: Some Tricky Questions," *Economy & Society*, Vol. 29, No. 1, February, pp. 146–59.

Akyus Y. (1998), *The East Asian Financial Crisis: Back to the Future?*, UNCTAD, Geneva.

Amin S., Arrighi G., Frank A.G. & Wallerstein I., eds (1982), *Dynamics of Global Crisis*, Monthly Review Press, New York.

Andersen E.S. (1992), "Approaching National Systems of Innovation from the Production and Linkage Structure," in Lundvall, B.A., ed., *National Systems of Innovation: Towards a Theory of Innovation and Interactive Learning*, Pinter Publishers, London.

Anderson P. (1997), "The Europe to Come," in Gowan, P. & Anderson P., eds, *The Question of Europe*, Verso, London.

Arestis P. & Chick V., eds (1995), *Finance, Development and Structural Change*, Edward Elgar, London.

Arestis P., McCauley K. & Sawyer M. (2001), "An Alternative Stability Pact for the European Union," *Cambridge Journal of Economics*, Vol. 25, No. 1, pp. 113–30.

Armstrong P., Glyn A. & Harrison J. (1991), *Capitalism since 1945*, Basil Blackwell, Oxford.

Arndt H.W. (1995), "External Economies in Economic Growth," *The Economic Record*, Vol. 31, November, pp. 192–214.

Arrighi G. (1978), *The Geometry of Imperialism*, New Left Books, London.

——(1994), *The Long Twentieth Century*, Verso Press, London.

Arrighi G. & Silver B.J., eds (1999), *Chaos and Governance in the Modern World System*, University of Minnesota Press, Minneapolis.

Arthur W.B. (1990), "Positive Feedbacks in the Economy," *Scientific American*, February, pp. 92–9.

Artis J.A. & Winkler B. (1997), "The Stability Pact: Safeguarding the Credibility of the European Central Bank," European University Institute, *Working Papers*, RSC No. 97/54, Florence.

Artis M. & Lee N., eds (1994), *The Economics of the European Union*, Oxford University Press, New York.

Atkinson A.B. & Brunetta R., eds (1991), *Economics for the New Europe*, Macmillan & Co., London.

Baran P.A. & Sweezy P. (1966), *Monopoly Capital*, Monthly Review Press, New York.

Blanden-Hovell R. (1994), "The EMS in Crisis," in Artis M. & Lee, N., eds, *The Economics of the European Union*, Oxford University Press, New York.

Block F. (1977), *Origins of Economic Disorder*, University of California Press, New York.

Boltho A. (1975), *Japan: an Economic Survey: 1953–75*, Oxford University Press, London.

——ed. (1982), *The European Economy*, Oxford University Press, New York.

Boltho A. (1993), "Western Europe's Economic Stagnation," *New Left Review*, No. 201.

Boyer R. (1992), "Technical Change and the Theory of Regulation," in Dosi G., Gianetti R. & Tonelli P.A., eds, *Technology and Enterprise in a Historical Perspective*, Clarendon Press, Oxford.

——(1996), "State and Market," in *States against Markets*, Boyer R. & Drache D., eds, Routledge, London.

——(2000), "Is a Finance-Led Growth Regime a Viable Alternative to Fordism? A Preliminary Analysis," *Economy & Society*, Vol. 29, No. 1, February, pp. 111–45.

Boyer R. & Drache D. eds (1996), *States against Markets*, Routledge, London.

Boyer R. & Petit P. (1991), "Kaldor's Growth Theories: Past, Present and Future," in Nell E.J. & Semmler W. eds, *Nicholas Kaldor and Mainstream Economics: Confrontation of Convergence?* St. Martin's Press, New York.

Braudel F. (1984), *Perspective of the World*, Vols 1–3, W. Collins, London.

Brett E.A. (1985), *The World Economy since the War: the Politics of Uneven Development*, Macmillan Press, London.

Business Week (1997), "Asia's Bad Debts," 24 February.

——(1997a), "Two Japans," 27 February.

Buzan B. (1988), "Japan's Future: Old History vs New Rules," *International Affairs*, Vol. 64, No. 4.

Carchedi G. (1997), "The EMU, Monetary Crises and the Single European Currency," *Capital & Class*, No. 63, Autumn.

——(2001), *For Another Europe*, Verso, London.

Chandler A.D. (1990), *Scale and Scope: the Dynamics of Industrial Capitalism*, Harvard University Press, Cambridge, Mass.

Chesnais F. (1992), "National Systems of Innovation, FDI and the Operations of MNEs," in Lundvall B.A. ed., *National Systems of Innovation: Towards a Theory of Innovation and Interactive Learning*, Pinter Publishers, London.

Chowdhury A. & Islam I. (1993), *The Newly Industrialising Economies of East Asia*, Routledge, London.

——(1997), *Asia-Pacific Economies: a Survey*, Routledge, London.

Clarke N. & Juma C. (1987), *Long-Run Economics*, Pinter Publishers, London.

Cline W.R. (1983), *International Debt: Systemic Risk and Policy Response*, Washington Institute for International Economics, Washington.

Coffey P. (1987), *The European Monetary System – Past, Present and Future*, Kluwer Academic Publishers, London.

Committee for the Study of Economic and Monetary Union (1989), *Report on Economic and Monetary Union in the EC* (The Delors Report), European Commission, Brussels.

Coombs R.W. (1981), "Innovation, Automation and the Long Wave Theory," *Futures*, October.

——(1987), "Long Waves, Depression and Innovation: Comment on Kleinknecht," *De Economist*, Vol. 135, No. 3.

Cumings B. (1984), "The Origins and Development of the North East Asian Political Economy: Industrial Sectors, Product Cycles and Political Consequences," *International Organization*, Vol. 38, No. 1.

Day R. (1976), "The Theory of the Long Cycle," *New Left Review*, No. 67.

Dixon C. & Drakakis-Smith D., eds (1993), *Economic and Social Development in Pacific Asia*, Routledge, London.

Dobb M. (1937), *Political Economy and Capitalism*, Routledge & Kegan Paul, London.

——(1973), *Theories of Value and Distribution*, Cambridge University Press, London.

Dore R. (1998), "Asian Crisis and the Future of the Japanese Model," *Cambridge Journal of Economics*, Vol. 22, No. 7, pp. 761–71.

Dosi G. (1983), "Technological Paradigms and Technological Trajectories," in Freeman C.F., ed., *Long Waves in the World Economy*, Francis Pinter, London.

—— ed. (1988), *Technical Change and Economic Theory*, Pinter Publishers, London.

Dosi G., Gianetti R. & Tonelli P.A., eds (1992), *Technology and Enterprise in a Historical Perspective*, Clarendon Press, Oxford.

Dosi G., Winter S. & Teece D.J. (1992), "Towards a Theory of Corporate Coherence," in Dosi. G., Gianetti R. & Tonelli P.A., eds, *Technology and Enterprise in a Historical Perspective*, Clarendon Press, Oxford.

Eatwell J., Milgate M. & Newman P., eds (1990), *The New Palgrave: Capital Theory*, Macmillan Press Ltd., New York.

Eatwell J. & Taylor L. (1999), "The American Stock-Flow Trap," *Challenge*, September/October.

Economist (1997), "The Asian Miracle: Is It Over?," 1 March.

——(1998), "Frozen Miracle," 7 March.

EEC Commission (1972), *Report to the Council and Commission on the Realisation by Stages of Economic and Monetary Union in the Community* (The Werner Report), Brussels.

Emerson M., ed. (1984), *Europe's Stagflation*, Clarendon Press, Oxford.

——ed. (1992), *One Market, One Money*, Oxford University Press, New York.

Emmanuel A. (1972), *Unequal Exchange: a Study of the Imperialism of Trade*, Monthly Review Press, New York.

Ferri P., ed. (1990), *Prospects for the European Monetary System*, St. Martin's Press, New York.

Fisher I. (1993), "The Debt-Deflation Theory of Great Depressions," *Econometrica*, Vol. 1, October.

Fitoussi J.P., ed. (1993), *Competitive Disinflation*, Oxford University Press, New York.

Freeman C.F., ed. (1983), *Long Waves in the World Economy*, Francis Pinter, London.

——(1994), "The Economics of Technical Change," *Cambridge Journal of Economics*, Vol. 18, pp. 463–514.

——(1995), "The National System of Innovation in Historical Perspective," *Cambridge Journal of Economics*, Vol. 19, pp. 5–24.

Freeman C. & Perez C. (1992), "Structural Crises of Adjustment, Business Cycles and Investment Behaviour," in Dosi G., Gianetti R. & Tonelli P.A., eds, *Technology and Enterprise in a Historical Perspective*, Clarendon Press, Oxford.

Fukuyama F. (1992), *The End of History and the Last Man*, Penguin, London.

Funabashi Y. (1988), *Managing the Dollar: From the Plaza to the Louvre*, Institute for International Economics, Washington.

Galbraith J.K. (1976), *The New Industrial State*, Penguin, London.

Galbraith, J. (1997), "Time to Ditch the NAIRU," *Journal of Economic Perspectives*, Vol. 11, No. 1, pp. 93–108.

Garvey G. (1943), "Kondratiev's Theory of Long Cycles," *Review of Economic Statistics*, Vol. 15, No. 4.

George S. (1988), *A Fate Worse Than Debt*, Penguin, London.

——(1991), *Politics and Policy in the European Community*, Oxford University Press, New York.

Gillman J.M. (1957), *The Falling Rate of Profit*, Dobson, London.

Gilpin R. (1975), *US Power and the Multinational Corporation*, Macmillan & Co, Ltd., London.

——(1979), "Three Models of the Future," in Modelski G., ed., *Transnational Corporations and World Order*, W.H. Freeman & Co., San Francisco.

——(2000), *The Challenge of Global Capitalism*, Princeton University Press, New York.

Giovannini A. (1990), "The Transition to European Monetary Union," *Essays in International Finance*, No. 178, November, Princeton University, New Jersey.

Giovannini A. & Spaventa L. (1991), "Fiscal Rules in the EMU: a 'No Entry Clause'," in Atkinson A.B. & Brunetta R., eds, *Economics for the New Europe*, Macmillan & Co., London.

Giovazzi F., Micossi S. & Miller M., eds (1988), *The European Monetary System*, Cambridge University Press, London.

Goodwin R.M. (1982), *Essays in Economic Dynamics*, Macmillan, London.

Gowan P. (1999), *The Global Gamble*, Verso Press, London.

——(2002), "After America," *New Left Review*, No. 13, Jan/Feb.

Gowan P. & Anderson P. eds (1997), *The Question of Europe*, Verso, London.

Grahl J. (2001), "Globalised Finance," *New Left Review*, No. 8, March/April.

Grahl J. & Teague P. (1989), "The Cost of Neo-Liberal Europe," *New Left Review*, No. 174.

——(2000), "The Regulation School, the Employment Relation and Financialization," *Economy & Society*, Vol. 29, No. 1, February, pp. 160–78.

Gramsci A. (1971), *Selections from Prison Notebooks*, eds Hoare Q. & Nowell Smith G., Lawrence & Wishart, London.

Guerrieri P. & Padoan P.C. (1986), "Neo-Mercantilism and International Economic Stability," *International Organization*, Vol. 40, No. 1.

——eds (1989), *The Political Economy of European Integration*, Simon & Schuster, London.

Halliday J. & McCormack J. (1973), *Japanese Imperialism Today*, Penguin, London.

Halevi J. (1992), "Asian Capitalist Accumulation: From Sectoral to Vertical Integration," *Journal of Contemporary Asia*, Vol. 22, No. 4.

——(1995), "The EMS and the Bundesbank in Europe," in Arestis P. & Chick V., eds, *Finance, Development and Structural Change*, Edward Elgar, London.

——(1996), "The Significance of the Theory of Vertically Integrated Processes for the Problem of Economic Development," *Structural Change and Economic Dynamics*, No. 7.

——(1998), "Accumulation, Breakdown Crises, Disproportionality, and Effective Demand," *Working Papers in Economics*, No. 98–16, December, Economics Department, University of Sydney, Sydney.

——(1998a), "The Accumulation Process in Japan and East Asia as Compared with the Role of Germany in European Post-War Growth," *Working Papers in Economics*, No. 98–04, University of Sydney, April.

Halevi J. & Lucarelli B. (2002), "Japan's Stagnationist Crisis," *Monthly Review*, Vol. 53, No. 9, Feb.

Halevi J. & Taouil R. (1998), "On a Post Keynesian Stream from France & Italy: the Circuit Approach," *Working Papers in Economics*, No. 98-08, July 1998, Economics Department, University of Sydney, Sydney.

Hall M. (1988), "The International Debt Crisis: Recent Developments," *Capital & Class*, No. 35.

Harcourt G.C. (1997), "Economic Theory and Economic Policy: Two Views," *Discussion Paper*, No. 369, Australian National University, Centre for Economic Policy Research, Canberra, Australia, July.

Harmes A. (2001), "Mass Investment Culture," *New Left Review*, No. 9 (new series), May/June.

Harrod R.F. (1933), *International Economics*, Macmillan, London.

——(1948), *Towards a Dynamic Economics: Some Recent Developments of Economic Theory and Their Application to Policy*, Macmillan, London.

Hatch W. & Yamamura K. (1996), *Asia in Japan's Embrace*, Cambridge University Press, New York.

Healey D. (1991), *Japanese Capital Exports and East Asian Economic Development*, OECD, Paris.

Henderson J. (1991), "The Rise of the State in the Economic Transformation of East Asia," in Dixon C. & Drakakis-Smith D., eds, *Economic and Social Development in Pacific Asia*, Routledge, London.

Henwood D. (1998), *Wall St.*, Verso, London.

——(1999), "The United States," *Monthly Review*, July.

Hilferding R. (1981), *Finance Capital*, Routledge & Kegan Paul, London.

Hirschman A.O. (1958), *The Strategy of Economic Development*, Yale University Press, New Haven and London.

Hodgson G.M (1999), *Evolution and Institutions*, Edward Elgar, London.

——(2001), *How Economics Forgot History*, Routledge, London.

Holland S., ed. (1983), *Out of Crisis: a Project for European Recovery*, Russell Press, London.

Hughes C.H. (2000), "Japanese Policy and the East Asian Currency Crises: Abject Defeat or Quiet Victory?," *Review of International Political Economy*, Vol. 7, No. 2, Summer.

Hymer S. (1975), "The Multinational Corporation and the Law of Uneven Development," in Radice, H., ed., *International Firms and Modern Imperialism*, Penguin Books, London.

International Monetary Fund (IMF) (1997), *World Economic Outlook: an Interim Assessment*, December, Washington, DC.

Itoh M. (1990), *The World Economic Crisis and Japanese Capitalism*, St. Martin's Press, New York.

——(2000), *The Japanese Economy Reconsidered*, Palgrave, New York.

Jarjoura G. (2000), "The Merhav–Pasinetti Approach to Industrialisation," *Journal of Contemporary Asia*, Vol. 30, No. 2.

Johnson C. (1982), *MITI and the Japanese Miracle*, Stanford University Press, Stanford, Calif.

——(1998), "Economic Crisis in East Asia: the Clash of Capitalisms," *Cambridge Journal of Economics*, Vol. 22, No. 6, pp. 653–61.

Junankar P.N. (1982), *Marx's Economics*, Philip Allen Pub., Oxford.

Kaldor M. (1978), *The Disintegrating West*, Allen Lane, London.

Kaldor N. (1939), "Speculation and Economic Activity," *Review of Economic Studies*, Vol. 7, No. 1–27, October.

Kaldor N. (1957), "A Model of Economic Growth," *Economic Journal*, Vol. LXVII, 1957.

——(1972), "The Irrelevance of Equilibrium Economics," *Economic Journal*, Vol. LXXXII, December, pp. 1237–55.

——(1985), *Economics without Equilibrium*, ME Sharp Inc., New York.

——(1996), *Causes of Growth and Stagnation in the World Economy*, Cambridge University Press, Cambridge.

Kalecki M. (1966), *Studies in the Theories of Business Cycles, 1933–39*, Oxford, UK.

——(1971), *Selected Essays on the Dynamics of the Capitalist Economy: 1933–70*, Cambridge, UK.

——(1972), "Political Aspects of Full Employment," in *The Last Transformation of Capitalism*, Monthly Review Press, New York.

——(1990), *Collected Works*, Vols 1 and 2, ed. Osiatynsky J., Clarendon Press, Oxford, London.

——(1990a), "The Problem of Effective Demand with Tugan-Baranovsky and Rosa Luxemburg," in Osiatynsky J., Vol. 2 *Collected Works*, Clarendon Press, Oxford, London.

Keen S. (1993), "Modelling Minsky's Financial Instability Hypothesis," *Discussion Paper 93/5*, School of Economics, University of New South Wales, Sydney.

——(2001), *Debunking Economics*, Pluto Press, Sydney, Australia.

Keynes J.M. (1930), *A Treatise on Money*, Vols 1 and 2, Macmillan & Co, London.

——(1936), *The General Theory of Employment, Interest and Money*, Macmillan & Co., London.

Kindleberger C.P. (1978), *Manias, Panics and Crashes*, Macmillan Press, UK.

——(1984), *A Financial History of Western Europe*, Allen & Unwin, London.

Kleinknecht A. (1981), "Observations on the Schumpeterian Swarming of Innovations," *Futures*, August.

——(1990), "Are there Schumpeterian Waves of Innovation?," *Cambridge Journal of Economics*, Vol. 14, No. 1, March.

Kondratiev N.D. (1935), "The Long Waves in Economic Life," *Review of Economic Statistics*, Vol. 17.

Korner P., Maass G., Siebold T. & Tetzlaff R. (1986), *The IMF and the Debt Crisis*, Zed Press, London.

Kosai, Y. (1986), *The Era of High-Speed Growth: Notes on the Postwar Japanese Economy*, translated by Jacqueline Kaminski, University of Tokyo Press, Tokyo.

Kosai Y. & Ogino Y. (1984), *The Contemporary Japanese Economy*, Macmillan Press, London.

Kriesler P. (1995), "Keynes, Kalecki and The General Theory," *Discussion Paper 95/39*, School of Economics, University of New South Wales, Sydney.

Kriesler P. & Halevi J. (1996), "Asia, Japan, and the Internationalization of Effective Demand," *Economie et Sociétés*, Série No. 10, 2–3.

Krugman P., ed. (1986), *Strategic Trade Policy and the New International Economics*, MIT Press, Cambridge, Mass.

——(1994), "The Myth of Asia's Miracle," *Foreign Affairs*, Nov/Dec, Vol. 73, No. 6.

——(1997), *What is Wrong with Japan?* (http:/web.mit.edu/krugman/www/nikkei.html)

——(1999), *The Return of Depression Economics*, Penguin, London.

Kunio Y. (1988), *The Rise of Ersatz Capitalism in S.E. Asia*, Oxford University Press, New York.
——(1994), *Japanese Economic Development*, Oxford University Press, New York.
Kruse D.C. (1980), *Monetary Integration in Western Europe: EMU, EMS and Beyond*, Butterworths, Boston, Mass.
Kuznets S. (1940), "Schumpeter's Business Cycles," *American Economic Review*, Vol. 30, June.
——(1953), *Economic Change: Selected Essays in Business Cycles, National Income and Economic Growth*, W.W. Norton & Co., New York.
Kwan C.H. (2001), *Yen Bloc*, Brookings Institution Press, Washington, DC.
Lall S. (1996), "Paradigms of Development: the East Asian Debate," *Oxford Development Studies*, Vol. 24, No. 2.
Landes D. (1970), *The Unbound Prometheus: Technological and Industrial Development in Western Europe from 1750 to the Present*, Cambridge University Press, London.
Lawson T. (1997), *Economics and Reality*, Routledge, London.
Lenin V.I. (1967), *The Development of Capitalism in Russia*, Progress Publishers, Moscow.
Leontief W. (1963), "The Structure of Development," *Scientific American*, Vol. CCIX, No. 3, September, pp. 148–66.
——(1986), *Input/Output Economics*, Oxford University Press, Oxford.
Lewis W.A. (1956), "Economic Development with Unlimited Supplies of Labour," *Manchester School*, No. 22, May.
Linge C. (1998), *The Rise and Decline of the Asian Century*, Macmillan, Melbourne.
Lipietz A. (1987), *Mirages and Miracles*, Verso, London.
List F. (1904), *The National System of Political Economy*, Longman, London.
Llewellyn J. & Potter S. (1982), "Competitiveness and the Current Account," in Boltho A. ed., *The European Economy*, Oxford University Press, New York.
Lucarelli B. (1999), *The Origins and Evolution of the Single Market in Europe*, Ashgate Publishers, London.
——(2002), "The East Asian Financial Meltdown," *Journal of Contemporary Asia*, Vol. 32, No. 4.
Lundvall B.A., ed. (1992), *National Systems of Innovation: Towards a Theory of Innovation and Interactive Learning*, Pinter Publishers, London.
Luxemburg R. (1971), *The Accumulation of Capital*, Routledge & Kegan Paul, London.
McCombie J.S.L. & Thirwall A.P. (1994), *Economic Growth and the Balance of Payments Constraint*, St. Martin's Press, London.
McEwan A. (1986), "International Debt and Banking: Rising Instability within the General Crisis," *Science & Society*, Vol. L, No. 2.
Maddison A. (1982), *Phases of Capitalist Development*, Oxford University Press, New York.
Magdoff H. & Sweezy P.M. (1987), *Stagnation and Financial Explosion*, Monthly Review Press, New York.
——(1989), *The Irreversible Crisis*, Monthly Review Press, New York.
Mandel E. (1980), *Long Waves in Economic Life*, Cambridge University Press, London.
——(1981), "Explaining Long Waves of Capitalist Development," *Futures*, August.

Mann M. (2002), "Globalisation, Global Conflict and September 11," *New Left Review*, No. 14, March/April.

Mansfield E. (1994), "Long Waves and Technological Innovation," *American Economic Association (Papers & Proceedings)*, Vol. 73, No. 2.

Marshall A. (1961), *Principles of Economics*, Macmillan, London.

Martin H. & Schuman H. (1997), *The Global Trap*, Pluto Press, Sydney.

Marx K. (1978), *Capital*, Vols. 1–3, Progress Publishers, Moscow.

Marx K. & Engels F. (1998), *The Communist Manifesto*, Verso, London.

Mayer M. (1974), *The Bankers*, Weybridge & Tulley, New York.

Mensch G. (1979), *Stalemate in Technology: Innovations Overcome Depression*, Cambridge University Press, London.

Metcalfe J.S. (1994), "Evolutionary Economics and Technology Policy," *The Economic Journal*, No. 104, July.

Michie J. & Smith J.G., eds (1999), *Global Instability*, Routledge, London.

Minsky H.P. (1982), *Inflation, Recession and Economic Policy*, Harvester Press, Brighton, UK.

Modelski G., ed. (1979), *Transnational Corporations and World Order*, W.H. Freeman & Co., San Francisco.

Modigliani F., Fitoussi J., Muro B., Snower D., Solow R., Steinherr A. & Sylos Labini P. (1998), "An Economists' Manifesto on Unemployment in the EU," *Banca Nazionale del Lavoro Quarterly Review*, Vol. LI, No. 206, September, pp. 327–61.

Monthly Review, eds (2002), "Slow Growth, Excess Capital and a Mountain of Debt," Vol. 53, No. 11, April.

Moon B.E. (1982), "Exchange Rate System, Policy Distortions and the Maintenance of Trade Dependence," *International Organization*, Vol. 36, No. 4.

Moravcsik A. (1991), "Negotiating the Single European Act: National Interests and Conventional Statecraft in the EC," *International Organization*, Vol. 45, No. 1.

Morris J., ed. (1991), *Japan and the Global Economy*, Routledge, New York.

Morris-Suzuki T. (1991), "Reshaping the Industrial Division of Labour: Japanese Manufacturing Investment in S.E. Asia," in Morris J., ed., *Japan and the Global Economy*, Routledge, New York.

Morroni M. (1992), *Production Process and Technical Change*, Cambridge University Press, New York.

Mundell R.A. (1961), "A Theory of Optimum Currency Areas," *American Economic Review*, No. 51.

Myrdal G. (1957), *Economic Theory and the Underdeveloped Regions*, Gerald Duckworth & Co. Ltd, London.

Nell E.J. & Semmler W., eds (1991), *Nicholas Kaldor and Mainstream Economics: Confrontation or Convergence?*, St. Martin's Press, New York.

Nelson R.R. (1987), *Understanding Technical Change as an Evolutionary Process*, Elsevier Science Publishers, Amsterdam.

Nelson R.R. & Winter G.W. (1982), *An Evolutionary Theory of Economic Change*, Harvard University Press, Cambridge, Mass.

Nordhaug K. (2002), "The Political Economy of the Dollar and the Yen in East Asia," *Journal of Contemporary Asia*, Vol. 32, No. 4.

North D.C. (1990), *Institutions, Institutional Change and Economic Performance*, Cambridge University Press, London.

Nurske R. (1956), "Balanced Growth on Static Assumptions," *Economic Journal*, Vol. LXVI, June, pp. 365–7.

OECD Report (1998), "Asian Financial Crisis," 19–20 Feb.

Okazaki T. & Okuno-Fugiwara M., eds (1999), *The Japanese Economic System and Its Historical Origins*, Oxford University Press, New York.

Omae K. (1998), *The Borderless World*, HarperCollins, London.

Osiatynsky J., ed. (1990), *Collected Works of Michal Kalecki*, Vols 1 and 2, Clarendon Press, Oxford, London.

Padoa-Schioppa T., ed. (1987), *Efficiency, Stability and Equity*, Oxford University Press, New York.

——(1988), "The Three Quartets," in Giovazzi F., Micossi S. & Miller M., eds, *The European Monetary System*, Cambridge University Press, London.

Parboni R. (1981), *The Dollar and Its Rivals*, New Left Books, London.

——(1983), "Reflections on Williamsburg," *New Left Review*, No. 141.

——(1986), "The Dollar Weapon: From Nixon to Reagan," *New Left Review*, No. 158.

Pasinetti L. (1981), *Structural Change and Economic Growth*, Cambridge University Press, New York.

——(1993), *Structural Economic Dynamics*, Cambridge University Press, New York.

——(1998), "European Union at the End of 1997: Who is in the Public Finance 'Sustainability' Zone," *Banca Nazionale del Lavoro Quarterly Review*, Vol. LI, No. 204, March, pp. 17–35.

——(1998a), "The Myth (or Folly) of the 3% deficit/GDP Maastricht Parameter," *Cambridge Journal of Economics*, Vol. 22, No. 1, pp. 103–16.

Pasinetti L.L & Scazzieri R. (1990), "Capital Theory: Paradoxes," in *Capital Theory*, in Eatwell, J., Milgate M. & Newman P., eds, *The New Palgrave: Capital Theory*, Macmillan Press Ltd, New York.

Pasinetti L.L. & Solow R.M., eds (1994), *Economic Growth and the Structure of Long-Term Development*, Macmillan, London.

Pavit K. (1984), "Patterns of Technical Change: Towards a Taxonomy and a Theory," *Research Policy*, Vol. 13, No. 6.

Petras J. & Rhodes R. (1980), "The Reconstitution of US Hegemony," *New Left Review*, No. 79.

Polanyi M. (1957), *The Great Transformation*, Routledge & Kegan Paul, London.

Pollin R. (1983), "A Theory of Financial Instability," *Monthly Review*, December.

——(2000), "Anatomy of Clintonomics," *New Left Review*, No. 3, May/June.

Porter M.E. (1990), *The Competitive Advantage of Nations*, Macmillan, London.

Radice H., ed. (1975), *International Firms and Modern Imperialism*, Penguin Books, London.

Reich R.B. (1991), *The Work of Nations*, Simon & Schuster, London.

Robinson J. (1962), *Essays in the Theory of Economic Growth*, Macmillan, London.

——(1979), "Solving the Stagflation Puzzle," *Challenge*, Vol. 22, November–December.

Romer P. (1986), "Increasing Returns and Long-Run Growth," *Journal of Political Economy*, No. 94.

——(1994), "The Origins of Endogenous Growth," *Journal of Economic Perspectives*, Winter.

Rosenberg N. (1982), *Inside the Black Box: Technology and Economics*, Cambridge University Press, London.

Rosenberg N. (1992), "Science and Technology in the Twentieth Century," in Dosi G., Gianetti R. & Tonelli P.A., eds, *Technology and Enterprise in a Historical Perspective*, Clarendon Press, Oxford.
Rosenberg N. & Frischtak C. (1984), "Technological Innovations and Long Waves," *Cambridge Journal of Economics*, Vol. 8, No. 1.
Ross G. (1992), "Confronting the New Europe," *New Left Review*, No. 191.
Rowthorn R.E. & Wells J.R. (1987), *Deindustrialisation and Foreign Trade*, Cambridge University Press, New York.
Sachs J. (1997), "The Wrong Medicine for Asia," *New York Times*, 3 November.
Saviotti P.P. & Metcalfe J.S., eds (1991), *Evolutionary Theories of Economic and Technological Change*, Harwood Academic Publishers, Geneva.
Schumpeter J.A. (1934), *The Theory of Economic Development*, Harvard University Press, Cambridge, Mass.
——(1939), *Business Cycles*, Vols 1 and 2, McGraw-Hill, New York.
——(1942), *Capitalism, Socialism and Democracy*, Unwin, London.
——(1947), "The Creative Response in Economic History," *Journal of Economic History*, Vol. 7, No. 2, November.
Sheridan K., ed. (1998), *Emerging Economic Systems in Asia*, Allen & Unwin, Sydney.
——(1998a), "Japan's Economic System," in Sheridan K., ed. *Emerging Economic Systems in Asia*, Allen & Unwin, Sydney.
Shiller R.J. (2000), *Irrational Exuberance*, Scribe Pub., Melbourne, Australia.
Smithin J. (1996), *Macroeconomic Policy and the Future of Capitalism*, Edward Elgar, London.
Solomou S. (1982), "Innovation Clusters and Kondratiev Long Waves in Economic Growth," *Cambridge Journal of Economics*, Vol. 10, No. 2.
Solow R. (1956), "A Contribution to the Theory of Economic Growth," *Quarterly Journal of Economics*, Vol. LXX, February, pp. 65–94.
——(1957), "Technical Change and the Aggregate Production Function," *Review of Economics & Statistics*, Vol. 39, pp. 312–20.
Spaulding R.M. (1991), "German Trade Policy in Eastern Europe, 1890–1990: Preconditions for Applying Trade Leverage," *International Organization*, Vol. 45, No. 3.
Spero J.E. (1977), *The Politics of International Economic Relations*, St. Martins Press, Inc., London.
Sraffa P. (1926), "The Laws of Return under Competitive Conditions," *The Economic Journal*, December.
Steindl J. (1976), *Maturity and Stagnation in American Capitalism*, Monthly Review Press, New York.
Sternberg F. (1963), *The Coming Crisis*, Richard Clay, London.
Steven R. (1991), "Structural Origins of Japan's FDI," in Morris, J., ed., *Japan and the Global Economy*, Routledge, New York.
Stiglitz J. (2002), *Globalization and Its Discontents*, Allen Lane, London.
Strange S. (1986), *Casino Capitalism*, Oxford Press, London.
——(1998), *Mad Money*, Manchester University Press, UK.
Stubbs, R. (1994), "The Political Economy of the Asia-Pacific Region," in Stubbs, R. et al., *Political Economy and the Changing Global Order*, Macmillan, London.
Swan T.W., (1956), "Economic Growth and Capital Accumulation," *The Economic Record*, Vol. 32, No. 63, pp. 334–61.
Sweezy P. (1946), *The Theory of Capitalist Development*, Dennis Dobson, London.

Sylos-Labini P. (1969), *Oligopoly and Technical Progress*, Harvard University Press, Cambridge, Mass.

——(1993), *Economic Growth and Business Cycles*, Edward Elgar, Brookfield, Vt.

Taggart-Murphy R. (2000), "Japan's Economic Crisis," *New Left Review*, No. 1 (second series), Jan/Feb.

Tarbuck K.J., ed. (1972), *Imperialism and the Accumulation of Capital*, Allen Lane, London.

Tew B. (1960), *International Monetary Co-operation*, Hutchinson & Co., Ltd, London.

Thirwall A.P. (1979), "The Balance of Payments Constraint as an Explanation of International Growth Rate Differences," *Banca Nazionale Del Lavoro Quarterly Review*, Vol. 128.

Thurow L. (1997), "Asia: the Collapse and the Cure," *New York Review*, 27 December.

Thygessen N. (1981), "Are Monetary Policies and Performances Converging?," *Banca Nazionale Del Lavoro*, September.

Tinbergen J. (1981), "Kondratiev Cycles and So-Called Long Waves: the Early Research," *Futures*, August.

Tipton F.B. (1998), *The Rise of Asia*, Macmillan, Melbourne.

Toner P. (1999), *Main Currents in Cumulative Causation: the Dynamics of Growth and Development*, Macmillan Press, Ltd, London.

Triffin R. (1961), *Gold and the Dollar Crisis*, Yale University Press, New York.

——(1978), "Europe and the Money Muddle Revisited," *Banca Nazionale Del Lavoro*, March.

——(1987), "The IMS (International Monetary System ... or Scandal) and the EMS," *Banca Nazionale Del Lavoro*, September.

Tsoukalis L. (1977), *The Politics and Economics of European Monetary Integration*, Allen & Unwin, Ltd, London.

——(1993), *The New European Economy*, Oxford University Press, New York.

UNCTAD (1996), *Trade and Development Report*, Geneva.

——(1996a), *World Investment Report*, Geneva.

Van Duijn J.J. (1981), "Fluctuations in Innovations over Time," *Futures*, August.

Van Ewijk C. (1981), "The Long Wave – a Real Phenomenon?," *De Economist*, Vol. 129, No. 3.

Veblen T. (1898), "Why is Economics Not an Evolutionary Science?," *The Quarterly Journal of Economics*, July, pp. 373–9.

Vernon R. (1966), "International Investment and International Trade in the Product Cycle," *Quarterly Journal of Economics*, May.

Wade R. (1990), *Governing the Market: Economic Theory and the Role of the Government in East Asian Industrialisation*, Princeton, New York.

Wade R. & Veneroso F. (1998), "The Asian Crisis: the High Debt Model vs the Wall St–Treasury–IMF Complex," *New Left Review*, March–April.

Wallerstein I. (1976), "Kondratiev Up or Kondratiev Down?," *Review*, No. 2.

Whittaker D.H. & Kurosawa Y. (1998), "Japan's Crisis: Evolution and Implications," *Cambridge Journal of Economics*, Vol. 22, No. 7.

Williams K. (2000), "From Shareholder Value to Present-Day Capitalism," *Economy & Society*, Vol. 29, No. 1, February, pp. 1–12.

Wood R.E. (1985), "Making Sense of the Debt Crisis," *Socialist Review*, Vol. 15, No. 3.

World Bank (1993), *The East Asian Miracle*, Policy Research Project, Oxford, USA.

Woronoff T. (1996), *The Japanese Economic Crisis*, Macmillan, London.

Yamamura K. (1986), "Caveat Emptor: the Industrial Policy of Japan," in Krugman P., ed., *Strategic Trade Policy and the New International Economics*, MIT Press, Cambridge, Mass.

Yamazawa I. (1990), *Economic Development and International Trade: the Japanese Model*, Resource Systems Institute, East-West Center, Honolulu, Hawaii.

Yoshikawa H. (2001), *Japan's Lost Decade*, International House of Japan, Tokyo.

Young A. (1928), "Increasing Returns and Economic Progress," *Economic Journal*, Vol. XXXVIII, pp. 672–86.

Index